Legilinguistic Translatology

Linguistic Insights

Studies in Language and Communication

Edited by Maurizio Gotti,
University of Bergamo

Volume 171

PETER LANG
Bern · Berlin · Bruxelles · Frankfurt am Main · New York · Oxford · Wien

Aleksandra Matulewska

Legilinguistic Translatology

A Parametric Approach to Legal Translation

PETER LANG
Bern · Berlin · Bruxelles · Frankfurt am Main · New York · Oxford · Wien

Bibliographic information published by die Deutsche Nationalbibliothek
Die Deutsche Nationalbibliothek lists this publication in the Deutsche Nationalbibliografie; detailed bibliographic data is available on the Internet at ‹http://dnb.d-nb.de›.

British Library Cataloguing-in-Publication Data:
A catalogue record for this book is available from The British Library, Great Britain

Library of Congress Cataloging-in-Publication Data

Matulewska, Aleksandra.
Legilinguistic translatology: a parametric approach to legal translation / Aleksandra Matulewska.
pages cm. – (Linguistic insights: Studies in language and communication; v. 171)
Includes bibliographical references.
ISBN 978-3-0343-1287-5
1. Law–Translating. I. Title.
K213.M39 2013
340'.14–dc23

2013004754

ISSN 1424-8689 pb.
ISBN 978-3-0343-1287-5 pb.
ISSN 2235-6371 eBook
ISBN 978-3-0351-0535-3 eBook

Hochfeldstrasse 32, CH-3012 Bern, Switzerland
info@peterlang.com, www.peterlang.com, www.peterlang.net

Printed in Switzerland

Contents

Acknowledgements

I am particularly grateful for advice, support, encouragement and inspiration provided by Prof. Jerzy Bańczerowski (Adam Mickiewicz University in Poznań, Poland). His pioneering research into axiomatic linguistics led me into this field. Prof. Jerzy Bańczerowski kindly read the first and the final drafts of this book and commented on it elaborately and I did my best to incorporate his valuable comments into the final work.

I am also greatly indebted to Prof. Feliks Zedler (Adam Mickiewicz University in Poznań, Poland) who kindly shared his knowledge in the field of insolvency law and also read the second draft of the book.

Next, I was introduced to legal translation by Piotr Tomasz Żebrowski whose professional approach and enthusiasm made me start research into this field and to whom I remain really indebted.

I would like to express my gratitude to Prof. Władysław Zabrocki for his valuable comments and critical remarks on formulating scientific theories.

I would also like to thank a number of people who have helped me in a variety of ways. I need to thank in particular Prof. Piotra Łobacz, Prof. Teresa Tomaszkiewicz, Prof. Piotr Wierzchoń and Prof. Jacek Witkoś for enabling me to attain this publication.

Finally, I give special thanks to my family for being so patient and understanding when I devoted more time to writing the book than to them.

At the same time I would like to apologize for any remaining inaccuracies which readers may find in this book as I am alone responsible for them.

Abbreviations

Chi.	Chinese
Eng.	English
Ger.	German
Fr.	French
L_i	source language
lit.	literal translation
L_j	target language
M	meaning
Po	postulate
Pol.	Polish
SLOT	source-language oriented translation
TLOT	target-language oriented translation
TL	target language
SL	source language
TEPIS	Polish Society of Specialised and Sworn Translators
STP	Association of Polish Translators and Interpreters
Gs	general statement
LSP	language for special purposes

Introduction

Purpose, scope and methodology of research

Legal translation is considered one of the most difficult tasks as far as translation of texts formulated in languages for special purposes is concerned. This is due to the fact that legal texts are rarely formulated in legal language only. Moreover, there is a wide variety of branches of law and text genres functioning in them. Finally, legal systems of different countries vary. Consequently some language pairs are easier to translate from and into, whereas others are more difficult and challenging. It happens so especially when the translator deals with, e.g., a common law / civil law language pair.

The translation of legal texts poses numerous problems encountered in the translational enterprise. The research has been inspired by numerous quandaries faced by translators of legal texts in Poland and abroad. The aim of this research is, on the one hand, to show how the existing theories of translation and linguistics may be adapted to legal translation and, on the other hand, to formulate a more formally advanced theory of legilinguistic translation. In other words, this work is to inquire into some difficulties which translators have to deal with while striving after securing translational equivalence.

With the purpose of making the process of legal translation accessible to investigation, I will resort to the parametrization of translational reality as an inalienable component of my translational theory being proposed here for consideration. My aim is to propose a more precise theory of legilinguistic translation which may enable us to clearly distinguish primitive terms and postulates. The latter specify the image (model) of the reality in question in terms of relevant dimensions used to characterize the following translational objects and relations:

(i) the impact of the author on the source text,
(ii) commissioner's impact on translation,

(iii) translator's competences,
(iv) source and target text properties,
(v) source and target communicative communities and their impact on rendered translations.

The dimensions secure a systematic examination of the translation reality and process.

In order to illustrate the practical application of the parametrization in legal translation, I will limit my discussion concerning translation approach to certain selected types of legal communicative communities which are amply exemplified. The research is based on data and information gathered during an in-depth case study of translations and parallel text corpora mainly in the field of civil law including insolvency and bankruptcy law. The proposed approach to a theory of legal translation will be illustrated with its practical implementation in the process of translation.

1. Legal Language and Translation

1.1. Introductory remarks

The 20th and the 21st centuries have witnessed a rapid development of studies on translation, not only of literary texts but also of specialized ones. What follows below is a short and by no means exhaustive summary of some translation theories and approaches applicable to general and legal translation. Some of them will be mentioned marginally which does not mean that they are less important, but they are less applicable to a theory presented in Part II of this work. Some Polish approaches to translation will be elaborated on in more detail as it has been assumed that they were published in Polish and due to the language barrier are less known to an international public (cf. e.g. F. Grucza 1981, Kielar 1973, 1996, Kierzkowska 2002).

1.2. General translatological foundations

1.2.1. Skopos theory

The theory of *skopos* and commission in translational action was developed by Vermeer (cf. Vermeer 1978, 1983, 1986, Reiss/Vermeer 1984). Vermeer's *skopos* theory is based on the aim and function of a source and target text and the translation circumstances including such elements as the client commissioning the action. The word *skopos* stands for the purpose of translation. The translation *skopos* is established on the basis of the function of the source text and the intended function of the target text.

> The aim of any translational action, and the mode in which it is to be realized, are negotiated with the client who commissions the action. A precise specification of aim and mode is essential for the translator. – This is of course analogously true of translation proper: *skopos* and mode of realization must be adequately defined if the text-translator is to fulfill his task successfully (Vermeer 2001: 221).

Vermeer points out that only translators who are experts in translational action and who are assisted by the client supplying them with every necessary and accurate information can properly identify the *skopos* of a text.

> The *skopos* theory thus in no way claims that a translated text should *ipso facto* conform to the target culture behaviour or expectations, that a translation must always *adapt* to the target culture. This is just one possibility: the theory equally well accommodates the opposite type of translation, deliberately marked, with the intention of expressing source-culture features by target-culture means. Everything between these two extremes is likewise possible, including hybrid cases. To know what the point of a translation is, to be conscious of the action – that is the goal of the skopos theory. The theory campaigns against the belief that there is no aim (in any sense whatever), that translation is a purposeless activity (Vermeer 2001: 231).

Vermeer also accurately notices that the change of *skopos* in translation may result in a different target text being produced by a translator.

1.2.2. Text typologies, translation and translative systems

For a very long time text typologies for the purpose of translation focus on the bipolar classifications (in general the typologies were based on the division of texts translated by the typology author and other texts). Hieronymus introduced the classification into biblical texts (to be translated *verbum e verbo*) and non-biblical texts (to be translated *sensum de sensu*). Later on the theorists of translation introduced the division into the translation of literary and non-literary texts (e.g. Leonardo Bruni, Pierre-Daniel Huet, Alexander Fraser Tytler). Pierre-Daniel Huet was one of the first scholars who recognized scientific translation next to literary translation (in Šarčević 2000b: 6). Huet believed “that scientific texts confront translators with particular demands” and “viewed scientific translation as one of the *foremost tasks of civilization* and one which had been *absurdly neglected* (in Steiner 1977: 265)” (Šarčević 2000b: 6). Schleiermacher, on the other hand, introduced the division into the translation of works of art (which referred to literary and scientific texts and was called *Übersetzen*) and wordly texts (which referred to business and other everyday life-related texts called *Dolmetschen*) (Šarčević 2000b: 6).

Fedorov (1953) distinguished the group of special purpose texts and, contrary to Schleiermacher, did not consider the translation of special purpose texts as inferior to the translation of works of art (literary texts). He was one of the first scholars who noticed that translation of LSP requires excellent knowledge of the field to which the text belongs. From about the mid-twentieth century more complex typologies appear in the theory of which many start accounting for the text function. Casagrande (1954) introduced the division into (i) pragmatic, (ii) aesthetic-poetic texts, (iii) ethnographic and (iv) linguistic texts. The term pragmatic texts referred to what Fedorov called special purpose texts. In the 1970s Reiss (1976) proposed the typology of texts based on their subject-matter and function at the same time. Following Bühler’s (1934) language typology, she distinguished informative texts (*sachorientierte informative Texte*), expressive texts (*senderorientierte expressive Texte*) and conative texts (*verhaltensorientierte operative Texte*) (Wille 2002: 91-92, Šarčević 2000b: 7). She later developed the typology of hybrid texts composed of mixture of those types. In Poland the research into specialised texts and their typologies has been carried out among others by F. Grucza (1994), S. Grucza (2004, 2007, 2008) and Lukszyn (2009).

In 1981 F. Grucza defined translation studies as the science investigating the processes taking place in a specific system, called a translative system. The translation process is rendered as a result of practical activities of a human being or a machine within the translative system (F. Grucza 1981: 10). F. Grucza presented two translative systems: a simplified one and a broadened one. In the broadened translative system the translator acts as an intermediary recipient and sender of the message.

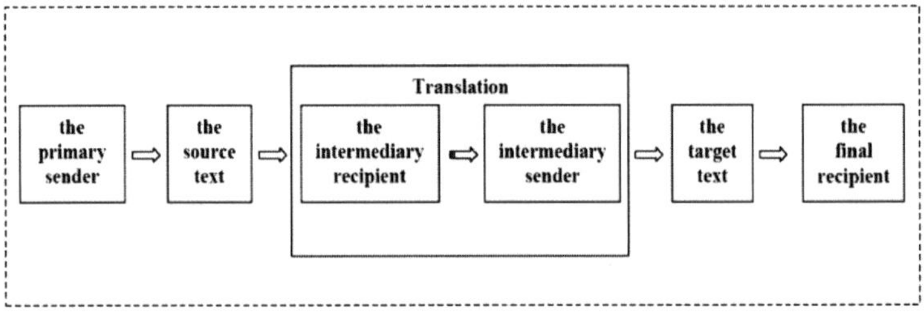

Figure 1. F. Grucza's translative system (1981: 10-11).

The continuous/uninterrupted line refers to the translative system proper, whereas the dashed line refers to the broadened translative system.

Furthermore, he stresses that translation is interdisciplinary as it involves among others linguistics, textology, psychology and physiology (F. Grucza 1981: 13).[1]

Additionally, F. Grucza (1981: 14) suggests the division of translation on the basis of text typology into translation of informative texts and literary (aesthetic) texts. In turn, translation of informative texts is divided into translation of popular texts and texts for occupational purposes.

F. Grucza (1985: 33) suggests the importance of translative system objects. The most important and central role is played by the translator and his translative properties. Next, he enumerates texts and as the last category the message sender and the message recipient. In

1 In the eighties and nineties of the 20th century Krings (1986), Kussmaul (1995), Hönig (1991) and Lörscher (1991) and F. Grucza (1981, 2007) in Poland investigated the application of psycholinguistics in translation. Many important observations have been made in the process of psycholinguistic research concerning for instance the translation decision-making process. Lörscher (1991) distinguished sign-oriented and sense-oriented translation. Kussmaul (1995) focused on translator's creativity and training. This approach was also recognized in Poland as very important. According to F. Grucza, the main aim of translation studies (called in Polish *translatoryka* – the name suggested by F. Grucza in 1976 during a conference devoted to translation and glottodidactics (F. Grucza 2007: 325)) is investigating the properties of translators and their mental processes affecting translation, rather than investigating the properties of texts (F. Grucza 2007: 326-327).

this paper he changes his stand on the role of text analysis in translation theory called in Polish *translatoryka* and accepts the necessity of analysing and investigating texts for the purpose of the theory of translation.

That translative system has been later modified by Kielar (1988). She suggested developing the translative system in reference to the sub-fields of translation and presented a teleological approach to translation.

There have been also other classifications of text types. For instance Kierzkowska (2002: 77-78) suggested the following division of legal texts: referential (denotative), performative, executive, informative, prescriptive (normative), expressive, phatic, appelative, etc.

Turning the translators' attention to the function of texts was a breakthrough. Theoreticians of translation after centuries of neglecting specialized translation or even treating it as inferior (Andresen 1974: 164, in Wilss 1977a: 129) started being interested in this sub-field of translatology in the twentieth century. Among the first ones were the representatives of the Leipzig School (Neubert 1973: 19, also Šarčević 2000b: 7, Pisarska/Tomaszkiewicz 1996). Šarčević (2000b: 7) points out after Möhn/Pelka (1977: 68) that pragmatic-oriented translation studies started gaining impetus in the late 1970s.

In 1982 Weber (1982: 227) suggested text typology based on Halliday's functional categories and distinguished the following text functions: "predominantly instrumental, regulatory, interactional, personal, heuristic, imaginative or representational". Šarčević (2000b: 8) acknowledges that first of all "a typology of LSP texts can be empirically adequate and formally consistent only if it is applicable to all types of special-purpose texts, including texts of the social sciences" and after Sager[2] she recognizes the need for the comprehensive model of communicative functions in special purpose texts. Special purpose texts are formulated in a language for special purposes which is defined as "[...] the means of linguistic communication required for conveying special subject information among specialists in the same subject" (Sager/Dungworth/McDonald 1980: 210). It is usually divided

2 Sager (1990) has distinguished informative, interrogative and directive communicative text functions.

into the language for occupational purposes and academic purposes (Kennedy/Bolitho 1991: 4-5; P. Robinson 1991: 2-5).

1.2.3. Parallel text comparison

Parallel source texts constitute a more trustworthy source of terminological, syntagmal and grammatical information than parallel texts in the form of the source text and its translation. As a rule, the former may serve the purpose of establishing textual-normative equivalence.

There are, however, some exceptions to the rule. For instance in the case of Polish-English translation (or to put it more generally translation from a civil law embedded source language into English) the legislation of Louisiana and Scotland may serve the purpose of establishing source-language oriented and relatively understandable significators. This happens because the legal systems of both Louisiana and Scotland derive from civil law traditions.

As will be mentioned when presenting the achievements of Kielar (1973, 1977) in the field of legal translation, although time-consuming, *parallel text comparison* is very helpful. What type of parallel texts do we have in mind? There are two types of parallel texts. The first type includes texts formulated in the source language and target language and belonging to the same genre. Delisle (1999: 166) defines such texts in the following manner:

> [...] a text that represents the same text type as the source text or text that treats the same or a closely related topic in the same subject field and that serves as a source for the *mots justes* and terms that should ideally be incorporated into the target text to ensure collocational cohesion.

The second type of parallel texts consists of collections of the source texts and their translations into the target language. The first type of parallel texts is usually used to establish connotative significators, whereas the second type depending on the translation orientation may serve the purpose of establishing any type of significators. The second type of parallel texts may also be very useful if they are of high quality.

Having two texts of a given genre formulated in two languages, the translator may find legal-system bound terminology, phraseology and formulaic sentences. Furthermore, if both languages in question belong to one legal system (e.g. two languages imbedded in civil law system based on the Napoleonic Code), the degree of resemblance of legal texts as far as their structure, content and even order of information are concerned, may be very high. But even in the case of documents formulated in languages belonging to two different legal systems (e.g. civil law and common law), such documents are very helpful. Neubert (1996: 101) states that:

> [...] parallel texts are texts produced by users of different languages under near-identical communicative conditions. [...] Parallel text files [...] are part and parcel of the material and mental equipment of the competent translator. This equipment is a vast database storing enormous experience. It is the key to an extensive knowledge of how texts are structured in the (text) world of different (communicative) cultures.

Parallel texts help establish equivalent pairs on the level of terms, phraseological units and formulaic sentences.

1.3. Equivalence in translation

1.3.1. Equivalence in general theory of translation

There have been numerous theories concerning providing equivalents for the purpose of translation[3]. Let us therefore discuss in more detail

3 As Wilss (1977a/2001: 135) accurately remarks: "Despite all theoretical efforts and all TE statements by translation practitioners, the discussion on TE so far has only scratched the surface of its apparently rather recalcitrant subject-matter. Van den Broeck is even more sceptical: 'The concept of translational equivalence itself, however fashionable this term may have become among students and scholars of translation, seems to represent a theoretical claim the a priori acceptance of which is misleading rather than fruitful' (1980: 84). No wonder that the TE concept is still characterized by relatively inoperative, difficult-to-harmonize concepts. This is obvious, if one looks at the current equivalence terminology. There one finds, among other terms, 'to-

some of those theories and approaches quoting just a few stands on the subject matter before we proceed with the procedures of providing equivalents which will be referred to in the subsequent chapters of this work.

Schleiermacher (1813 in Lefevere 1992/2004: 149) states that the translator has just two options which nowadays are called source-language oriented translation (leaving the author in peace) or the target-language oriented translation (leaving the reader in peace) and according to him all intermediary solutions are unacceptable as they pose the threat of miscommunication.

The two methods presented by Schleiermacher are also referred to as foreignization and domestication.

Jakobson (1959/1966) has introduced the term *equivalence in difference* which means that the task of the translator is to create the target language message which would be equivalent to the source language message (in other words "[...] translation involves two equivalent messages in two different codes"). Moreover, Jakobson stresses the fact that languages differ not because of what they may express, but because of what they must express. In general, he assumes that the translator may translate the message by finding adequate equivalents, and if there are no equivalents available in the target language, he may create them by coining neologisms, or resorting to semantic shifts, different types of borrowings (e.g. loanwords or loan-translations) as well as circumlocutions (cf. Jakobson 1959 in Bukowski/Hydel 2009: 43-49).

Nida introduced the concept of formal and dynamic equivalence. He defines formal equivalence as source-oriented[4] and dynamic

---

tal equivalence' (Albrecht 1973), 'functional equivalence' (Jäger 1973), 'equivalence in difference' (Jakobson 1966), 'retention (maintenance) of translation invariance on the content level' (Kade 1968a), 'equality of textual effect' (Koller 1972), 'illusionist vs. anti-illusionist translation' (Levy 1969), 'closest natural equivalent' (Nida 1964), 'formal correspondence vs. dynamic equivalence' (Nida 1964), 'stylistic equivalence' (Popović 1976), 'functional invariance' (Roganova 1971), 'communicative equivalence' (Reiss 1976), 'pragmatic appropriateness of translation' (Kopczyński 1980), and 'text-pragmatic equivalence' (Wilss 1980 b)."

4 "A formal equivalence (or F-E) translation is basically source-oriented; that is, it is designed to reveal as much as possible of the form and content of the original message. In doing so, an F-E translation attempts to reproduce several

equivalence as target-oriented. Translation oriented towards dynamic equivalence is aimed at achieving the receptor response and naturalness to the target text recipient[5].

Nida and Taber (1982: 14, 22-28) in their later work *The Theory and Practice of Translation* use the terms dynamic equivalence and formal correspondence. Dynamic equivalence is achieved by applying terms which are *functionally equivalent* (Nida/Taber 1982: 14). Furthermore, they give priority to dynamic equivalence over formal correspondence (Nida/Taber 1982: 22-28).

Equivalence was of immense interest for representatives of the Leipzig School (Kade 1968, Jäger 1973, 1975 and Neubert 1968b) as well as *Übersetzungswissenschaft* (Wilss 1977b, Reiss 1976, Koller 1972, 1979). Kade (1968b) in his paper distinguished four types of equivalence (in Pisarska/Tomaszkiewicz 1996: 21, 162-162):

(i) *totale Äquivalenz* (*total equivalence*: ideal equivalence or in other words 1:1 correspondence at the formal and semantic level between two languages),

(ii) *fakultative Äquivalenz* (*optional equivalence*: one-to-many correspondence when the source language unit has several equivalents in the target language, e.g., in German: *Spannung,* in English: *voltage, tension, suspense, stress, pressure*),

(iii) *approximative Äquivalenz* (*approximate equivalence*: the meaning of a SL unit is divided between or may be expressed by us-

---

formal elements, including: (1) grammatical units, (2) consistency in word usage, and (3) meanings in terms of the source context. The reproduction of grammatical units may consist in: (a) translating nouns by nouns, verbs by verbs, etc.; (b) keeping all phrases and sentences intact (i.e. not splitting up and readjusting the units); and (c) preserving all formal indicators, e.g. marks of punctuation, paragraph breaks, and poetic indentation." (Nida 2004b: 165).

5 "One way of defining a D-E translation is to describe it as 'the closest natural equivalent to the source-language message.' This type of definition contains three essential terms: (1) *equivalent*, which points toward the source-language message, (2) *natural*, which points toward the receptor language, and (3) *closest*, which binds the two orientations together on the basis of the highest degree of approximation. [...]. Basically, the word natural is applicable to three areas of the communication process: for a natural rendering must fit: (1) the receptor language and culture as a whole, (2) the context of a particular message, and (3) the receptor-language audience." (Nida 2004b: 166-167)

ing two TL equivalents, e.g. in Polish *palec*, in English: *finger, toe*), and

(iv) *Null-Äquivalenz* (*zero equivalence*: the source language unit does not have a target language equivalent, e.g. in English: *equity*, in Polish: no equivalent).

Furthermore, Kade (1968) claimed that LSP texts are best for achieving exact reproductions of the semantic content of the translandive texts. Nowadays, however, it is claimed that translators should aim at reproducing informative content of the source text (Šarčević 2000b: 65).

Koller (1979) developed Kade's four levels of equivalence into five levels. Moreover, he also dealt with the related concept of correspondence. In his approach correspondence relates to the concept of *langue* / linguistic systems, whereas equivalence relates to concrete *parole* / source language and target language pairs and contexts. Koller (1979 in Pisarska/Tomaszkiewicz 1996: 163, 170) describes five levels of equivalence which have to be met in order to be able to talk about textual equivalence, namely:

(i) *denotative Äquivalenz* (*denotative equivalence* when the translation conveys the extralinguistic information),

(ii) *konnotative Äquivalenz* (*connotative equivalence* when the translation features the same style as the original at the level of sociolect, register, etc.),

(iii) *textnormative Äquivalenz* (*text-normative equivalence* when the translation reflects editorial norms prescribed for texts of a given category),

(iv) *pragmatische Äquivalenz* (*pragmatic equivalence* when the translation is adapted to the knowledge of the recipient so he can understand it), and

(v) *formal-ästhetische Äquivalenz* (*formal equivalence* which is different than Nida's formal equivalence because it occurs when the translation produces the same aesthetic effect as the original).

Moreover, Koller (1979) also suggests developing a hierarchy of equivalence requirements depending on the communicative context in which the translation is to function. The hierarchy should be prepared on the basis of source text analysis.

Jäger (1975 in Kielar 1988: 70-74), on the other hand, claimed that there are two types of equivalence that is to say:

(i) communicative equivalence which is realized when the average communicative value of the source text is preserved in translation, and

(ii) functional equivalence which is realized when the average functional value (which is understood here as the sum of the functions of linguistic signs, the sum of their meanings) of the source text is preserved in translation.

Finally, Šarčević (2000b: 236) refers to the term functional equivalence and points out that the existence of that sort of equivalence between the source and target languages does not mean that the concepts may be used for the purpose of translation. She also elaborates on the meaning of the term functional equivalence in different theories of general translation (cf. Wilss 1977a, 1977b; Reiss/Vermeer 1984; Reiss/Snell-Hornby/Kadric 1995), legal translation (cf. Kerby 1979, Gémar 1995–II and 1987, Groffier/Reed 1990, Weston 1991, de Groot 1991) and comparative law (cf. Bartels 1982) (in Šarčević 2000b).

Komissarov (1973, 1980 in Kielar 1988: 74-76, 2003a: 99-102) who analysed a vast corpus of English-Russian translations has, in turn, distinguished five levels of equivalence

(i) equivalence on the level of the communicative goal (the lowest / minimal degree of semantic similarity of the content of the target text message with the source text message),

(ii) equivalence on the level of the situation (the higher degree of similarity as not only the communicative goal must be achieved but also the situation referred to in the target text must be identical with the source text situation, even though it is not so evident at first sight as the target message may be expressed in other words than the source text message),

(iii) equivalence on the level of message / of method of description of the situation (besides making the target text equivalent at the two abovementioned levels that is the level of the communicative goal, the situation described, the way in which the situation is described is very similar),

(iv) equivalence on the level of utterance (besides making the target text equivalent at the three abovementioned levels that is the level of the communicative goal, the situation described, and the manner of describing the situation, the grammatical and lexical structures are also partly identical, i.e. their differences result only from the differences between the systems of the two languages), and finally

(v) equivalence on the level of words (the maximum possible similarity which is achieved by making the target text equivalent also at the four abovementioned levels).

House (1977 in Kielar 1988: 65-67, 2003: 93-95), who favours semantic and pragmatic equivalence, turns attention to the impact of the text genre and function on translation. As she considers translation *a cross-linguistic sociocultural practice* (House 1988: 63) she states that the translation is the process of replacing the translandive text with a translative text which must be functionally equivalent. Moreover, she introduces the concept of overt and covert translation. What is characteristic of an overt translation is the fact that the target text must overtly be a translation, its recipients need to realize that they read the translation, whereas the covert translation should be functionally equivalent to the source text. Furthermore, she states that functional equivalence which may have different forms and types is achieved when the translative text reflects the same situational context as the translandive text (House 1988: 63-64)[6].

Catford (1965 in Pisarska/Tomaszkiewicz 1996: 160-161) distinguishes formal correspondence and textual equivalence. Formal correspondence refers to any TL category, which occupies the same or nearly the same place in the system hierarchy of the target language as the given source language category occupies in the source language, whereas textual equivalence is achieved when the source text or its part are considered interchangeable in a given situation with the target text or its part or as Catford (1965: 27) states textual equivalent is:

---

6 "[...] the most important requirement for translation equivalence is that a translation have a function equivalent to that of its original, and that 'functional equivalence' (in its different form and types) can be established and evaluated by referring original and translation to the context of situation enveloping two texts, and by examining the interplay of different contextual factors both reflected in the text and shaping it."

> [...] any TL form (text/portion of text) which is observed to be equivalent of a given SL form (text/portion of text) as well as SL and TL texts or items are translational equivalents when they are interchangeable in a given situation. (Catford 1965: 49)

In order to achieve textual equivalence the identity of contextually relevant features must occur.

Text-pragmatic equivalence introduced by Wilss (1977a/2001: 135) is a sort of functional equivalence as he states that:

> *Text-pragmatic* is here understood within a semiotic framework of reference as a term describing and regulating the communicative relations between SLT and TLT.

Baker (1992), who stresses that she applies the term equivalence for the sake of convenience (1992: 5-6), differentiates equivalence (i) at the level of words, (ii) above word level, (iii) at the grammatical level, (iv) at the textual level that is (a) at the level of thematic and information structures as well as (b) at the level of textual cohesion and finally (v) at the pragmatic level.

Dzierżanowska (1990: 109), in turn, distinguishes three levels of equivalence: (i) equivalence at the level of a text, (ii) equivalence at the level of a translative unit and (iii) equivalence at the level of a word. Equivalence at the level of a text is the situation in which the translator manages to create the target text which expresses the contents and is the formal equivalent of the source text. Textual equivalence is achieved sometimes by splitting long sentences into shorter ones to make the target text more comprehensible and readable for the target text recipient. Equivalence at the level of a translative unit, on the other hand, is the quest for collocations, that is to say, the translator must find the equivalent of the main element of the translative unit, and then start looking for its collocations or looking for equivalents determined by the meaning of the unit in a given micro-context (Dzierżanowska 1990: 109-111). Finally, equivalence at the level of a word may be established by using bilingual and monolingual dictionaries. First, it is necessary to determine the meaning of the word. Next the translator starts looking for its equivalents. If equivalents cannot be found, he may resort to six methods of translating *untranslatable* words: (i) direct borrowings in the source language spelling form, (ii) direct borrowings with transcript spelling, (iii) calques sometimes supplemented with explanatory footnotes or descriptions, (iv) neologisms, (v) descriptive translation and finally (vi) translation by grammatical substitution for instance by replacing a noun modifier with a modifying sentence (Dzierżanowska 1990: 111-113).

F. Grucza (1999: 3) also turns his attention to some other equivalence-related problems of specialised translation:

> The sources of these problems stem from the deficiencies in a communicative potential of given languages: All natural languages are defective in many respects. It is common knowledge that it is not easy to express oneself in those languages in an unambiguous way and that in many cases it is not possible at all. Even the authors of scientific texts often fail to achieve this. Unanimity poses many problems to the authors of legislative texts. Even if they try hard to achieve it, they rarely succeed. It usually happens that on the one hand, in a given language, users including translators have more than one equivalent (word, grammatical category, syntactic structure, etc.) at their disposal; but on the other hand, there may also be no adequate equivalent. In the first case translators must make creative choices, while in the second case the translators themselves must create an adequate equivalent or adopt a foreign one. However, in a situation like the present one, that is in the situation of a mass import of different western ideological (political, economic, administrative, structural, cultural) and material *goods*, a translator must perform work which is comparatively much more creative than the one performed in a relatively ideologically and materially balanced world. (trans. by A. M.)

Klaudy (2003) differentiates three types of equivalence which must be met in order to render a communicatively equivalent translation, that is to say:

(i) referential equivalence which is achieved when the target text refers to the same segment of reality, to the same facts, events and phenomena as the source text,

(ii) contextual equivalence which is achieved when individual sentences occupy the same position in the whole of the target text as their correspondents in the whole of the source text, and

(iii) functional equivalence which is achieved when the target text plays the same role in the community of target text recipients as the source text in the community of source text recipients (depending on the text type the target text may need to transfer the same information, provoke the same / similar emotions, etc.).

1.3.2. Equivalence in legal translation

In general, the approaches concerning equivalence in legal translation are based on the abovementioned equivalence theories. Gémar (2006: 76), for instance stresses that "[...] difficulties arise because the legal norms (or rules) and concepts do not correspond". Tessuto (2008: 286) states that legal concepts are strictly bound with specific legal systems[7]. Furthermore, Tessuto (2008: 286) stresses that "As well as being socio-culturally determined, they are subject to moral values and traditions of the country concerned at a particular point in time".

There are scholars who actually stress the impossibility of finding target language oriented equivalents. For instance, Kjaer (2007: 84) says that legal translators can only try to achieve partial equivalence due to the differences between legal languages which are deeply-rooted in national legal systems. Moreover, in the case of authentic texts the term *absolute equivalence* is introduced which is supposed to be achieved by the EU translators as "[...] each authentic text is supposed to have identical meaning" (Kjaer 2007: 84) as translations are not treated as translations but as original texts having the force of the law. Many other theorists and practitioners of legal translation share this point of view (cf. de Groot 1991: 157 on the impossibility of achieving absolute equivalence and Šarčević 2000b). De Groot (1991: 157) also points out that legal problems are resolved differently in different countries and this affects the process of translation and equivalence[8].

---

7 "[...] intrinsically bound up with the national legal systems and principles in which they are formulated' and 'continually redefined by the legal community, making it more difficult for language users (e.g. lawyers, translators, ...) when a word and concept with an established core of meaning is stretched beyond its ordinary use". Tessuto (2008: 286)

8 "It regularly occurs that legal problems in different legal systems are resolved in very different ways – through very different legal institutions [...] The required equivalence must not only be a *functional* one, but also must be well founded in terms of the technical structure of the legal system." (de Groot 1991: 157)

Goddard (2009: 180) stresses that:

> Approaches to problems of equivalence include, e.g.: simply not to translate the word or phrase; devise a loanword; or use circumlocution, in the sense of roundabout expression or indirect description [...].

and he also quotes Blomqvist (2006:308 in Goddard 2009: 180, footnote 121) who states that as a rule those solutions should be supplemented with some explanatory comments (definitions) to make the reader understand them correctly and such comments are not appreciated by the readers[9]. Šarčević (2000a) shares the same opinion.

Pieńkos (1999: 119) claims that translation is not the search for identical meaning but a quest for situational equivalency and he opts for functional equivalency, which is the most useful and effective in legal translation.

Kierzkowska's model of pragmatic translation of legal terminology (2002: 95-96) provides four types of equivalence which should be applied depending on the translation strategy adopted by the translator on the basis of determination of the type of the recipient and the function of the text. She gives the following definitions of those types of equivalence:

(i) denotative equivalence is the relationship between two statements or terms in two different legal languages each of which implies the other, and at the same time both are associated with the source-language legal reality,

(ii) connotative equivalence is the relationship between two statements or terms in two different natural legal languages each of which implies the other, and at the same time the concepts of the source-language legal reality are associated with the relevant concepts of the target-language legal reality,

(iii) pragmatic equivalence is the relationship between two statements or terms in two different natural legal languages each of

9 "Unless the context makes it absolutely clear as to what the term refers to, all these three solutions will need some explanatory remarks. These solutions are also bound to give rise to disapproving comments from the readers and in particular the legal community. Unfortunately for the sensible veteran translator, there are no other options for solving the equivalence problem."

which implies the other, and the target-language concept is imposed by the target-text recipient or the person who has initiated the translation process, and finally

(iv) textual-normative equivalence is achieved when the translator applies the linguistic and textual norms typical of a given text genre in a given target language.

Textual-normative equivalence must always be achieved no matter which type out of (i) – (iii) above is applied by the translator at other text levels.

Šarčević (2000b: 238-239), on the other hand, enumerates three situations: near equivalence, partial equivalence and non-equivalence. Near equivalence is the case

> [...] when concepts A and B share all of their essential and most of their accidental characteristics (intersection) or when concept A contains all of the characteristics concept B, and concept B all of the essential and most of the accidental characteristics of concept A (inclusion) [...]. In the majority of cases functional equivalents are only partially equivalent. Partial equivalence occurs when concepts A and B share most of their essential and some of their accidental characteristics (intersection) or when concept A contains all of the characteristics of concept B but concept B only most of the essential and some of the accidental characteristics of concept A (inclusion). [...] If only a few or none of the essential features of concepts A and B coincide (intersection) or if concept A contains all of the characteristics of concept B but concept B only a few or none of the essential features of concept A (inclusion), then the functional equivalent can no longer be considered acceptable. In such cases, one speaks of non-equivalence. Furthermore, non-equivalence also occurs in cases where there is no functional equivalent in the target legal system for a particular source concept. In such cases one speaks of exclusion.

For the purpose of this work the division into near, partial and non-equivalence will be used.

1.4. Legal language and legal translation in brief

1.4.1. Legal language as a language for special purposes

Legal language is definitively a language for special purposes (Mattila 2006: 3), or as Cao (2007: 8) puts it "[...] language for special purpose (LSP) in the context of law, or language for legal purpose (LLP)", but legal texts are usually formulated in more than one language for special purposes. It happens so because law regulates different spheres of our lives, and in order to be precise must resort to specialised terms used in given fields (cf. Choduń 2006a: 26, also 2006b, 2007). Moreover, scholars dealing with legal language note that within legal language we may distinguish sub-languages used to formulate texts on a given branch of the law (Mattila 2006: 3).

At the same time Mattila (2006: 106) states that: "Legal language differs from most other languages for special purposes in that it describes a metaphysical phenomenon. Law does not exist in the physical world". The language of law has a very long history. Many scholars have shown interest in various aspects of the language. For a very long time the language of the law has been criticized for its incomprehensibility and isolating character (cf. Rodell 1939, Bryant 1962, Mellinkoff 1963, 1982 in Yankova 2004: 5).

Hexner (1941) points out that:

> Different extra-legal views frequently make difficult a common understanding of even very simple legal concepts. Thus, political and legal doctrine furnishes a striking analogy to the ziggurat tower of Babel. The confusion of tongues and expressions in this particular field is disconcerting and causes unexpectedly important effects.

Still the problems connected with the division of the language of the law or legal language (as both terms on numerous occasions are used interchangeably in pertinent literature) into sub-genres have not been solved. Lawyers have their own classifications which often cannot be applied to a linguistic analysis of the language in question. Moreover, in different countries different classifications are adopted in which different criteria are taken into account.

Legal language has been called differently by different scholars and lawyers. Mellinkoff (1963) favours the name *the language of the law*, Tiersma (1999) uses the term *legal language*, Cornu (1990: 17) writes in French about *langage du droit*. In Poland, in turn, the first work devoted solely to legal language was written by B. Wróblewski in 1948. B. Wróblewski (1948) distinguished two types of the language of the law namely *język prawny* which was defined as the language of legislators / statutory instruments and *język prawniczy* which was used to discuss, describe, and analyse statements in the language of the law and which was called by him the language of lawyers (legal doctrine). Basing their works in legal translation on B. Wróblewski's (1948) distinction, Kielar (1977) suggested the following English equivalents for those two terms: *the language of the law* for the former and *the lawyers' language* for the latter, whereas Roszkowski (1999) wrote about *the language of the legislator* understood as *język prawny* and *the juristic language* as *język prawniczy*.

Previously, legal doctrine used various names referring to the professions practiced by lawyers (therefore they wrote about the language of judges, notaries, advocates, etc. (B. Wróblewski 1948: 5).

Similarly as B. Wróblewski and his predecessors, Gémar (1995-II: 116-122) distinguishes six subdivisions of the legal language that is (i) the language of the legislator, (ii) the language of judges, (iii) the language of the administration, (iv) the language of commerce, (v) the language of the private law and (vi) the language of scholarly writings (doctrine). Gémar recognizes that his classification refers to one legal system (the French one). Therefore, one has to assume that in every legal system the divisions into sublanguages may be different (cf. the division into sub-genres suggested by Mattila (2006: 4), e.g. the language of notarial profession typical of continental Europe countries, etc.). Moreover, with the development of the law (including international and supranational law), national and international legal relations, the language also develops and the divisions into legal language and its subdivisions evolve. Furthermore, the classifications of legal language made by lawyers may differ from those made by linguists. B. Wróblewski's division of *lingua legis* has been modified by Zieliński (1999), who in turn, introduces several sub-categories of this language for special purposes. Let us now present the division of Polish legal language developed on the basis of B. Wróblewski's bipartite division into *język prawny* and *język prawniczy* by Zieliński (1999: 50-72).

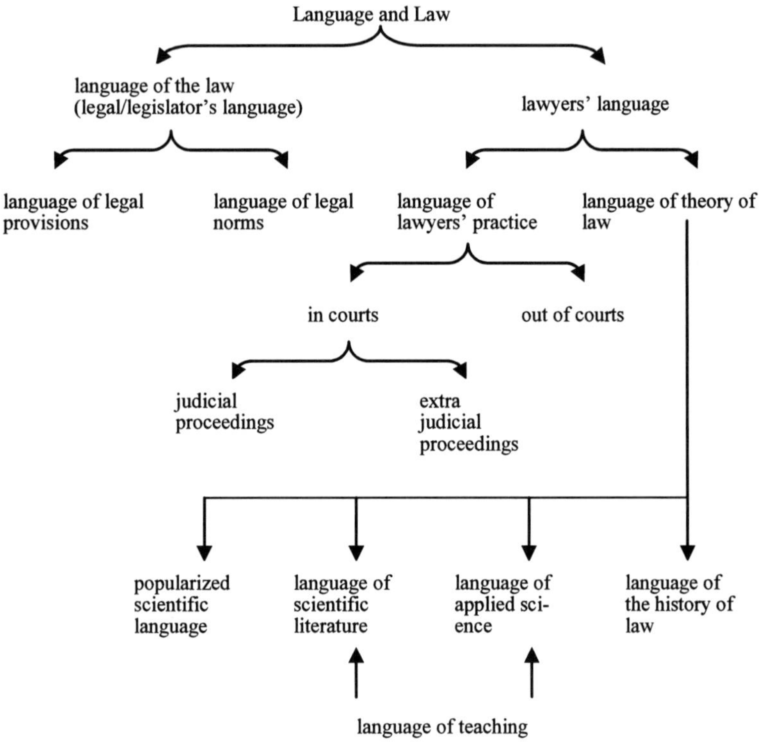

Figure 2. Typology of legal languages by Zieliński (1999: 50-72, figure in Jopek-Bosiacka 2010: 20, cf. Polish version in Jopek-Bosiacka 2006: 18-20).

Zieliński (1999: 63) stresses that the division of the language of the legislator into the language of statutory provisions and the language of legal norms has been introduced by Ziembiński (1960). Additionally, Zieliński (1999: 71-72) has also introduced the classification of circum-legal languages encompassing:

(i) the official language (*język urzędników*)[10], including a hybrid case of the language used by the Polish Ombudsman,
(ii) language of auxiliary fields of legal studies such as legal logic, criminology, victimology, forensic medicine, forensic psychiatry, etc.
(iii) the language of politicians and journalists discussing legal matters, and
(iv) the language of citizens discussing legal matters.

Jopek-Bosiacka (2006: 20, cf. also 2010: 18-20) considers the division sufficient for the purposes of legal translation.

Matulewska (2007: 27-28) introduces the term *lingua legis* as the name for:
(i) the legal language (used to create all legal texts), and
(ii) the legal meta-language used to discuss them.

She stresses that legal language and legal meta-language may be further subdivided for instance into languages in which different genres of legal documents are formulated and corresponding legal meta-languages used to talk about such texts. Finally apart from the language of legislator, we may talk about the language of (i) texts in legal communication which are legally-binding, or create a new or change an already existing legal situation of the parties, (ii) texts which are not legally-binding but may potentially become (e.g. a bill, a draft of a contract draft, etc.), and (iii) texts formulated in quasi-legal language. Quasi-legal language may be easily confused by translators with legal language as it resembles legal language but the meanings of the terms used in texts formulated in quasi-legal language often diverge from their legal meaning.

The approach to the classification of legal language in English literature is however different. In general, lawyers and linguists divide legal language in accordance with (i) the text genre criterion or (ii) the author criterion (cf. Solan 1984, Melinkoff 1963, Tiersma 1999). Garner (2002) writes about legal style rather than legal language.

10 For more on the official language cf. Malinowska 1999, 2004a, 2004b.

Cao (2007: 9) talks about legal language which includes (i) the language of the law, (ii) the language about the law and (iii) the language used in other legal situations, and puts emphasis, similarly as Kielar (1973, 1977), on its normative nature:

> [...] legal language is a normative language. It is related to norm creation, norm production and norm expression (Jori 1994). This means that the language used from law or legal sources is largely prescriptive. The normative language of law derives from the fact that law has the basic function in society of guiding human behaviour and regulating human relations. [...] the language used in law to achieve its purpose is predominantly prescriptive, directive and imperative. Laws are written in language the function of which is not just to express or convey knowledge and information, but also to direct, influence or modify people's behaviour, whether it be a legal enactment, judicial pronouncement or a contract. (Cao 2007: 13)

On the other hand, Mattila (2006: 4) divides legal language into subgenres such as the language of (i) legal authors, (ii) legislators, (ii) judges, (iv) administrators, (v) advocates, (vi) notarial profession, etc.

Galdia (2009: 91) recognizes the typology of legal texts based on the text author composed of:

- Language of statutes (language of legislation)
- Language of legal decisions including fact description
- Language of the legal doctrine
- Language used by lawyers in professional discussions and pleadings
- Language used by laypersons in legal contexts (testimony, comments on legal decisions)
- Language used by administrative clerks.

At the same time he acknowledges that in accordance with traditional linguistics it is possible to divide legal texts into:

> [...] narration, description, exposition, argumentation, instruction. More advanced typologies include informative, appellative or declarative texts. One can classify one legal text as belonging to several types [...]. (Galdia 2009: 91)

Moreover, Galdia (2009: 90) claims that:

> [...] the legal language is mostly perceived as a professional register, i.e. a specific language use based on ordinary language in communicative situations which take place within social (judicial) institutions.

Šarčević (2000b: 8-9) acknowledges that different types of legal texts assume different functions and therefore all typologies based on Bühler's language typology (that is Reiss, Newmark, Habermas) are misleading as they either characterise legal texts as informative or conative. Therefore, she suggests applying the legal theory classification into regulatory (prescriptive) and informative (descriptive) functions (Šarčević 2000b: 11). On the basis of those two functions, she distinguishes three groups of legal texts that is (i) primarily prescriptive (e.g. statutory instruments including statutes, conventions, treaties and other regulations as well as contracts), (ii) primarily descriptive but also prescriptive (e.g. judicial decisions, pleadings, briefs, appeals, petitions, requests, etc.) and (iii) purely descriptive (e.g. writings of legal scholars: legal opinions, law textbooks, articles, etc.) (Šarčević 2000b: 11). Cao (2007: 9-10), in turn, suggests distinguishing four main varieties of written legal texts that is: (i) legislative texts, (ii) judicial texts produced in the judicial process, (iii) legal scholarly texts, and finally (iv) private legal texts.

Considering the criterion of the author as prevailing we may adopt the following classification of the genres of the language of law:

(i) the language of the legislator,
(ii) the language of judges,
(iii) the language of notaries,
(iv) the language of advocates (barristers),
(v) the language of legal authors,
(vi) the language of administrators, etc.

Considering the criterion of the text genre (cf. Mattila 2006, Galdia 2009: 91) as prevailing we may adopt the following classification of the genres of the language of law:

(i) the language of statutory instruments,
(ii) the language of petitions,
(iii) the language of judgments and court decisions,
(iv) the language of testaments,
(v) the language of powers of attorney,

(vi) the language of legal opinions,
(vii) the language of law reports,
(viii) the language of contracts, etc.

No matter which classification we adopt, we have to agree with Maley (1994: 11) who states that:

> In all societies, law is formulated, interpreted and enforced [...] and the greater part of these different legal processes is realised primarily through language. Language is the medium, process and product in the various arenas of the law where legal texts, spoken or written, are generated in the service of regulating social behaviour.

1.4.2. Legal linguistics

The need for legal linguistics has also been noted for a long time. Bautro (1935: 12) notices that:

> The point, however, is that we need the description of the relationships between jurisprudence and linguistics as well as the idea of *legal linguistics*, and especially its main part, namely *legal semantics*. We accept not only a possibility, but also a necessity to form and conduct them. We think that in this way the research on law will be deepened, and the understanding and the formulation of its structure and functioning as well as its logics and action will be facilitated. Moreover, we expect that then we will gain the proper foundation, examination and material for the legal theory and practice. Semantics (and linguistics in general) and logistics (that is logic) while interacting, will manage to elucidate all legal processes, all legal views, and in general logical structure of the world of human thoughts and acts in law. (Trans. A. M.)

However, the first publications devoted solely and specifically to legal linguistics were published in 2006 (Mattila) and 2009 (Galdia). This is mostly due to the fact that in order to analyze legal language one must know both the law and linguistics. Numerous works have been published on various aspects of the language of the law in Poland by both linguists (cf. Lizisowa 1986, 1995, Jadacka 2002) and lawyers (cf. Malinowski 2006, Gizbert-Studnicki 1972, 1978, 1979, 1986, J. Wróblewski 1956, 1984, 1987, Wronkowska/Zieliński 1993, 1997). But hardly any is written by the authors representing both professions (cf. Pieńkos 1999, 2003, Jopek-Bosiacka 2006, 2010) and many of them would greatly benefit from the mutual cooperation between lawyers and linguists. The same refers to bilingual dictionaries which often reflect the profession of the author (cf. Polish-English and English-Polish dictionaries by Bar 1986 H. Jaślan/J. Jaślan 1991, Ożga 1998, Pieńkos 2002, Łozińska-Małkiewicz/Małkiewicz 2005, Myrczek 2006, Ożga 2006, Gordon 2008) and do not answer complex needs of translators.

For the purpose of this volume legilinguistics (also called here legal linguistics) is a discipline which deals with the research into *lingua legis* (the language of law).

> Legal linguistics examines the development, characteristics and usage of legal language. Studies in this discipline may equally concern vocabulary (notably terminology), syntax (relationships between words), or semantics (the meaning of words) of the language. (Mattila 2006: 11)

1.4.3. Legal translation

In accordance with classifications of legal language presented above, legal translation is classified according to various criteria. Having distinguished the various types of legal texts, Šarčević (2000b: 11) distinguishes three main types of text-function oriented legal translation: (i) primarily prescriptive (referring to the translation of statutory instruments including statutes, conventions, treaties and other regulations as well as contracts), (ii) primarily descriptive but also prescriptive (translation of judicial decisions, pleadings, briefs, appeals, petitions, requests, etc.) and (iii) purely descriptive (translation of writings of legal scholars: legal opinions, law textbooks, articles, etc.) (Šarčević 2000b: 11).

It is possible to divide legal translation into (i) the translation of enforceable law (such as statutory instruments and (ii) non-enforceable law (such as legal scholarly works) (Cao 2007: 8) or divide it in accordance with the subject matter: translating (i) statutory instruments both domestic and public, (ii) private legal documents, (iii) legal scholarly works, (iv) case law (Cao 2007: 8). Finally, Cao (2007: 10-12) suggests dividing legal translation into three categories in compliance with the purpose of the target text, that is to say: (i) legal translation for normative purposes, (ii) legal translation for informative purposes and (iii) legal translation for general legal or judicial purposes.

Kielar was a trailblazer in the field of legal translation in Poland. Her research focused on translation of statutory texts mostly. She was interested in Polish-English legal translation and as a result of her research she published two monographs (in 1973 and 1977) and a number of articles on the subject.

The first monograph was devoted to the methods of providing equivalents for Polish statutory terms. She has introduced the contrastive method in establishing equivalents of legal terms based on comparative legal studies proper. Analysing the problem of providing equivalents for Polish legal terminology she suggested the following procedure:

(i) establishing pertinent features of the Polish legal institution,
(ii) searching for a similar institution in the English legal system, next analysing its relevant features in order to determine whether the Polish and English terms are equivalent,
(iii) in case of finding no equivalents in the English legal system, coining descriptive equivalents (Kielar 1973: 19).

The terminology which is analysed by Kielar is considered in two situations: (i) in a specific textual context which is a tool enabling selection of a proper equivalent and (ii) in the context of a given legal system with which the terminology is bound (Kielar 1973: 19-20). She formulated the double-context method designed to find "[...] adequate TL equivalents of Polish legal terms by an analysis of relevant linguistic co-text and cultural and historical context" (Kielar 1977: 37).

Her approach involved the usage of parallel texts understood not as the source text and its translation but as two texts of the same genre formulated in the source and target languages. She stated that:

> [...] in translation the relevant SL and TL data are to be confronted, but not on equal footing: the SL text is to be studied in terms of the TL usage in view of the unidirectionality of translation. [...] the decomposition in content transfer involves the confrontation of relevant realia and law-created relationships expressed in the SL in terms of the TL. (Kielar 1977: 37)

She claimed that: "[...] how to designate realia foreign to the TL receptor poses serious problems. The most important issue, however, is specialized terminology in translation" (Kielar 1977: 36). Despite that view, her second monograph was devoted not only to the problem of providing equivalent terms in legal translation, but to provide adequacy also at the stylistic and grammatical level. Additionally, she noted the ubiquitous trend of source-language oriented translation reflecting source language terminology, grammatical and stylistic devices and criticised it as not justified and not conveying the sense of the message. She advocated using target language devices at the stylistic and grammatical level to express the intended meaning in statutory instruments. Therefore she recommended applying in translation the TL word order, rather than following source language word order (Kielar 1977: 39, 48). Next, she was a supporter of following target language stylistic patterns typical of the target text of the same genre (Kielar 1977: 90-94, 127-130):

> In the course of textual recomposition in the TL certain TL-oriented adaptations are to be made to turn a crude version into a more refined rendition which incorporates TL stylistic features typical of the register. (Kielar 1977: 39)

For instance she criticised the usage of indicative mood to express deontic modality in statutes translated into English and recommended the usage of mandatory *shall* (Kielar 1977, cf. also Kielar/Miler 1993). Discussing advantages and disadvantages of source language and target language translation orientation she stressed that:

> The tension in the translation of statutes issues from a simultaneous gravitation toward the SL and the TL as regards form and content. The SL orientation highlights the original message itself and its local colour, the TL orientation reflects the need of speaking to the TL receptor in terms of his own social, cultural and linguistic background and experience. (Kielar 1977: 36)

Taking about legal translation, Kielar stresses the importance of the successful translation of the message for specific recipients:

> A text is usually translated with a prospective audience in view. The reason is obvious: to attain successful communication the prospective receptor should be approached in terms of his linguistic, social and cultural behavioural patterns. (Kielar 1977: 36)

At the terminological level, she distinguishes various needs and the necessity to apply the equivalent adapted to the needs of the recipient. Thus, if the text is translated for lawyers, the translator must be aware that they are interested in both similarities and differences between legal systems in question. Therefore, she recommends using TL-oriented equivalents whenever possible. "With the assumption that the TL receptor ought to be approached in terms of his culture and experience, dynamic equivalents seem to attain the highest degree of adequacy" (Kielar 1977: 119).

Descriptive and modified target language equivalents are the next step on the scale, serving the purpose of stressing the differences between the source language term and the target language term. To stress existing differences which cannot be rendered by using the two abovementioned methods, she recommends coining a translational equivalent. Finally, she also admits that in some cases it is possible to use a TL adapted self-explanatory literal rendition. The latter is considered better. Formal equivalents and/or literal translations are acceptable "[...] when the text is meant as material for comparative studies" (Kielar 1977: 95). However, she also warns that "[...] certain literal abstract TL renditions are meaningless" (Kielar 1977: 96).

Despite advocating TL oriented approach, Kielar noted the need to preserve the systemic background of a translated statutory instrument in order not to *produce a distorted picture* (Kielar 1977: 39). And consequently she noticed that:

> Each legal term is defined by direct and indirect interconnections prevalent in the system of which it is part. Equivalence between a Polish legal term and a relevant English term can be established with the content as *tertium comparationis*. Legal science provides information on the technical aspects of the legal institutions being confronted in this connection, and on their place in the legal system. Hence what we obtain are in fact quasi-equivalents, representing approximately corresponding values. (Kielar 1977: 153)

Thus, she recognizes the impossibility of rendering the same meaning in the course of legal translation. She advances "[...] a functional pattern modified imitation method applicable to interlinguistic and interlegal confrontations made for translation purposes" (Kielar 1977: 153).

To sum up, she focused on:

> [...] intrasystemic and transsystemic confrontations of legal relationships and a comparison of statutory texts as sources of lexical and grammatical patterns to imitate. By *intrasystemic* we mean *pertaining to a given system of law*, by *transsystemic* we mean *involving confrontation with an element in another system of law*. (Kielar 1977: 37)

As already mentioned, in contrast to many scholars of that time, she advocated preserving adequacy at all levels, rather than concentrating on terminological level solely. At the same, time Kielar also analysed equivalents suggested in available translations. Let us stress once again that Kielar was the first Polish scholar who started investigating legal translation.

Kierzkowska (2002)[11] has based her model of pragmatic translation of legal terms on F. Grucza's translative system, Vermeer's theory of *skopos* and translation steps of Delisle et al. (1999). She has described the *skopos* hand at the discourse disc reflecting the eight discs representing issues affecting the decision-making process of translators and the process of translation.

Kierzkowska (2002: 88) in her model specifies three types of recipients:

(i) close recipients who know or want to know the source-language culture (e.g. business people, lawyers, translators, interpreters),
(ii) distant recipients who do not know or want to know the source-language culture (e.g. tourists), and
(iii) self-determined recipients who use their own terminology.

In the above-mentioned example, the German minority living in Poland would belong to the first group of recipients, namely, close recipients as they would be interested in how the Constitution of the Republic of Poland affects their lives. However, the English translation would rather serve informative purposes as there is no English-speaking minority in Poland which would be affected by the Polish Constitution. Self-determined recipients are usually institutions, e.g. the European Union, imposing their own terminology, which is to be applied by the translator.

---

11 The following description of Kierzkowska's model of pragmatic translation of legal texts has been already published in Matulewska (2007).

Furthermore, Kierzkowska (2002: 90) describes four categories of usage imperatives which are imposed on translators giving the following examples:

1. international usage:
   - *Eng. immovable property* *Pol. nieruchomość*
2. national usage:
   - *Eng. real property* *Pol. nieruchomość*
3. local translation usage:
   - *Eng. real estate* *Pol. nieruchomość* and
4. imposed usage:
   - *Eng. realty* *Pol. nieruchomość*

The translative terminological usage imperative depends on the legal reality in which the recipients of the text function.

The terminology which may be considered to be international is usually gathered, published and accepted by international organizations. In the case of legal vocabulary it is usually possible to create databases containing terminology referring to public and private international law. Such legal terminology can be found in IATE, which is a special terminology database of the European Union. The international terminology is not directly connected to national terms, that is, legal vocabulary used by the European Union is coined in such a way as not to evoke connotations with British or American legal reality.

The national terminology in countries with one official language is hard to determine as there are no parallel legal texts in at least two languages which would be binding (authoritative) under the law of a country. An attempt was made to create a Polish national terminology base by TEPIS. The terminological databases published by the TEPIS Publishing House are called POLTERM Glossaries. They are supposed to constitute an integral part of the Polish System of Unified Terminology POLTERM (Kierzkowska et al. 1992, Kierzkowska 1994, Borkowski 2011) recommended by the International Organization of Unification of Terminological Neologisms affiliated with the United Nations. They are created on the basis of the sources provided by Polish Ministries and institutions. Even though the idea deserves to be highly praised, unfortunately for translators those glossaries seem to be used mostly by TEPIS members.

What is characteristic of local usage is the fact that it is created in a spontaneous, uncontrollable way. Equivalents created in such a way catch on even if they are rather quasi-equivalents. They quickly become nationwide as far as their usage is concerned and the attempts to replace them with better equivalents usually fail. Kierzkowska (2002: 94) gives an example of such a situation in Poland which is the usage of the term *real estate* as an equivalent to Polish *nieruchomość*, while more appropriate in many contexts would be, e.g. *immovable property* because of the roots (Roman law and Napoleonic Code) as well as the fact of its being used by the European Union.

A self-determined recipient expects the terminology imposed by institutions usually in the form of glossaries of equivalent terms. In such a case the work of translators is simplified because they are only expected to apply given terminology.

Once the function of a text has been established, the type of recipients, and the imperative of terminology usage determined, Kierzkowska (2002: 199) suggests that the next step consists of determining the type of equivalence according to the type of translation recipient. The *Model* suggests that the translator apply denotative equivalence for *close recipients* and adopt connotative equivalence – wherever possible – for *distant recipients*. The author proposes to apply pragmatic equivalence for *self-determined recipients*. The *Model* also assumes that, wherever possible, connotative equivalence (*natural equivalents*) should be allowed on condition that a given pair of *potential equivalents* shows a satisfactory degree of similarity to the respective pair of concepts, each of which belongs to a different legal system.

Contrary to other research, Šarčević's new approach to legal translation (2000b) is no longer meaning oriented. What her translation approach intends to achieve is the equivalence of the legal effect of the authoritative source language and target language texts. Although she focuses mostly on cases of bilingual and multilingual countries, in which the function of the source text is the same as the one of the target text, her approach is also applicable to translation in other contexts (e.g. intersystemic legal translation). But she notes that as plurilingual countries have one legal system, translation into the official languages used in them is less complicated as translandive and translative language signs designate the same objects and concepts (Šarčević 2000b: 15).

At the same time she stresses that: "When the same language is used in several states, provinces or cantons, this leads to terminological incongruency within the same language as each regional law has its own system of reference" (Šarčević 2000b: 15).

Šarčević claims that legal translation is in fact an act of communication within the mechanism of the law. As such it refers to the communication between the message sender and message receiver, both of which are specialists in the field.

Apart from text producers she, similarly as F. Grucza, differentiates text receivers. The receivers are divided into two groups: actual and intended receivers (Lyons 1977: 34 in Šarčević 2000b: 59) or in other words direct and indirect addressees (Kelsen 1979: 40 in Šarčević 2000b: 59). "Since legal communication is first and foremost a form of specialized communication, it follows that the actual or direct addressees of legislative texts must also be specialists" (Šarčević 2000b: 59).

The next participant of the act of interlingual legal communication is the translator who "[...] must be thoroughly familiar with legal hermeneutics, in particular with the methods of interpretation" (Šarčević 2000b: 60-61).

The text is another element present in Šarčević's approach. She stresses the importance of the division into authoritative texts and non-authoritative texts. Texts are presumed authoritative if they are binding. "Legal instruments translated exclusively for information purposes are non-authoritative: they are not vested with the force of law and are non-binding" (Šarčević 2000b: 19). If the text of the translation is authoritative it should not be called the target text but authenticated translation (Šarčević 2000b: 64). Authenticated translations *have the same communicative function* as the source legal instrument (Šarčević 2000b: 64). When analysing plurilingual legal texts she remarks that equal meaning is rather unattainable and "[...] the authentic texts of a single instrument are presumed to have the same meaning until proven otherwise" (Šarčević 2000b: 67).

She also acknowledges the importance of the role played by text in translation as "[...] the meaning of legal texts is determined primarily by legal context". Thus the core of the new approach to legal translation is the text as the unit of translation rather than terminology as such because "[...] legal translation is not a process of transcoding, i.e., translating a string of words from one language into another. As in other areas of translation, the basic unit of legal translation is the text, not the word" (Šarčević 2000b: 5).

Moreover, the legal system to which the source and target languages refer are crucial and that is why "When dealing with legal texts, it is always necessary to determine according to which legal system the text, parts thereof, or even individual institutions and concepts are to be interpreted." (Šarčević 2000b: 67).

As has already been noted above, when translating from and into the same legal system, the chances of attaching the same meaning to the text are greater due to the same system of reference. But when the legal system of the source text differs from the legal system of the target text, the translator has to account for the conflicting system of reference. As a result, "[...] the receivers are bound to attach different meanings to the same text if they are interpreted according to different systems of reference" (Šarčević 2000b: 69) and if the system of reference is the same no one can guarantee the intended meaning interpretation (Šarčević 2000b: 69).

One must also account for the social, economic, political and ideological context in which the text has been created. A high level of cultural context may lead to untranslatability (Hegenbarth 1982: 60 in Šarčević 2000b: 70). Therefore, the translators should aim at producing legal texts equal in legal effect (Šarčević 2000b: 71). Consequently, to produce a text that leads to the same results in practice, the translator must be able:

> [...] to understand not only what the words mean and what a sentence means, but also what legal effect it is supposed to have, and how to achieve that legal effect in the other language" (Schroth 1986: 55-56; cf. Šarčević 1989: 286-297; also Lehto 1985: 156). [...] the translator should strive to produce a text that is equal in meaning and effect with the other parallel texts, whereby the main emphasis is on effect. [...] Since the success of an authenticated translation is measured by its interpretation and application in practice, it follows that the translator can best preserve the unity of the single instrument by striving to produce a text that will be interpreted and applied by the courts in the same manner as the other parallel texts of that instrument, particularly the original. This is known as uniform interpretation and application. Thus it can be said that the goal of legal translation is to produce a text that will preserve the unity of the single instrument by guaranteeing uniform interpretation and application. To this end, the translator must

> produce a text that has the same normative intensity as the other parallel texts. (Šarčević 2000b: 72)

The above rule may be applied to the translation when the source and target texts have the same function: "Perfect can be said to occur in the mechanism of the law when the authentic texts of a single instrument are interpreted and applied uniformly as intended by the legislator" (Šarčević 2000b: 73).

Therefore, legal translation is the process of interpretation striving after revealing the intended meaning and legal effect, it aims at resolving ambiguities and avoiding textual inconsistencies and finally should end with determining the highest common meaning.

Moreover, although Šarčević (2000b) states that legal communication takes place between professionals, the author of this work favours Mattila's opinion (2006: 3) who claims that:

> For example, a law normally requires compliance of all the people, while a court judgment relates, first and foremost, to the parties involved in the case. Thus, legal language is not an instrument aimed solely at internal communication within legal profession.

Furthermore, we agree that: "[...] language use in law differs as the context of use is changing" (Galdia 2009: 30) and the consequences of the change of context may be very important. Moreover "[...] the analysis of the language used in legal texts (written as well as oral) requires substantial knowledge of law. This requirement can be fulfilled through diligent legal studies" (Galdia 2009: 34) and translators must know the rules of interpretation but they are not required to interpret legal texts in the same way as judges or other lawyers do it (cf. Šarčević 2000b). Nevertheless, "[...] the professional legal competence is necessary to interpret legally relevant language use" (Galdia 2009: 41) and to translate legal texts successfully.

As shown by theoretical and practice-oriented investigations, the author realizes that some important works may have been omitted or treated marginally. It does not mean that the author finds them less important or not worth mentioning, but in the present world with the number of publications in the field, and in the light of the so-called information flood the limits of this work have not allowed for taking into account all publications devoted to legal translation, not to mention general theories of translation. Presenting the state-of-the-art in legal translation and legal language solely would require writing a separate volume of 500 pages or more. Let us just mention a few authors researching legal translation in Poland and abroad.

One of the milestones of legal translation is undoubtedly the already quoted book by Šarčević (2000b). The author also published numerous articles on the topic (Šarčević 1988a, 1988b, 1988c, 1989, 2000a). Cao is the author of many books on legal translation and law (especially from an English-Chinese perspective), but the most pertinent one is *Legal Translation* (2007).

Alcaraz and Hughes (2002) wrote a very valuable handbook: *Legal Translation Explained.* Apart from that, Alcaraz wrote numerous papers on Spanish-related legal translation problems.

There are numerous articles on the topic, e.g. Kussmaul (1984, 1995), Pommer (2008), Rayar (1992, 1993, 1999a, 1999b).

One cannot forget Bhatia's (et al. 2003, 2008, 2010) input into the field of legal translation as well.

Peter Lang Publishing House publishes a series *Linguistic Insights* edited by Maurizio Gotti (cf. Bathia/Candlin/Gotti (eds) 2003, Bhatia/Engberg/Gotti/Heller 2005, Ch. Williams 2005/2007, Wagner/Cacciaguidi-Fahy (eds) 2006, Bhatia/Candlin/Evangelisti Allori (eds) 2008, Gotti/Ch. Williams (eds) 2010, Giannoni/Frade (eds) 2010).

The scholar dealing with legal language and legal translation in Bulgaria is Yankova, among others the author of the book on Bulgarian-English translation of statutory instruments (2004).

There is also elaborate literature in French (for instance: Gémar 1987, 1995, 2006, Lerat 1995, Houbert 2010) and German (e.g. Sandrini 2009)

In Poland, one cannot fail to mention scholars investigating legal translation between the following language pairs: (i) Polish-English: Kielar (1973, 1977, 1979, 1996), Kierzkowska (1991, 1993, 1996, 1997, 2002, 2005, 2011), Jopek-Bosiacka (2006, 2010), Biel (2007), Witczak-Plisiecka (1999, 2009), Goźdź-Roszkowski (1999, 2012), Piotrowska (2007), (ii) Polish-German: Kubacki (2008), Polish-Chinese: Grzybek (2009a, 2009b, 2010), (iii) Polish-Hungarian: Kaczmarek (2009, 2010, 2011), (iv) Polish-Greek: Gortych (2009), (v) Polish-Spanish: Nowak (2009), and many others.

Moreover, Tryuk (2006, 2007) investigates community interpreting also in legal settings.

There are also publications of organizations gathering court interpreters and legal translators (e.g. FIT publications, or in Poland TEPIS and Translegis publications).

Adam Mickiewicz University publishes a journal titled *Comparative Legilinguistics. A Journal for Legal Communication* (Bańczerowski/Matulewska (eds) 2009, 2010a, 2010b, 2010c, 2011, Matulewska ed. 2011 a, 2011b, 2011c, 2012a, 2012b).

2. Legilinguistic Translatology[12]

2.1. Introductory remarks on translatology

For a very long time translation was considered to be a practical action only. Translatology as a discipline was not considered a science. This approach changed with the emergence of the linguistic trend in translation studies (Jakobson 1959, Nida 1964, etc.). Right now translation studies are a subdiscipline of applied linguistics, with the research domain of translation studies (also called translatology) being translational reality. In the past, translators mainly focused on translative texts but the development of translational theories brought to our attention also other important objects of this reality which is now acknowledged to comprise not only translative texts but also translandive texts, the author of the translandive text, translators, their actions as well as other entities pertinent to the translation process (e.g. the commissioner mentioned for the first time by Vermeer or recipients of a translative text for whom Luther consciously adapted his translation of the Bible). Additionally, it should be borne in mind that the hierarchy of objects may depend on the type of translation and translational situation as translation is the process of ensuring interhuman communication (cf. Popovič 1977, Hatim 1997 (2001a), Tabakowska 1993, 1999, 2001, 2009, Kielar/Lewandowska 1999, Kierzkowska 2002, etc.), which should be effective. Therefore, the effectivity of translation is also a very important factor, which is dependent among others upon the quality of translation.

To be more explicit, translation may be divided into:

(i) translatology, or in other words a theory of translation or a science of translation, and
(ii) translational practice.

---

12 Chapter 2 contains some grounds levelled in the paper by Bańczerowski/Matulewska (2012) which, have been extended significantly and more focused on legilinguistic translatology.

There are various subdivisions of translatology depending on the applied criteria. First of all, there is:
(i) theoretical, and
(ii) practical translatology.

Theoretical translatology is to be understood as the class of theories about translational reality, whereas *practical translatology* formulates translational directives derived from postulates formulated within the former. Finally, *translational practice* is the application of such directives.

A translation theory aspiring to project a general image of the whole translative reality should be universal (adaptable to the needs of various translation domains). Such a universal character of translatology should favour the formulation of more specific theories penetrating various language pairs and language domains (e.g. various languages for special purposes). To put it in other words, the division of theories of translation into general ones and particularistic ones (technical translation, legal translation, translation of poetry, etc.) is based on the criterion of the range of application of such theories.

Therefore, it should be assumed that translatology may be divided into:
(i) general, and
(ii) particular translatology.

Consequently, *general translatology* should give a holistic view of translative reality, whereas *particular translatology* should focus on a specific translative domain.

A legilinguistic translatology is thus a kind of a particular translatology which focuses on legilinguistic translative reality.

The aim of this work is to make a modest contribution to a particular translatology, namely a legilinguistic translatology by surveying a fragment of legilinguistic translative reality but in a tentative and preliminary way. The conceptual structure and propositional content of legilinguistic translatology will be offered for consideration. I shall present a theoretical and a practical legilinguistic translatology and translational practice based on the proposed theory of translation. The former will be encoded in its (i) primitive and defined terms and

(ii) postulates and their consequences. The latter, in turn, will provide directives that is to say sentences which designate translative actions and signify the properties of such actions.

Let us now briefly outline the framework of legilinguistic translatology in more detail.

2.2. Legilinguistic translatology

Legilinguistic translatology, on the one hand, is a subdiscipline of translatology (a particular translatology) and consequently applied linguistics, and on the other hand, it may be considered a subdiscipline of legal linguistics (cf. Galdia 2009, Mattila 2006), and consequently a part of legal theory.

Legilinguistic translatology is the science about the translation of legal texts. The subject matter of legilinguistic translatology is therefore constituted by the intersection of translational reality and legal reality. This intersection will be called here legilinguistic translational reality.

Legilinguistic translational reality is comprised of legal translandive and translative texts, legal translators and their actions, translation commissioners, authors of translandive texts, communicative community recipients of translative texts and possibly other entities relevant to legal translation.

Recipients of legal translative texts are called communicative community recipients (or members) because legal translation is a kind of legal communication occurring among human beings.

Legilinguistic translatology may be divided into:

(i) legilinguistic theoretical, and
(ii) legilinguistic practical translatology.

Legilinguistic theoretical translatology may be conceived as a class of theories about legal translational reality. In other words, it is a class of theories which inquire into, describe and explain various aspects of legal translational reality. Therefore, there may be theories focusing on a specific object of such a reality (e.g. a legal translator or a legal text, etc.).

Legilinguistic practical translatology, in turn, provides rules (called here directives) on how to perform translational actions in given circumstances (it designates actions) and signifies the properties of such actions informing whether they would lead to intended results or not.

2.3. Theoretical legilinguistic translatology

Legilinguistic theoretical translatology, if formally advanced as a deductive system, is composed of four component parts:

(i) the terminological one,
(ii) the propositional one
(iii) the explanatory one, and finally
(iv) the confirmatory one.

Within the *terminological component* of a translational theory the following could be distinguished:

(i) primitive terms (which are terms which may be described as they are undefinable, or in other words their intuitive sense may be explained), and
(ii) defined terms (terms provided with definitions).

The theory operates with those terms and they constitute the conceptual content of the theoretical legilinguistic translatology.

Theorems, in turn, constitute the *propositional content* of theoretical legilinguistic translatology. They are simply statements which refer to properties of entities (objects) existing in legilinguistic translational reality. The propositional component is comprised of two types of theorems (statements) on various aspects of the translational reality, that is to say:

(i) axioms (called here postulates), and
(ii) their consequences.

The former, being true and obvious, do not need any proofs, whereas the latter are theorems which are proved on the basis of postulates, definitions or other consequences.

Primitive and defined terms and postulates (Po) and their consequences form the class of theorems of a given theory.

Entities are facts, events, relations, states, etc. By observing translation reality entities we acquire translative knowledge, which enables us to formulate theorems of different levels of generality.

Consequently, theorems may be divided into:

(i) general theorems (general statements) expressing generalizations about relevant properties of entities, and
(ii) singular theorems (singular statements).

General theorems refer to classes of facts, classes of affairs, classes of states, classes of relations, etc., that is to say they express generalizations about abstract translational entities. Consequently, they provide us with the general principles of legilinguistic translation. *Singular theorems*, on the other hand, refer to less abstract or singular empirical entities. In other words, singular theorems refer to individual facts, affairs, states, relations, events, etc.

Both types of theorems describe the legilinguistic translational reality in terms of general and singular principles of translatology respectively. As a theory is justified by the formulated theorems, they constitute a deductive justification of a given theory.

As far as theorems are concerned they may be divided into various subgroups. For instance, theorems referring to already mentioned translation effectivity signify anystic modality (term introduced in Bańczerowski/Matulewska (2012) and referring to an effective accomplishment of an action). They will be called anystic theorems here and corresponding anystic directives will be derived from them. There are three main types of anystic theorems, that is to say, theorems signifying three main anystic modal meanings:

(i) possibility,
(ii) necessity,
(iii) impossibility.

A theorem signifying the meaning of Translational Anystic Possibility informs that there is at least one corresponding translative significator for a given translandive unit. A theorem signifying the meaning of Translational Anystic Necessity informs that there is only one corresponding translative significator (equivalent) for a given translandive unit. A theorem signifying the meaning of Translational Anystic Impossibility informs that there is no corresponding translative significator for a given translandive unit.

Finally, the *explanatory component* consists in explanations referring to translational reality and its fragments (that is to say singular entities, e.g. objects, facts, actions, etc.) and made on the basis of observations of that reality. The data acquired and confirmed in the process of translational reality observation constitute translational knowledge.

The explanatory component is formulated in terms of an explanation scheme deriving from the hypothetical-deductive method and composed of two parts:

(i) an explanans, and
(ii) an explanandum.

The *explanans* must be composed of at least one general statement and one singular statement with the former in the form of an implication and the latter referring to a singular entity and being an empirical manifestation (exemplification) of the antecedent of the former. The *explanandum*, in turn, is a singular statement which constitutes an empirical manifestation of the succedent (postcedent or consequent) of the general statement. To put it in other words, explanans and explanandum are intertwined as the former explains the latter, and the latter may be deduced from the former. To sum up, a general statement is a general law which is necessary for the derivation of the explanandum and a singular statement must have the empirical content or in other words a singular statement is a statement of antecedent conditions as it must be a logical consequence of the explanans, or in other words it is a singular fact that exemplifies the succedent of the general statement. Therefore, the explanans constitutes an explanation for a given explanandum (empirical fact).

The *confirmatory component*, in turn, has the form of verifiable empirical material. As such is the domain of research into corpora in translation and will not be discussed in more detail in this work.

To sum up, the theory of legilinguistic translation will be composed of the following component parts:

(i) terminological one (constituted by primitive and defined terms),
(ii) propositional one (constituted by postulates, theorems and axioms),
(iii) explanatory one (constituted by explanation schemes), and finally
(iv) confirmatory one (in the form of verifiable empirical material).

The legilinguistic theoretical translatology may also be divided into the following subdisciplines:

(i) general theoretical legilinguistic translatology, and
(ii) particular theoretical legilinguistic translatology.

General theoretical legilinguistic translatology provides general principles of legilingusitic translation (general theorems) whereas a *particular theoretical legilinguistic translatology* provides particular principles of legilingusitic translation (particular theorems, that is to say theorems which apply to, e.g., a given pair of languages or a given type of legal texts).

2.4. Practical legilinguistic translatology

Practical legilinguistic translatology[13] will provide the translator with a set of directives (rules). Directives are derived from corresponding theorems which are formulated within the theoretical legilinguistic translatology.

Directives are simply sentences which:

(i) designate translational actions, and consequently
(ii) signify properties of such actions.

---

13 Practical legilinguistic translatology is the second component of translatology understood here as a theory of translation and should not be mixed with translational practice.

In the case of practical legilinguistic translatology directives designating actions are sentences which will be carried out to achieve the intended translative goals and purposes (effectivity of translational actions). Furthermore, such sentences will also inform or instruct the translator whether the suggested action will lead to the intended results or not. Such directives derived from theorems signifying anystic meanings, elaborated on above, will be called anystic directives.

Translational actions, in turn, are operations of calculation of translative text homosignificators for the corresponding translandive text units for the purpose of rendering translation of a translative text for a given community of recipients.

Translational actions may be:

(i) required,
(ii) recommended,
(iii) permitted, or
(iv) prohibited.

A required translational action is the one which has to be carried out to attain a desired translational goal. Sometimes the attainment of a goal will require the performance of more than one translational action. A respective directive will be referred to as a directive of requirement.

A recommended translational action is one of a few available courses of action which in given circumstances is more beneficial than the others. A respective directive will be referred to as a directive of recommendation.

A permitted translational action is subject to certain circumstances, which means that it will be executed only if some particular circumstances intervene, otherwise it will not be applicable. A respective directive will be referred to as a directive of permission.

A prohibited translational action, in turn, will be the action which will not lead to the attainment of the desired results, and therefore will be considered an ineffective translational action. A respective directive will be referred to as a directive of prohibition.

A directive unconditionally requiring a performance of a certain (required) action will derive from a theorem signifying the Anystic Necessity, a directive permitting or recommending the performance of a certain action will derive from a theorem signifying the Anystic

Possibility, a directive prohibiting a performance of a certain action will derive from a theorem signifying the Anystic Prohibition. It should be stressed here that requirement, recommendation and permission refer to translationally effective actions whereas prohibition to translationally ineffective ones.

Finally, the directives which require, recommend, permit or prohibit certain actions will apply to whole texts (general directives) or their parts (particular directives).

As a rule, a sequence of directives will have to be followed in order to translate a text. *Translational algorithms* are certain sequences of directives (steps) which must be followed to attain the desired translational goal.

Legilinguistic practical translatology may also be divided into the following subdisciplines:

(i) general practical legilinguistic translatology, and
(ii) particular practical legilinguistic translatology.

General practical legilinguistic translatology provides general directives of legilingusitic translation applicable to any pair of languages whereas a *particular practical legilinguistic translatology* provides directives of legilingusitic translation applicable to a given pair of languages or a given type of legal texts. Consequently, every particular translatology will have its foundations in general translatology, or to formulate it differently, will incorporate it. Additionally, a particular translatology will formulate translational grammars for given pairs of languages. A *translational legilinguistic grammar* is understood here as a translational theory for a particular pair of legal languages constituting a theoretical foundation for rendering translative texts translationally equivalent with the corresponding translandive texts formulated in a legal language.

2.5. Legilinguistic translational reality

Since the author will concentrate on translation serving the purposes of legal communication (legilinguistic translation), it is necessary to briefly describe legal communication reality. This reality is the space in which legal communication is performed. In this reality, in turn, certain entities exist, which are necessary for the communication process to occur. The entities include the following:

(i) the author of the source text,
(ii) the source text (translandum or translandive text),
(iii) the communicative community to which the author of the source text belongs,
(iv) the commissioner who commissions the translation,
(v) the translator who renders the translation,
(vi) the translator's communicative community,
(vii) the target text (translatum or translative text), and
(viii) the communicative community of target text recipients.

Those entities have certain properties, which affect the process of legal communication and consequently translation (which may be a part of the legal communication process).

2.6. Primitive and defined terms

The following main primitive terms have been chosen for the purpose of illustrating the theory of legilinguistic translatology:

(i) the set of texts (*Txt*),
(ii) the set of translandive texts (*Tld*),
(iii) the set of translative texts (*Tlt*),
(iv) the set of parallel texts (*Ptxt*),
(v) the set of lingual units (*Lun*),
(vi) the set of significators (*Sg*),
(vii) the set of equivalents (*Eq*),
(viii) the set of translandive text authors (*Tta*),
(ix) the set of translators (*Tr*),
(x) the set of commissioners (*Tc*),
(xi) the set of recipient communicative communities (*Tcc*), and
(xii) the set of translationally relevant dimensions (parameters) (*DTR*).

The first seven primitive terms refer to the main objects of translational reality. Those main primitive terms may subsequently be described by their properties. The sets of properties of those primitive terms will be grouped in the corresponding translationally relevant dimensions which will be described in more detail in the subsequent chapter devoted to the parametrization of legilinguistic translation. The set of communicative communities of recipients of translandum (*Tcc*) will also be elaborated on in more detail later on in subsequent chapters of this work. However, the list of communicative communities provided here is by no means exhaustive and serves only illustration purposes.

The *set of translationally relevant dimensions* can be classified into six groups of dimensions, being respectively related to already mentioned translational reality objects, namely:

a) the source-text author,
b) the translandum, translatum and their component parts,
c) the commission and commissioner,
d) the translator,
e) the communicative community of translation recipients.

The relevant dimensions will be described in more detail in chapter 3, but in brief dimensions are comprised of homogeneous properties comparable with each other and excluding one another. Some dimensions may be merged in hyper-dimensions, with respective dimensions transforming into properties of such a hyper-dimension. Each object may take on only one property out of each relevant dimension to the effect that objects of translational reality are characterized in terms of those properties.

Nevertheless, it should be borne in mind that *a translandive text* is a text which is translated, and *a translative text* is a text which is produced as a result of translation. The terms *translandive text* and *translative text* will refer to any lingual unit being on object of the operation of translation and every lingual unit being rendered as a result of translation respectively. Such lingual units may thus include not only whole texts of a given legal genre but also words, phrases, and sentences appearing in them.

Apart from them we may also distinguish the *set of parallel texts* (*Ptxt*) which will be understood here as texts of the same genre created as originals in both the source and target languages used for the purpose of searching for potential target language equivalents for translandive lingual units.

The *set of lingual units* (*Lun*) refers to words, collocations, and sentences of the translandive and translative text out of which translandive and translative texts are composed.

The *set of significators* (*Sg*) refers to lingual units which signify the meaning of M in the source and target languages. The difference between a lingual unit and a significator is that a lingual unit may be semantically empty, whereas a significator must signify some meaning. Significators represent extralingual entities. Such entities are coded. Codes are understood here as any languages or distinct varieties of a language. Thus extralingual units may be coded in languages by means available in a given language, that is to say, they may be coded lexically, grammatically or lexico-gramatically (cf. Bańczerowski/Grzelak 2012).

The *set of equivalents* (*Eq*) refers to words, collocations, and sentences in the target language which fulfil the requirements of Postulates 8-19 discussed below and thus are considered permissibly complementary or sufficiently convergent to be used in the process of formulating a communicatively effective translative text corresponding to the translandive text. In other words equivalents are such lingual units which are bound by the relation of translational equivalence.

Also some relations constitute a group of primitive terms:

(xiii) the relation of translatability (*trb*),
(xiv) the relation of translatability for a given communicative community (*trbcc*),
(xv) the relation of translatability for a given period of time (*trbt*),
(xvi) the relation of translatability for a given commissioner (*trbc*),
(xvii) the relation of designation (*dsg*),
(xviii) the relation of signification (*sgf*),
(xix) the relation of homosignification (*hsgf*),
(xx) the relation of translational equivalence (*treq*),
(xxi) the relation of translational convergence (*trcv*),
(xxii) the relation of translational complementarity (*trcm*),

(xxiii) the relation of translational divergence (*trdv*),
(xxiv) the relation of translational incommensurability (*trincom*),
(xxv) the relation of equitranslativity,
(xxvi) the relation of a not greater degree of translative equivalence ($\leq^{eq}_{tlt}$),
(xxvii) the relation of a smaller degree of translative equivalence ($<^{tr}_{eq}$).

The following abbreviations will also be used:

T_i – a variable ranging over a set of translandive texts (also called source texts),
T_j – is a variable ranging over a set of translative texts (also called target texts),
S – is a variable ranging over a set of legal text sentences,
S_i – is a variable ranging over a set of translandive sentences (also called source text sentences),
S_j – is a variable ranging over a set of translative sentences (also called target text sentences),
G – is a variable ranging over a set of text genres (e.g. a statutory instrument, a testament, etc.),
CC – is a variable ranging over a set of communicative communities of target (translative) text recipients, that is to say people to whom the translative text is addressed,
C – is a variable ranging over a set of commissioners,
P – is a variable ranging over a set of properties from a given dimension,
D – is a variable ranging over a set of dimensions,
X – is a given translandive lingual unit, and
Y is a given translative lingual unit.

The following brief explanations of the above mentioned terms will be provided to ensure the correct understanding of them.

The *relation of translatability* (*trb*) will connect two heterolingual texts, out of which one being a translandive text and the other one a translative text. As mentioned above, translation is an operation as a result of which a translative text is rendered, and consequently, a translandive text is understood here as an object on which translation operates. Hence, it is a relation binding at least two allolingual units, that is lingual units of at least two different languages. The formula *X trb Y* shall be read as: *X* is translatable as *Y*, or *Y* is a translative unit for a translandive unit *X*.

A given lingual unit of a translandive text may be translated into another language in a number of ways depending on the linguistic potential of a given target language and other factors affecting the process of translation (which will be illustrated with examples in part III of this monograph). In keeping with this we may further discern subrelations of translatability, e.g. (i) the relation of translatability for a given communicative community, (ii) the relation of translatability for a given period of time, (iii) the relation of translatability for a given commissioner, etc. Analogously, the formula *X trbcc Y* will be read as: *X* is translatable as *Y* for a given communicative community *CC*, or *Y* is a translative unit for a translandive unit *X* understandable for a given communicative community. Again, the formula *X trbt Y* will be read as: *X* is translatable as *Y* in a given period of time *CC*, or *Y* is a translative unit for a translandive unit *X* proper in a given period of time. Finally, the formula *X trbc Y* will be read as: *X* is translatable as *Y* for a given commissioner *CC*, or *Y* is a translative unit for a translandive unit *X* understandable for a given commissioner.

The *relation of designation* and the *relation of signification* bind lingual signs which will be called here meaningful units, with the corresponding entities of extralingual reality.

> The entities in question exhibit various properties. These properties are nothing else but entities of a certain kind. The lingual signs may simultaneously designate and signify. By means of designation, extralingual entities are grasped as certain wholes, whereas by signification their properties are reflected upon; and these properties are, in turn, conceived of as meanings signified by the lingual units designating these entities. Thus, the relation of signification connects lingual units with the corresponding meanings. If these units signify identical meanings with respect to translationally relevant dimensions, they will be said to be bound by the *relation of homosignification*. What is more, these units may be tautolingual or heterolingual, and homosignification may be relativized to certain meanings only. A meaning being signified may be *lexified* or *semified*. In the former case it is conveyed by lexical morphemes, and in the latter by semical (grammatical) morphemes. (Bańczerowski/Matulewska 2012)

Translational equivalence, as already discussed, is understood in various ways in different translation theories and approaches. Despite the fact that it has been used by numerous scholars, its meaning remains rather obscure and seems to be conditioned by the type of translation under scrutiny. In this research the *relation of translational equivalence* will bind a translandive text with a corresponding translative text. With regard to the meaning of a text given above, this relation may also bind translandive and corresponding translative lingual units exhibiting a certain meaning, also called significators. As will be argued below, this relation will be relativized to a set of translationally relevant dimensions of a lingual (semantic, pragmatic) and extralingual nature. The formula T_i $treq_D$ T_j will be read as: a translative text T_j is translationally equivalent to a translandive text T_i with respect to a set D of translational dimensions.

On account of types of equivalence distinguished by Šarčević (2000b) and other researchers in legal and specialized translation (cf. Alcaraz/Hughes 2002, Baker 2007, and others), it seems necessary to discern two subrelations within the relation of translational equivalence, viz: (i) the *relation of translational convergence* (*trcv*) and the *relation of translational complementarity* (*trcm*). The formula T_i $trcv_D$ T_j will be read as: a translative text T_j is translationally convergent with a translandive text T_i with respect to a set D of translational dimensions; and analogously the formula T_i $trcm_D$ T_j will be read as: a translative text T_j is translationally complementary to a translandive text T_i with respect to a set D of translational dimensions.

In general, in order for two texts T_i and T_j to be translationally convergent in respect to a given dimension, both texts must take on the same property from a given dimension. If two texts T_i and T_j take on different properties from a given dimension, they are translationally complementary relative to this dimension. If two texts T_i and T_j take on different properties from a given dimension, and take on the same property from a more abstract but not too abstract hyperdimension, then they are permissibly complementary.

Bringing to our attention the classification of equivalence by Šarčević (2000b), for the translative unit Y to be considered sufficiently equivalent to a translandive unit X, both a translandive unit and a translative unit must be either (i) at least translationally convergent relative to all essential dimensions and most secondary (accidental) dimensions (sufficient near equivalence), or (ii) at least translationally convergent relative to some essential dimensions and complementary relative to other essential dimensions and most secondary dimensions respectively (sufficient partial equivalence). Therefore, convergence in respect to all essential (relevant) dimensions presupposes sufficient near equivalence (in terms of this theory the term *sufficient convergence* is used as it nearly never happens that lingual units of a source language and a target language are convergent relative to all essential and secondary dimensions) whereas convergence in respect to most essential dimensions and complementarity in respect to other essential dimensions presuppose sufficient partial equivalence (in terms of this theory called permissible complementarity). Again, it may be said that the relation of translational convergence reflects the idea of the coincidence of two texts in all or nearly all relevant translational dimensions. If two texts T_i and T_j are convergent in respect to a given dimension, they are indistinguishable or do not differ in respect to such dimension. Hence, sufficient convergence, for obvious reasons, will be more desired than permissible complementarity. Complementarity, in turn, as occurring when two texts take on different properties from the same dimension essentially entails (i) the *relation of translational divergence* with respect to a hypo-dimension (that is to say a dimension in respect to which the texts T_i and T_j take on different properties) and (ii) the *relation of translational convergence* in respect to a property taken from a more but not too abstract hyper-dimension than the hypo-dimension.

It should be remembered here that we deal with two levels of convergence and complementarity. The first level is the *trcv* or *trcm* in respect to a given dimension, and the other level is the *trcv* or *trcm* in respect to a set of all relevant translational dimensions. Thus, it may happen that a translandive unit is convergent with a given translative unit in respect to only a few relevant dimensions and in respect to other relevant dimensions it is divergent, and hence still not sufficiently translationally equivalent. The formula $T_i \, trdv_D \, T_j$ will be read as: a translative text T_j is translationally divergent with a translandive text T_i with respect to a set D of translational dimensions

That is why dimensions include not only meaning related properties but also pragmatic properties of lingual units. Consequently, we may talk about equivalence in respect to a given dimension and in respect to a set of all relevant dimensions. Finally, apart from convergence, divergence and complementarity, we may also distinguish the *relation of translational incommensurability* which occurs when one text assumes a determined property from a given dimension and the other text an indetermined property. Incommensurability makes the texts incomparable in respect to a given dimension or set of dimensions. The formula T_i $trincom_D$ T_j will be read as: a translative text T_j is translationally incommensurable with a translandive text T_i with respect to a set D of translational dimensions

Finally, translational convergence includes homosignification as a relation binding two lingual units conveying identical meanings. But convergence is a wider concept than homosignification as it encompasses also pragmatic and extralingual factors of translational enterprise. Analogously, complementarity embraces heterosignification as a component part of the relation of divergence. The relations described above will be illustrated with examples later on. To sum up, the level of equivalence depends on the number of dimensions in respect to which both a translandive text and a translative text assume the same properties, or to put it in other words, the more relevant properties the translandive text and the translative text have in common, the more equivalent they are.

A pair of translative texts (T_j, T_k) may be bound with a translandive text T_i by one out of three already listed relations, that is to say:

(i) the relation of equitranslativity,
(ii) the relation of a smaller degree of translative equivalence,
(iii) the relation of a not greater degree of translative equivalence.

The *relation of equitranslativity* binds two translative texts (T_j, T_k) with a translandive text T_i in the event when the degree of translative equivalence is equal between two pairs (i) T_l and T_j as well as (ii) T_i and T_k.

The *relation of a smaller degree of translative equivalence* also binds two translative texts (T_j, T_k) with with a translandive text T_i in the event when text T_j is translationally equivalent with text T_i to a higher degree than text T_k to T_i. Out of the relation of a smaller degree of translative equivalence the *relation of a higher degree of translative equivalence* may be derived as it is a logical consequence that if the text T_j is translationally equivalent with text T_i to a higher degree than text T_k to T_i, then T_k is translationally equivalent with text T_i to a smaller degree than text T_j. Therefore, there is no formal need to distinguish the relation of a higher degree of translative equivalence as it is unavoidably embedded in the relation of a smaller degree of equivalence.

The degree of equivalence may be calculated in terms of the translational distance between a translandive text and a translative text in terms of the number of dimensions from which both texts take on the same properties (in respect to which they converge) and the number of dimensions in respect to which they diverge and consequently in respect to which more abstract dimensions they are complementary. However, it should be remembered that the number of dimensions is a preliminary criterion to calculate the distance. A hierarchy of importance of particular dimensions will be taken into consideration as some of them are of primary importance, some are of secondary importance, and others may be of marginal importance or even may be irrelevant. The application of non-equal weighting of dimensions should be taken into account; however, at this stage of research it cannot be done, as it requires more extensive corpora analysis and hence a closer examination of this problem will not be attempted here. Moreover, it should be determined whether the weights should be based on statistical results of corpora analysis (a statistical method) or on expert opinions (a participatory method), or a combination of both. Finally, it seems justified, when determining a hierarchy of dimensions to include pragmatic aspects which may result in various dimension hierarchies in various communicative situations.

The communicative aspect of legilinguistic translational practice is very important as texts are being rendered for certain recipients (communicative communities). In order to ensure effective communication the needs, expectations and knowledge of recipients must be accounted for in the process of translation. Three relations will be proposed here to apprehend such pragmatic aspects, that is to say:

(xxviii) the relation of translative comprehension (*trcp*),
(xxix) the relation of translational adaptation for (*trap*),
(xxx) the relation of translative adjustment (*tradj*), and
(xxxi) the relation of translative acceptability (*tracc*).

The relation of *translative comprehension* holds between a recipient of a translative text and this text itself when the recipient understands the translative text. The relation may apply to the whole text or its parts (e.g. sentences, terms, etc.).

The *relation of translative adaptation* binds a translandive text T_i, a translative text T_j, and a recipient community C subject to the adjustment of T_j to the needs of this community resulting from the differences between source and target legal systems. Therefore, if T_j has been adjusted to the requirements of the community C resulting from legal reality in which such community functions, then the relation of translative adaptation holds. Finally, it should be stressed here that it is possible to create for one translandive text T_i various tautolingual translative texts differing from each other as a result of adaptation to the requirements of various tautolingual communities (cf. Po. 18 below).

The *relation of translative acceptability* binds a recipient and a translative text. A translative text is acceptable if it meets the recipient's communicative needs, purposes, and other expectations. This relation may hold between the whole text and a recipient as well as only a part of text and a recipient. Finally, it may happen that the translandive text and the corresponding translative text will be equivalent but not acceptable for the recipient as a result of insufficient or even absent translative adaptation.

The *relation of translative adjustment* binds a translandive text T_i, a translative text T_j, and a recipient community C subject to the adjustment of T_j to the needs of this community resulting neither from the differences between source and target legal systems, nor from meeting comprehension and acceptability requirements. Translative adjustment occurs when the translator transforms translandive grammatical structures into translative ones. Such adjustment process will be frequently encountered in case of translation between pairs of languages from different language families (having differing grammatical systems) (cf. Wojtasiewicz 1957, reprinted in 2005).

In translation we shall distinguish between:

(xxxii) translational procedures,
(xxxiii) translational methods, and
(xxxiv) translational strategies.

Translational procedures will be referred to as procedures of providing (establishing) equivalents for target text at the level of words and syntagms (cf. Newmark 1988: 81-93, Delisle et al. 1999: 191, Wilss 1977a: 110-111). The procedure will depend on the equivalence type required by translation recipients (cf. Šarčević 2000b). I shall describe below some possible translation procedures but shall limit myself to those which are most frequently applied to legal translation, admitting at the same time that there are also other solutions available.

According to Newmark (1988: 81) translation methods apply to whole texts and they include word-for-word translation, literal translation, faithful translation, semantic translation, adaptation, free translation, idiomatic translation, communicative translation, etc. (Newmark 1988: 45-47). In this work, however, a *translational strategy* (or in other words an approach) will be applied to the whole text which is to be translated, whereas the *translational methods* will be applied to sentences of which the text is composed, as it is assumed that in order to produce one target text several different methods may be applied due to the varying degrees of semantic and grammatical isomorphism between given language pairs (a source language and target language pair).

Strategies, in turn, refer to the translation orientation, that is to say we may distinguish two types of main strategies:

(i) source-oriented strategies and

(ii) target-oriented strategies.

A source-oriented strategy means that the translator makes the translative text resemble the translandive text as much as possible by choosing procedures stressing differences between the source and target legal realities and literal or near-literal translation methods.

A target-oriented strategy means that the translator chooses procedures stressing similarities between the source and target legal realities and idiomatic or near-idiomatic translation methods.

Therefore, in compliance with Delisle et al. (1999: 191), a translation strategy will be a global approach to a text or in other words:

> [...] a coherent plan of action adopted by translators based on their intention with respect to a given text. The translation strategy applies globally to any given text and is distinguished from ad hoc decisions such as those regarding the applica-

> tion of various translation procedures. Depending on the situation, translators may adopt a strategy of adaptation or of literal translation, or they may change the text type or modify it as a function of the perceived needs of the target audience. In the latter case, for instance, a translator can decide that a summary of a text will suffice instead of a full translation. (Delisle at al. 1999: 192)

For the purpose of this study we shall refer to procedures as the procedures of arriving at sufficient equivalents. We may distinguish the following defined terms[14] referring to procedures:

a) functional equivalent,
b) denotative equvalent,
c) modified functional equivalent,
d) neologism, and
e) cultureless equivalent.

Functional equivalents also called in pertinent literature connotative (Kierzkowska 2002: 95) or dynamic equivalents, are significators, which replace the source language legal reality translative units with target language terms associated by target recipients with similar entities existing in the target language legal reality.

(1) skarga pauliańska → revocatory action

(2) stół sędziowski → the bench

Denotative equivalents (Kierzkowska 2002: 95), called in pertinent literature formal equivalents, are translative significators for the source language legal reality translative units, which are not associated or not directly associated by target recipients with similar entities existing in the target language legal reality. In other words, such significators inform the recipient that the element of reality in question is different from the reality known to the recipient. The different types of borrowings described above constitute sets of denotative significators.

Joseph (1995: 23) stresses that most texts are translatable because even if terms of the source language and target language are not absolutely equivalent they are still sufficiently equivalent *for most*

14 Some of them have already been discussed in Matulewska 2007.

translation purposes. He compares the meaning of words to fuzzy blots and states that "[...] the blots of L1 may rarely correspond exactly to those of L2" and "[...] law, or at least some areas of it, requires those blots to shed their fuzz and become point-like" (Joseph 1995: 23).

Sometimes the degree of resemblance between the meaning of a source text translative unit and its target text significator is sufficient to satisfy the needs of a given communicative community for which the target text is translated. However, if the disparity between the meaning of a source text translative unit and its target text significator is too great to satisfy (i) the needs of a given communicative community or (ii) the needs of all members of a given communicative community for which the target text is translated, it is usually necessary to modify the target text significator (in the case of partial equivalents) or to coin a new significator. The procedures of modification of the semantic content of the partial target text significator include the following which are also defined terms of our theory:

a) expansion,
b) restriction,
c) two terms or more for one, and
d) the intension or extension of the meaning by pre- or post-modification.

Expansion, restriction, supplying two terms or more for one and the intension or extension of the meaning by pre- or post-modification are methods of significator modification usually resulting from different segmentation of reality by users of different languages. The well-known examples of types of *snow* distinguished by Eskimos or types of *fog* in Britain, which do not have connotative significators in many languages may serve as an illustration of the problem here. The same situation may be observed in legal reality. There are numerous instances in which legislators in different legal systems for some purposes consider different segmentation of reality necessary or sufficient.

Expansion is the situation in which for a given communicative community it is possible to use as a target text significator a hypernym for the source text translative unit, e.g.:

(3) company → spółka

(4) hipoteka → mortage

whereas *restriction* is the situation in which it is possible to use as a target text significator a hyponym for the source text translative unit, e.g.:

(5) spółka → partnership

(6) lease → dzierżawa

Two terms or more for one is the situation in which for a given communicative community it is possible to use as a target text significator a set of hyponyms for the source text translative unit, which together constitute the meaning sufficiently equivalent to the meaning of the calculated source text unit:

(7) spółka → partnership and company

(8) mortgage → zastaw and hipoteka

(9) powołać do spadku → give, devise and bequeath

The *intension* or *extension* of the meaning *by pre- or post-modification* is the situation in which the significator obtained in the course of the application of the translation algorithm is near or partial and not sufficiently equivalent to some members of the communicative community but sufficiently equivalent to others. The degree of disparity may be important and should be stressed. In such cases the translator may use a modified approximate connotative significator in the target text, e.g.:

(10) Urząd Stanu Cywilnego → *Polish* Vital Statistics Office

(11) Urząd Stanu Cywilnego → *Polish* Birth, Death and Marriage Register

(12) Birth, Death and Marriage Register → *brytyjski* Urząd Stanu Cywilnego

(13) Insolvency Act → Ustawa prawo upadłościowe i naprawcze *dla Anglii i Walii*

(14) the Supreme Court → Sąd Najwyższy *Stanów Zjednoczonych Ameryki*

(15) hipoteka → mortgage *encumbering an immovable property*

(16) *pełnomocnictwo do doręczeń* → power of attorney *for document service*

(17) kurator (dla osoby ubezwłasnowolnionej częściowo) → guardian *of a partially incapacitated person.*

The translator may identify system-bound terms only by establishing the meaning of the source text signs and comparing them with target text signs. Moreover, it is necessary to compare the terms with possible significators from the same branch of law. Smith (1995: 187) points out that:

> [...] recognizing a case of absent terminology requires constant comparison between the legal systems of the source and the target languages, as well as being familiar with up-to-date legal literature. [...] In the global legal world, where legal traditions and cultures differ so much that one system uses a legal concept completely unknown or even alien to another system, equivalency must also include cultural equivalency.

The most popular methods of providing significators in the form of *neologisms* for system-bound terms include:

a) different types of borrowings (exotics, loanwords, loanblends, loanshifts (calques), international terms),
b) definition, intension, extension,
c) other types of neologisms.

Haugen (1950: 212) states that: "[...] borrowing is the attempted reproduction in one language of patterns previously found in another".

Exotics (Fisiak 1961a: 108) are borrowings the spelling of which is preserved in the target-language. Such concepts are strictly connected with the source-language culture and constitute significators for translative units unknown in a target-language legal reality.

(18) know-how → know-how

(19) copyright → copyright

(20) gmina → gmina

(21) Sejm → the Sejm

Apart from exotics we may distinguish other types of borrowings with different degrees of morphemic importation and/or substitution. Borrowings which "[...] show morphemic importation without substitution" (Haugen 1950: 62) are called loanwords, e.g.:

(22) Sejm → the Seym

(23) powiat → poviat

(24) dealer → diler

(25) developer → deweloper

Next, borrowings which show both morphemic substitution and importation are called loanblends (Haugen 1950: 62) or hybrids, e.g.:

(26) proxy agent → agent proxy.

And finally, words which "[...] show morphemic substitution without importation" (Haugen 1950: 62) are called loanshifts, *calques*, semantic loans or loan translations, e.g.:

(27) Secretary of State → Sekretarz Stanu

(28) common law → prawo powszechne

(29) sędzia-komisarz → judge-commissioner

(30) Ministerstwo Spraw Zagranicznych → Ministry of Foreign Affairs

Some borrowings are incorporated by different languages and therefore they start functioning as *international terms*, e.g.:

(31) bank → bank (from Italian)

(32) bankructwo → bankruptcy (from Italian)

(33) teokracja → theocracy (from Greek)

It is possible to provide significators for system-bound translative units by conveying the meaning in the form of a definition (a descriptive equivalent). Such a significator may include the source text translative unit (exotic) or not. One is able to distinguish here definitions by intension (incomplete definitions) and extension (complete definitions) (Patryas 1997).

> In applying intension, a non-exhaustive set of characteristics or properties by which the entity described by a term in the source language may be determined and identified in the target language is enumerated. Thus, the intension of *spółka komandytowa* is the set including the following features: *partnership, limited partner, general partner*. In extension, an exhaustive list of characteristic features by which the entity described by a term in the source language may be determined and identified in the target language is enumerated. This type of definition may be applied to a legal meaning of *ryby* [*fish*] in Polish statutory texts where the name is used to refer to *fish* and *crayfish*. (Matulewska 2007: 146)

Definitions may be: incorporated in the text as descriptive significators or provided in the form of a translator's additional comment in (i) brackets, (ii) a footnote or (iii) a special glossary at the end of the translated text.

(34) judge-commissioner (a person who manages and supervises the course of the bankruptcy proceedings in Poland under the Polish Act on Insolvency and Rehabilitation)

Such equivalents give the target text recipient some background knowledge concerning elements of legal reality unknown to him. If they are accompanied by exotics they simultaneously serve the purpose of facilitating further inquiries.

All the above-mentioned methods of providing equivalents for system-bound terms are neologisms. However, there are also *neologisms*, which do not have to be borrowings, e.g.:

(35) assured shorthold tenancy → najem krótkoterminowy z gwarancją odzyskania posiadania

Cultureless significators, on the other hand, are deemed to be terms deprived of the system-bound character and used by various international institutions to describe a certain set of properties typical of many legal realities. Such significators often refer to Roman law or in the case of the European Union are created by attaching a new cultureless meaning to well-known English concepts, e.g. *mortgage* as a method of encumbering only immovable property.

In general one may distinguish two types of Latin-based equivalents in the language of the law that is to say: (i) assimilated borrowings and (ii) unassimilated borrowings. What is typical of assimilated borrowings from Latin is the fact that they penetrate into different legal languages and they often preserve their meaning derived from Roman law.

Unassimilated Latin terms are typical of Polish non-statutory language. Yet despite the fact that the common law system has not been so influenced by Roman law as the civil law system there are numerous unassimilated Latin borrowings in British and American statutory instruments. Unassimilated Latin terms in the European Union legislation are also found.

Polish and English legal realities differ significantly. Nevertheless, Latin still functions in both languages and may serve as a bridge that facilitates the finding of dynamic equivalents.

The fact that unassimilated words and expressions are used in both Polish and English can be very helpful from the translators' point of view.

The term, which may be used to illustrate the procedure of using Latin to find dynamic equivalents, is the noun *zobowiązanie* (L. *obligatio*), which in Polish civil law may include the following types of obligations:

(36) zobowiązanie w świetle prawa cywilnego,

(37) zobowiązanie umowne, and

(38) zobowiązanie z deliktu.

The Latin equivalents for those three terms are respectively the following:

(39) obligatio civilis,

(40) obligatio ex contractu, and

(41) obligatio ex delicto.

Not only are the Latin syntagmas used in English legal texts but also legal dictionaries enable translators to find dynamic equivalents, which are as follows:

(42) civil obligation,

(43) contractual obligation, and

(44) tortious obligation.

There are of course branches of law which are especially vulnerable to the influence of Latin, and thus Latin is an especially convenient tool serving the purpose of providing equivalents. Among such branches of law one may enumerate the law of succession and the law of contracts.

Thus, connotative equivalents are usually associated with target-text oriented translation and denotative ones with source-language oriented translation. Additionally, there are also some hybrid solutions possible oscillating between those two extremes.

2.7. Translational postulates

The set of tentative translational postulates (Po) offered for consideration below reflects some aspects of the propositional content of a theory. In general, postulates may be divided into two main groups, namely: (i) general translatological postulates and (ii) particular translatological postulates applicable to legilinguistic translatology only. Apart from that we may distinguish postulates referring to specific objects or aspects of translational reality.

Postulates referring to translatability

Po 1 – Postulate of the heterolinguality of translatability

Any two texts bound by the relation of translatability are heterolingual.

Po 2 – Postulate of translatability

Every text of one language is translatable into a corresponding text of another language.

Po 3 – Postulate of genre preservation

If two legal texts are bound by the relation of translatability, they have to be of the same genre.

Po 4 – Postulate of the asymmetry of translatability

If text T_i is translatable as text T_j, then it does not mean that text T_j is completely translatable as text T_i.

Po 5 – Postulate of the non-transitivity of translatability

If text T_i is translatable as text T_j, and text T_j is translatable as text T_k, and each of these texts is in a different language, then text T_i is not necessarily translatable as text T_k.

Po 6 – Postulate of the absence of complete homosignification

No two heterolingual texts bound by the relation of translatability are completely homosignificative.

Po 7 – Postulate of the translational distance

The translational distance between texts T_1 and T_n, being, respectively, the first and the last member of a translatability chain (that is, a finite sequence made up of heterolingual texts and such that every preceding text T_i is bound by the relation of translatability with the directly succeeding text T_j) is directly proportional to the length of this chain, that is, a linear distance between T_1 and T_n within this chain.

Postulates referring to equivalence

Po 8 – Postulate of translational equivalence and translatability

If text T_j is sufficiently equivalent to text T_i, then text T_i is translatable into T_j.

Po 9 – Postulate of translational equivalence

If heterolingual texts T_i and T_j are sufficiently translationally equivalent, then they are sufficiently translationally convergent or permissively translationally complementary.

Po 10 – Postulate of translational convergence

If heterolingual texts T_i and T_j are sufficiently translationally convergent (*tr*-convergent), then they are translationally equivalent.

Po 11 – Postulate of translational convergence and homosignification

If heterolingual texts T_i and T_j are translationally convergent (sufficiently *tr*-convergent), then they are sufficiently homosignificative (*hsgf*) (that is, they coincide with respect to the relevant translational dimensions). Thus translational convergence presupposes *hsgf*.

Po 12 – Postulate of homosignification and non-divergence

If two heterolingual texts T_i and T_j are sufficiently homosignificative also with respect to the considered meaning M and are not excessively divergent, then they are translationally equivalent.

Po 13 – Postulate of permissible translational complementarity

If heterolingual texts T_i and T_j are permissibly translationally complementary relative to dimension D, then they are translationally divergent relative to D, and they are translationally convergent relative to dimension Δ, and Δ is not too distant a hyperdimension for D, that is Δ being more abstract than D but not too abstract. (Another approach to a permissible translational complementarity of two texts would take into consideration that they are translationally convergent in a greater number of relevant dimensions than the number of those dimensions in which they diverge).

Po 14 – Postulate of translational quasi-equivalence

If two texts T_i and T_j are translationally quasi-equivalent, then they are translationally divergent and at the same time impermissibly translationally complementary.

Po 15 – Postulate of translational incomparability

If heterolingual texts T_i and T_j are translationally incomparable relative to the considered set of *tr*-dimensions D, then they are translationally incommensurable but not complementary relative to D.

Po 16 – Postulate of translational comparability

If two heterolingual texts T_i and T_j are characterizable with respect to a common set of translational dimensions, then they are translationally comparable. (This is irrespective of whether they converge, oppose or are complementary relative to these dimensions).

Po 17 – Postulate of the homosignification of translative texts relative to translandum

If each of two different tautolingual translative texts T_j and T_k is sufficiently homosignificative with translandive text T_i, then T_j is sufficiently homosignificative with T_k.

Po 18 – Postulate of the situational dependence of translational equivalence

Even if translative text T_j is sufficiently translationally equivalent in one translative situation to text T_i, it is not necessarily translationally sufficiently equivalent to text T_i in another translative situation.

Po 19 – Postulate of the translational feasibility

If text T_i is translatable as text T_j, then T_j is translationally equivalent to T_i or T_j is translationally quasi-equivalent to T_i (thus, there are no non-translatable texts).

Postulates referring to providing translative equivalence

Po 20 – Postulate of terms as translandive and translative lingual units

If a translandive lingual unit is a term, then a translative lingual unit is either a functional equivalent, or a modified functional equivalent or a neologism.

Po 21 – Postulate of near equivalence (intersection)

If a translandive lingual unit and its potential functional equivalent in the target language are sufficiently convergent in respect to all essential dimensions and most secondary dimensions, then they are sufficiently equivalent in respect to a set of relevant dimensions.

Po 22 – Postulate of near equivalence (inclusion of a translative unit in a translandive unit)

If a translandive lingual unit is convergent in respect to all of the properties of a translative unit and the translative unit is convergent in respect to all of the essential and most of the secondary properties of the translandive unit, then they are sufficiently equivalent in respect to relevant dimensions.

Po 23 – Postulate of near equivalence (inclusion of a translandive unit in a translative unit)

If a translative lingual unit is convergent in respect to all of the properties of a translandive unit and the translandive unit is convergent in respect to all of the essential and most of the secondary properties of the translative unit, then they are sufficiently equivalent in respect to relevant dimensions.

Po 24 – Postulate of partial equivalence (intersection)

If a translandive lingual unit and its potential functional equivalent in the target language are sufficiently convergent or permissibly complementary in respect to all essential properties from relevant dimensions and some secondary properties, then they are not sufficiently equivalent in respect to a set of relevant dimensions unless the translative unit is modified to diminish the distance between the units or a sufficiently equivalent term is coined.

Po 25 – Postulate of partial equivalence (inclusion of a translative unit in a translandive unit)

If a translandive lingual unit shares all of the properties of a translative unit and the translative unit only most of the essential and some of the secondary properties of the translandive unit, then they are not sufficiently equivalent in respect to relevant dimensions unless the translative unit is modified to diminish the distance between the units.

Po 26 – Postulate of partial equivalence (inclusion of a translandive unit in a translative unit)

If a translative lingual unit shares all of the properties of a translandive unit and the translandive unit only most of the essential and some of the secondary properties of the translative unit, then they are not sufficiently equivalent in respect to relevant dimensions, unless the translative unit is modified to diminish the distance between the units.

Po 27 – Postulate of non-equivalence (intersection)

If a translandive lingual unit and its potential functional equivalent in the target language are sufficiently convergent or permissibly complementary in respect to only a few essential properties, then they are not sufficiently equivalent in respect to a set of relevant dimensions.

Po 28 – Postulate of non-equivalence (intersection of secondary dimensions)

If a translandive lingual unit and its potential functional equivalent in the target language are sufficiently convergent or permissibly complementary in respect to only secondary properties, then they are not sufficiently equivalent in respect to a set of relevant dimensions.

Po 29 – Postulate of non-equivalence (inclusion of a translative unit in a translandive unit)

If a translandive lingual unit shares all of the properties of a translative unit and the translative unit only a few of the essential properties of the translandive unit, then they are not sufficiently equivalent in respect to relevant dimensions.

Po 30 – Postulate of non-equivalence (inclusion of a translandive unit in a translative unit)

If a translative lingual unit shares all of the properties of a translandive unit and the translandive unit only a few of the essential properties of the translative unit, then they are not sufficiently equivalent in respect to relevant dimensions.

Po 31 – Postulate of zero equivalence (lack of similarity between source and target legal realities)

Absolute legal system divergence occurs when there is no functional equivalent in the target legal system for a particular translandive unit which is sufficiently convergent or permissibly complementary in respect to any dimensions.

Po 32 – Postulate of collocations as translandive and translative lingual units

If a translandive lingual unit is a collocation, then a translative lingual unit is based on a functional equivalent.

Po 33 – Postulate of texts as translandive and translative lingual units

If a translandive lingual unit is a text composed of sentences, then a translative lingual unit conforms to the grammatical rules of structuring texts of a given genre in a target text.

Po 34 – Postulate of translation in the absence of a corresponding translative text genre

If a translandive lingual unit is a text composed of sentences and there is no corresponding genre of text in the translative legal reality, then a translative lingual unit shall conform to the grammatical rules of structuring texts of a closest hyper-genre in respect to the translative text existing in a translative legal reality.

Postulates referring to translational adaptation

Po 35 – Postulate of the adaptive preservation of translatability

If text T_i is translatable as T_j, and T_j is translationally adapted as T_k, then T_i is translatable as T_k.

Po 36 – Postulate of adaptation and comprehension

If a translative text has been adapted to the requirements of the recipient, then the recipient understands this text.

Po 37 – Postulate of acceptability and comprehension

If a translative text is acceptable to the recipient, then this text is also understandable to the recipient and preserves the intended meaning of the translandive text sufficiently accurately.

Postulates referring to the translator

Po 38 – Postulate of translator and comprehension

If *h* translated text T_i as text T_j, then *h* understands both these texts.

Po 39 – Postulate of translator's idiolect impact on translation

If the translandive text is translated by different translators, then each translative text produced by a different translator is potentially different linguistically from each other.

Po 40 – Postulate of the time of translation impact on translation

If the translandive text is translated at different times, then each translative text produced at different time is potentially different linguistically from each other.

Po 41 – Postulate of translator's experience and knowledge impact on translation

The more experienced and knowledgeable the translator is in the field of translation, the higher quality translations he potentially renders.

Po 42 – Postulate of the impact of the time factor on translation

The more time the translator devotes to rendering translation, the higher quality translations he potentially produces.

Po 43 – Postulate of the impact of the observation of translation steps on the quality of translation

If the translator fails to observe the steps of translation, the lower quality of translation he produces with each non-observed step.

Postulates referring to the commissioner

Po 44 – Postulate of commissioner's impact on translation

The more willing to share information on the communicative community of recipients the commissioner is, the higher degree of adjustment and adaptation of translation to the requirements of such community the translator potentially achieves.

Postulates referring to recipients of translative texts

Po 45 – Postulate of a specialist as a recipient of a translative text

If a recipient of a translative text is a specialist in the field of law, then the recipient expects a higher degree of precision revealing legal system differences in the process of legal communication.

Po 46 – Postulate of a non-specialist as a not legally affected recipient of a translative text

If a recipient of a translative text is not a specialist in the field of law, then the recipient expects a lower degree of precision in the process of legal communication when the recipient's legal status is not directly affected by the contents of the translative text.

Po 47 – Postulate of a non-specialist as a legally affected recipient of a translative text

If a recipient of a translative text is not a specialist in the field of law, then the recipient expects a higher degree of precision in the process of legal communication when the recipient's legal status is directly affected by the contents of the translative text.

Po 48 – Postulate of a recipient of a translative text operating in translandive legal reality

If a recipient of a translative text is to operate in the translandive legal reality, then the recipient expects a higher degree of precision revealing legal system differences in the process of legal communication.

General legilinguistic translatological postulates

Po 49 – Postulate of interdisciplinarity of legilinguistic translation

Legilinguistic translation is interdisciplinary as it intersects law, linguistics and usually some other field.

Po 50 – Postulate of the impact of legal system differences on translation

The more differences there are between the legal system reflected in a translandive text and a legal system of the target language, the more difficult the process of translation is.

[Numerous/most translation difficulties result from differences between the source language legal system and the target language legal system.]

Po 51 – Postulate of legal effect (consequences) of plurilingual legislation

If the translandive text and translative text belong to the set of plurilingual legislation, then the translation is considered effective if the translandive text and translative text have the same legal effect (consequences).

Po 52 – Postulate of legal effect of the translandive text and informative content of the translative text

If the translandive text is binding, then the translative text is communicatively successful if it conveys the informative content about the legal effect (consequences) of the translandive text

Po 53 – Postulate of legal effect of the translative text and informative content of the translandive text

If the translative text is binding and the translandive text is informative, the translative text is communicatively and legally successful if it conveys the informative content about the intended legal effect (consequences) of the translandive text.

Po 54 – Postulate of communicative effectiveness

If a translative text is comprehended in the desired way, then the communication is effective.

Po 55 – Postulate of the impact of the quality of translandive text on the quality of translative text

The lower the quality of a translandive text is, the more difficult it is to render a high quality translative text.

Po 56 – Postulate of the effect of language potential on translation
Numerous translation difficulties result from differences in the communicative potential of the source and target languages, especially when the potential of the latter is limited in comparison with the former.

The above list may be treated as tentative postulates for general theoretical translatology.

Although Jakobson (1959) distinguishes interlingual, intralingual and intersemiotic translation, the present study will employ a narrower approach in the wake of which the relation of translatability shall always hold between two allolingual texts (Po 1), that is a translandive text T_i formulated in L_i and a translative text T_j formulated in L_j. Translation is understood here as an operation of mapping a translandive text T_i formulated in L_i onto a corresponding translative text T_j formulated in L_j.

When dealing with translation it is necessary to assume that all texts are translatable at least to some extent. Postulate 2 presupposes that even if 1:1 translation may not be possible, some translational approximation of every (legal) text is feasible. Such approximation may not always result in the achievement of full equivalence but still may be translationally acceptable for its recipients. Finally, in the event of the lack of suitable lingual unit in the target language for a translandive lingual unit, the translator may apply procedures (or techniques) of providing significators (cf. Vinay/Darbelnet 1966, Kielar 1973, 1977, Šarčević 2000b, Alcaraz/Hughes 2002, Kierzkowska 2002, Newmark 1982, 1988, 1991, *etc.*) which especially at the initial stage of use may be only quasi-equivalent (cf. Po 13).

Postulate 3 informs about the need to preserve the text genre in the process of legal translation. All transformations which are made in the process of translation shall not result in the change of the genre.

Under postulate 4 translatability is not symmetrical as a relation. It is especially visible in the case of translating a text formulated in terms of one legal language system into a text formulated in terms of another legal language system. It stems from the fact that the meanings of translandive and translative lingual units are hardly identical (cf. earlier remarks on the lack of full equivalence in legal translation). For instance, although the term *korporacja* may be translated into English as *corporation*, it will not always be the other way round, as in the case of the American legal system it may also be translated as *spółka kapitałowa*, which under the British legal system is called *company*.

Postulate 5 refers to the observed phenomenon of message distortion risk resulting from re-translation (translating a text from a translation through a pivot language or the so-called relay-translation). In general, the length of the translatability chain is directly proportional to the risk of message distortion, or to put it in other words, the risk of distortion increases with the length of the translatability chain (under Po 17) (on the quality of translation and retranslation cf. Hejwowski 2004, Kopczyński/Kizeweter 2009, and others).

Postulate 6, analogously to postulate 2, refers to the approximation of translatability at the level of homosignification. (cf. Jospeh 1995: 23, Smith 1995: 187, Šarčević 2000b: 15, 236, 238-239)

Postulate 7 touches upon the problem of retranslation (also called indirect translation or intermediate translation) in the process of which each next retranslation is more distant from the initial translandive text (cf. inter alia Toury 1980, 1995(2001), Gutt 1991, 2000(2004b), Sperber/Wilson 1986, Hickey 1998 (2001), J. Williams/Chesterman 2002 (2007), Dollerup 2006(2007), Hatim/Munday 2004, Bańczerowski/Grzelak 2012 in press). Although not recommended in translational practice, it is still rendered due to different limitations for instance resulting from the lack of bilingual dictionaries within a given pair of languages, political and religious reasons, restricted access to the original source text, etc. However, the translator should be aware of the increased risk of meaning distortions which occur in retranslations.

Postulate 8 refers to the already mentioned problem of the lack of full equivalence or correspondence of legal institutions existing in different countries with differing legal systems (cf. Šarčević 2000b: 238-239, Kunz 1995, Rayar 1993). Consequently, the term sufficient translational equivalence is introduced which is understood here as an appropriate degree of equivalence between a translandive text and a corresponding translative text which entails among others the fulfilment of the requirement of comprehension and acceptability by the recipient communicative community.

Postulates 9-13 refer to the translational convergence and complementarity. Those two relations are crucial for the purpose of achieving sufficient translational equivalence. Let us illustrate them through a few examples.

In accordance with Postulate 9 if two allolingual units are sufficiently translationally equivalent, they are either sufficiently translationally convergent or permissibly complementary. In Polish *spadkodawca* refers to both *a testator* (that is a person who draws up a testament) and *an intestate* (that is a person who fails to draw up a testament). In Poland the former is called *spadkodawca testamentowy* and the latter *spadkodawca ustawowy*. In British and American statutes, however, there is also one more term used to name both, that is *the deceased*, which may be considered an equivalent for *spadkodawca*. But it should also be borne in mind, that the Polish legislator in the Civil Code, Book IV, titled Succession uses the term *zmarły* (a person who died). *Zmarły* and *the deceased* are convergent and hence sufficiently equivalent. The pair *spadkodawca* and *the deceased* is, on the other hand, complementary, as the term *the deceased* has a broader meaning than *spadkodawca*. The Polish term is used with reference to the law of succession only, and the English one may be encountered in texts devoted to many branches of law. Finally, the pairs *a testator* and *spadkodawca testamentowy* as well as *an intestate* and *spadkodawca ustawowy* are convergent and sufficiently equivalent (under Po 10). As stated in Postulate 11 if terms are convergent, they must be homosignificative, whereas in the event of complementarity we deal with inclusion, that is a situation in which the meaning of hypernym includes the meaning of hyponym. Moreover, permissible complementarity is the situation in which we may use the pair hypernym-hyponym as sufficient equivalents for legal communication purposes, for instance when the context clearly indicates that the text refers to the law of succession, the English-Polish pair *the deceased – spadkobierca* may be deemed sufficiently equivalent. Convergence may also be achieved by supplying in the translandive text two hyponyms (or more) if they exhaust the meaning of the translandive lingual unit, or the other way round, e.g. (i) the English terms *fingers and toes* for the Polish noun *palce* (which if not postmodified by indicating the limb to which they are attached may mean both) or (ii) the English noun *lease* which may be translated into Polish as *najem* and *dzierżawa*. As stated above, homosignification is a narrower term than convergence. Therefore homosignificative terms may be considered translationally equivalent only if they do not diverge excessively. For instance, they may diverge in respect to the dimension of lect. If one of the terms is a technical term, used in the language of the law only, and the other one is homosignificative but used in the colloquial language, they are homosignificative but not necessarily considered sufficiently equivalent in a given communicative situation. For instance the English term *adoption* is homosignificative with two Polish terms, namely *adopcja* and *przysposobienie*, but the latter is a legal term whereas the former is used in common speech. In the event of translating Birth, Death and Marriage certificates into Polish only *przyposobienie* would be considered sufficiently equivalent, but when interpreting in the courtroom for a person not knowing legal language it may be the other way round. All in all, *adopcja* and *przysposobienie* diverge in respect to the dimension of lect (Po 12) and converge in respect to other dimensions so the relevance of that dimension in a particular translational situation will be a determining factor in deciding which of the two would be sufficiently equivalent (Po 13). Apart from that, we may have terms which are considered homosignificative in colloquial language but not in the language of the law.

Complementarity and convergence are relations which are strictly related with dimensions, therefore some more examples may be found in subsequent chapters.

Under Postulate 14 if two texts diverge, that is to say, one of them assumes an indetermined property from translationally relevant dimension and the other one a determined property, they are impermissibly translationally complementary and thus quasi-equivalent. It means that if we cannot determine the property assumed by the text, we cannot compare them (Po 15). For instance, if a translandive text is of unknown genre, and we cannot determine the branch of law to which it belongs (for instance due to the fact that it has been partially destroyed and what the translator has at her disposal is just a preserved fragment) it may be impossible to find an equivalent for a polysemous translandive term. Among such English polysemous terms we may enumerate *claim*, *estate*, and many others (cf. examples from subsequent chapters). To sum up, it is a situation when the translator is unable to state complementarity impermissible and the more so permissible between the considered lingual units of a translandive and translative texts.

Postulate 15 may also refer to texts which due to numerous translational problems (errors or mistakes) including omissions, additions and other meaning distortions are comparable but ineffective translationally to such an extent that they may be misleading or even incomprehensible for the recipient community.

On the other hand, postulate 16 refers to situations in which a translandive text is comparable with a translative text. Such situations take place when both texts in respect to a given set of dimensions either converge, or are complementary. Even if they diverge in respect to one dimension, they can still be comparable in respect to some relevant hyper-dimension in reference to which they are complementary or other relevant dimensions in respect to which they converge. Analogously, incommensurability may refer to one dimension only and in the event of other dimensions convergence or complementarity may occur enabling us to arrive at sufficient convergence or permissible complementarity irrespective of incommensurability relative to one dimension.

Under Po 17, despite the lack of complete homosignification, we may still encounter two translative texts which are sufficiently homosignificative with one and the same translandive text. Even if those translative texts have been adapted and adjusted to different communicative communities of recipients they are still sufficiently homosignificative in respect to each other.

Additionally, it is acknowledged that translative texts must be situation sensitive (under Po 18 referring to situational dependence of translatability) which means that there is no one universal version of translative text suitable for all communicative occasions, or to put it in other words, one translative text which is sufficiently translationally equivalent in onc communicative situation, may not be deemed sufficiently equivalent in another. Therefore, due to the fact that legal translation serves communicative purposes, there is a need to adjust and adapt it to the requirements of the recipient communicative community as well as make it comprehensible and acceptable for such recipients.

In general, in order to talk about translation we need to assume that translation is feasible, possible of performance. Therefore, postulate 19 refers to the relation of equivalence (Po 9 and others) and quasi-equivalence (Po 14) where texts diverge.

If a translational unit is a term (Po 20), then the translator has at his disposal three main procedures of providing sufficient translative equivalents that is to say applying a functional equivalent (if it is sufficiently convergent with the translandive term), modifying such an equivalent to make it sufficiently equivalent or coining a neologism (for instance in the form of a borrowing or a descriptive equivalent, etc.).

Under Po 21 if a translandive lingual unit and its potential functional equivalent in the target language are convergent in respect to all essential and most secondary properties (or in other words share all of their essential and most of their accidental characteristics), then they are sufficiently equivalent in respect to a set of relevant dimensions and such a translative unit may be considered sufficiently equivalent to be used in the target text. It should be stressed here that relevant dimensions are such dimensions which are vital for conveying the content of the message to the communicative community of translation recipients. Therefore, properties from a dimension important for one community (and thus relevant) may not be important for another and thus irrelevant. Among such sufficiently equivalent pairs we may enumerate the English term *contract of sale* and its Polish functional equivalent *umowa sprzedaży*. Both terms assume the same properties from dimensions described in more detail in chapter 3 (among others the branch of law which is contract law, lect, etc.). Whereas, the pair *contract of sale* and *kontrakt sprzedaży* would not be considered sufficiently equivalent for legal translation purposes as they are only complementary in respect to the dimension of lect as the former assumes the property of legal lect and the latter of colloquial or economic lect. So if the dimension of the lect is considered relevant and the property taken on from it essential, then either under Po 24 the Polish term must be modified or under Po 27 another term which would be sufficiently equivalent must be found or coined.

Under Po 22 if a translandive lingual unit contains all of the characteristics of a translative unit and the translative unit all of the essential and most of the accidental characteristics of the translandive unit, then they are sufficiently equivalent in respect to relevant dimensions.

Under Po 23 if a translative lingual unit contains all of the characteristics of a translandive unit and the translandive unit all of the essential and most of the accidental characteristics of the translative unit, then they are sufficiently equivalent in respect to relevant dimensions.

Po 24 states that if a translandive lingual unit and its potential functional equivalent in the target language are sufficiently convergent or permissibly complementary in respect to all essential properties from relevant dimensions and some secondary properties (or in other words share all of their essential and some of their accidental characteristics), then they are not sufficiently equivalent in respect to a set of relevant dimensions unless the translative unit is modified to diminish the distance between the units.

Under Po 25 if a translandive lingual unit contains all of the characteristics of a translative unit and the translative unit only most of the essential and some of the accidental characteristics of the translandive unit, then they are not sufficiently equivalent in respect to relevant dimensions unless the translative unit is modified to diminish the distance between the units.

Under Po 26 if a translative lingual unit contains all of the characteristics of a translandive unit and the translandive unit only most of the essential and some of the accidental characteristics of the translative unit, then they are not sufficiently equivalent in respect to relevant dimensions, unless the translative unit is modified to diminish the distance between the units.

Postulate 22 may be illustrated with the pair *syndyk* and *trustee in bankruptcy*. *Syndyk* is the Polish term used in insolvency law to refer to the person who administers and liquidates the estate of the insolvent debtor no matter whether the debtor is a natural or legal (artificial) person. On the other hand, *trustee in bankruptcy* in England and Wales is a person who performs similar functions but only in reference to the debtors who are natural persons. Therefore, if the property of the type of person to which the proceedings apply in which a given official takes part is secondary for the translation recipient, then the terms may be considered sufficiently equivalent (Po 22). However, if that property is relevant for translation recipients, then under postulate 25 we need to make up for the translative distance between the terms by modifying the translative term, for instance in the following manner: *trustee in bankruptcy for natural and legal persons*. If the translandive unit would be the English term *trustee in bankruptcy* and the translative one *syndyk*, then analogously we would apply postulate

23 if the dimension in question was of secondary importance or postulate 26 if it was of importance. In the event of postulate 26 we would need to modify the functional equivalent in Polish, e.g. *syndyk ustanawiany dla osób fizycznych*.

Postulates 27-31 refer to non-equivalence. Under Po 27 if a translandive lingual unit and its potential functional equivalent in the target language are sufficiently convergent or permissibly complementary in respect to only a few essential properties (or in other words share only a few of their essential characteristics), then they are not sufficiently equivalent in respect to a set of relevant dimensions. Consequently, under Po 28 if a translandive lingual unit and its potential functional equivalent in the target language are sufficiently convergent or permissibly complementary in respect to only secondary properties (or in other words share none of their essential characteristics), then they are not sufficiently equivalent in respect to a set of relevant dimensions.

Among such non-equivalent pairs (Po 27) we may enumerate the English term *common law* and the frequently applied improper equivalent in Polish *prawo zwyczajowe*. Both terms refer to the system of law which developed in Europe. However, as Sczaniecki (1985: 217-218) remarks, the common law system cannot be treated as a customary law, because from the Middle Ages this legal system was unified and applied nationwide in the form of precedents created by the Crown Courts. At the same time, a customary law was applied locally by a given community inhabiting a given territory, often limited to a village or a group of villages. Thus, *common law* and *prawo zwyczajowe* taking on the same properties from only a few relevant dimensions cannot be treated as sufficiently equivalent.

A similar situation occurs when a translandive unit and a translative one share only secondary properties, that is to say their referential and pragmatic meanings diverge in respect to essential properties from relevant dimensions.

Postulate 29 states that if a translandive lingual unit contains all of the characteristics of a translative unit and the translative unit only a few of the essential characteristics of the translandive unit, then they are not sufficiently equivalent in respect to relevant dimensions. Consequently, Po 30 states that if a translative lingual unit contains all of the characteristics of a translandive unit and the translandive unit only a few of the essential characteristics of the translative unit, then they are not sufficiently equivalent in respect to relevant dimensions.

Postulates 29 and 30 are again cases of inclusion of the translative term in the translandive one and the other way round respectively. Such a situation takes place in the case of the term *office holder* used in insolvency law in England and Wales and any possible type of an office holder appearing in the Polish legal system. As in Polish there is no term which would encompass the broad meaning of the English one we deal in this case with the relation of hypernym-hyponym. The English hypernymic term contains the Polish hyponimic terms but nevertheless the differences between the English and Polish insolvency law make the terms too distant to be considered sufficiently equivalent. In such a case the translator must coin a term which would convey the intended message to its recipients. Analogously, the Polish term *syndyk* mentioned earlier and the term *office holder* would also be insufficiently equivalent under postulate 30.

Under Po 31 absolute legal system divergence occurs when there is no functional equivalent in the target legal system for a particular translandive unit which is sufficiently convergent or permissibly complementary in respect to a minimal set of relevant dimensions. Such a case exists when in the target language legal reality there is no object which would correspond to the source language legal reality object. The English term *equity* is an example of such objects not existing in the Polish legal system or the French term *bail commercial* not existing in the English legal system. Again, if that is the case, the translator must resort to methods of coining equivalents for non-equivalent terminology.

On the other hand, if a translational unit is a collocation (Po 32), the collocation applied in the translative text will be based on the functional equivalence, no matter whether the collocation is weak, strong, fixed or idiomatic so as to provide natural sounding speech and writing (cf. e.g. Kielar 1977, Kierzkowska 2002). Postulate 33, on the other hand, informs about the need to render grammatically correct translative texts and to apply structures typical of a given genre (cf. e.g. Kielar 1977, Kielar/Miler 1993, Kierzkowska 2002, Newmark 1988 (2007), 1991 (2006)). Although in literary translations infringing collocations may be considered a planned action of the text author, in the case of legal translation such deficiencies indicate the lack of specialized professional knowledge and either provokes unpleasant comments or leads to losing a client or even if results in the distortion of meaning or ambiguity may lead to far more unpleasant consequences such as being faced with disciplinary proceedings (cf. Kubacki 2008). The knowledge of collocations reveals a degree of competence of the translator. The only exception from this rule would be translation for the purpose of linguistic analysis of a translandive text or translation which aims at revealing the idiolect of an author for the purpose of forensic linguistic analysis. However, even if such a word-for-word translation were required, it would still most probably be accompanied by an idiomatic translation needed in the process of legal communication. The problem may also occur when it is impossible to establish natural equivalents (terms, collocations, grammatical structures) due to the lack of a corresponding genre of texts in the target language (Po 34). In such a case, the translator should resort to the closest hyper-genre in respect to the source text, so as to render a grammatically natural sounding target text or alternatively a hypo-genre.

The next three postulates (35-37) refer to the relation of adaptation. First of all, the translation stages actually require translational adaptation. It is commonly accepted that the translator should first read the text and understand it. Next, he should establish equivalents (usually at the level of words, collocations and grammatical structures typical of a given genre). The third stage is the process of rendering translation where text T_j is produced. Next, text T_j is compared with text T_i in order to make sure that nothing has been left untranslated or distorted by the translator. Finally, the translator should read text T_j and transform it into text T_k to adapt it translationally (by for instance removing syntactical calques from the source language, improving it stylistically, etc.). This final version of a translative text called here T_k is a translative text corresponding to translandive text T_i. Apart from grammatical and stylistic adaptation, the adaptation to the requirements of the recipient is necessary (Po 36) so as to make the text understandable for the recipient. In such a case the translator has to take into consideration the knowledge and needs of recipients. Such adaptation may require the translator, e.g. to supply borrowings with bracket descriptive equivalents or footnotes with some background information, etc. Also the translator's comments placed in brackets concerning the translandive text and required under the Polish Code of

Sworn Translators and Interpreters (Kierzkowska 1991, 2005, 2011) fall under this category of text adaptation (information about watermarks, photographs, emblems, corrections made on the document, presence or absence of stamps and seals, etc.). Finally, postulate 37 deals with the need to produce a translation which will be understandable for the recipient and which reveals the intended meaning. Only if those two conditions are met, we may assume that the text is acceptable to the recipient.

It should also be stressed that adaptation may be understood here as adjustment to legal system (Šarčević 2000b) or cultural adaptation (Gutt 2004a) or adaptation in the process of proofreading, revising and editing done either by the translator or by an independent proofreader, reviser or editor) (cf. Tabakowska 1999, 2009).

One of the prerequisites in the field of legal translation for the translator is to understand the translandive text (Po 38). This postulate however, will not be discussed in more detail, as this problem has been elaborated on when talking about the relation of comprehension.

Postulates 39-43 are actually self-explanatory and describe what has been noticed a long time ago, that is to say that apart from very short messages, translations rendered by different translators diverge from each other, still being sufficiently equivalent to the translandive text. Even the same translator rendering translation of the same text at different times (Po 40) due to the linguistic potential of the target language renders stylistically divergent target texts (Po 39). The problem of the impact of the time provided for translation (Po 42) as well as the knowledge and experience of the translator (Po 41) will be elaborated on when discussing relevant dimensions in chapter 3.

Steps of translation mentioned in postulate 32 have already been listed when discussing postulates 35-37. Non-observance of those steps results in different types of errors and mistakes which may occur in translative texts. It should be stressed here that for instance the omission of the stage of comparing the translandive text with the translative one results most frequently in the so-called translational errors and mistakes, that is such problems which are spotted only when we compare the original with its translation (including information omission, addition, distortions of the meaning, etc), whereas the last stage which consists in proof-reading the text results in the so-called linguistic errors and mistakes that is to say problems which are detectable when reading the translative text (cf. Pisarska/Tomaszkiewicz 1998, Kozłowska 2002, Hejwowski 2004, Matulewska/Nowak 2006).

From the translator's point of view, the commissioner is the best source of information on the translation recipients, their needs, expectations and knowledge (Po 44). Therefore, the degree of adjustment and adaptation of translation depends also on the information obtained from the commissioner (for more on the topic see chapter 3).

The next group of postulates (45-48) accounts for the requirements of translative text recipients, who depending on their degree of professional knowledge and effect of translation on their legal situation need to be provided with translations revealing (i) differences (Po 45, 47, 48) or (ii) similarities (Po 46) between the legal systems in question.

Postulate 49 reflects what has been noticed by scholars dealing with legal linguistics and legal translation, that is to say that legal translation intersects applied linguistics, translatology, theory of law, comparate law and other fields as well (cf. Kielar 1973, 1977, Pieńkos 1999, Šarčević 2000b, Kierzkowska 2002, Mattila 2006, Galdia 2009, Jopek-Bosiacka 2010, and many others).

In general, the more differences may be observed between the source legal system and the target legal system, the more problems may be encountered with finding sufficient equivalents and making the translative text meet the needs and requirements of its recipients (Po 50). Additionally, in compliance with the opinion of Šarčević (2000b), the situation gets even more complicated when the translator operates within a plurilingual legal environment (Po 51) where both the translandive text and a translative one must have not the same meaning but the same legal effect which means that the legal consequences of translations will be the same as that of originals (Po 52) as all texts are treated as authoritative. Finally, if the target text is not binding, the target text is considered sufficiently equivalent if it informs the recipient about legal consequences of the source text (Po 53). Finally, postulate 54 states that the translator should aim at producing the translative text which will be comprehended in a desired way in accordance with the intention of the information sender. It should be stressed here that the information sender does not need to be the author of the text as it may also be the commissioner.

The quality of the source text is of vital importance as far as translation is concerned (Po 55) because the higher the quality of the translandive text is, the easier the job of the translator is as well. Texts burdened with numerous grammatical and stylistic mistakes are hard to translate and the time required to understand them is longer, thus the time needed for translation extends as well. In extreme cases ambiguous translandive texts may even turn out to be hard to comprehend and if that is the case translators usually resort to literal translation which results in rendering low quality translation. Such a situation may also happen when the translator for some reasons is unable to consult the author of the text to have the ambiguities clarified.

Finally, the linguistic potential of each language definitely affects the process of translation (Po 56). Problems resulting from potential differences may be encountered not only when the target language has a more limited potential than the source language (when the translator will be required to resort to techniques/procedures of providing equivalents for non-equivalent terminology and phraseology) but also when the source language has a more limited potential than the target language (when the translator needs to reveal more information in the translative text than is revealed in the translandive text cf. for instance Jakobson 1959/1966, 2009).

As stated above, postulates may refer to

(i) general translatology (laws referring to all types of translation and possible combinations of languages), for instance postulates 1, 2, 3, and
(ii) particular translatology (laws referring to all types of translation but limited to a given pair of languages),
(iii) general legilinguistic translatology (laws referring to all possible combinations of languages but limited to legal translation), for instance postulates 35 and 36 which deal with adaptation understood here as taking into account differences between legal systems as well as postulates 38-48 referring to legal communication participants, and
(iv) particular legilinguistic translatology (laws referring to a given pair of legal languages).

Finally, we may also distinguish postulates referring to specific aspects of general and particular legilinguistic translatology, for instance translation of lingual units conferring/expressing the meaning of deontic modality. It should be remembered that legilinguistic translatology is interdisciplinary (Po 49) (cf. Toury 1995 (2001): 53). Therefore, apart from strictly translation process related postulates, there are also legilinguistic postulates describing the legilinguistic reality. Among such postulates we may list the following:

Po 57 – If sentence *S* expresses unconditional obligation, then the action is required at any time and in any circumstances.
Po 58 – If sentence *S* expresses conditional obligation, then the action is required but subject to some additional circumstances which must occur in order for the action to be required (obligatory).
Po 59 – If sentence *S* expresses conditional obligation with an exclusion, then the action is required unless the obligation excluding circumstances occur.

The above postulates may be applicable to all texts in all languages in which the meaning of obligation is conveyed. However, the postulates may be limited to a given translandive language:

Po 60 – If sentence S_i in L_i expresses unconditional obligation, then the action is required at any time and in any circumstances.
Po 61 – If sentence S_i in L_i expresses conditional obligation, then the action is required but subject to some additional circumstances which must occur in order for the action to be required (obligatory).
Po 62 – If sentence S_i in L_i expresses conditional obligation with an exclusion, then the action is required unless the obligation excluding circumstances occur.

And *mutatis mutandis* to a corresponding translative language:

Po 63 – If sentence S_j in L_j expresses unconditional obligation, then the action is required at any time and in any circumstances.
Po 64 – If sentence S_j in L_j expresses conditional obligation, then the action is required but subject to some additional circumstances which must occur in order for the action to be required (obligatory).

Po 65 – If sentence S_j in L_j expresses conditional obligation with an exclusion, then the action is required unless the obligation excluding circumstances occur.

Finally, we may further limit our postulates to texts of a given genre G, formulating the following laws:

Po 66 – If sentence S_i in L_i in a text T_i of genre *G* expresses unconditional obligation, then the action is required at any time and in any circumstances.

Po 67 – If sentence S_i in L_i in a text T_i of genre *G* expresses conditional obligation, then the action is required but subject to some additional circumstances which must occur in order for the action to be required (obligatory).

Po 68 – If sentence S_i in L_i in a text T_i of genre *G* expresses conditional obligation with an exclusion, then the action is required unless the obligation excluding circumstances occur.

And *mutatis mutandis* corresponding translative language postulates may be formulated:

Po 69 – If sentence S_j in L_j in a text T_j of genre *G* expresses unconditional obligation, then the action is required at any time and in any circumstances.

Po 70 – If sentence S_j in L_j in a text T_j of genre *G* expresses conditional obligation, then the action is required but subject to some additional circumstances which must occur in order for the action to be required (obligatory).

Po 71 – If sentence S_j in L_j in a text T_j of genre *G* expresses conditional obligation with an exclusion, then the action is required unless the obligation excluding circumstances occur.

Having formulated such laws on (translandive) and (translative legilinguistic) reality based on parallel text analysis, we may develop directives for translators of a given pair of languages, informing them how they must or may or may not translate a translandive sentence S_i in L_i in a text T_i of genre *G* into a corresponding translative sentence S_j in L_j in a text T_j of genre *G*. This procedure will be referred once again when presenting the explanation scheme developed for the purpose of this tentative theory.

The postulates provided above are intended to illustrate the complexity of legilinguistic translational reality and for obvious reasons are by no means exhaustive. Finally, it should be reminded here that each directive (formulated within practical legilinguistic translatology) derives from at least one postulate.

2.8. Explanation scheme

The problem of making translative decisions bothers not only translators and commissioners but also translation recipients. They frequently ask themselves a question how to translate expression *X* from one language into another and the next question that follows is why *X* is translatable into another language in that manner. The explanation scheme included below is to illustrate that decision-making process in the light of the theoretical foundations presented so far.

The explanation scheme proposed here due to the complex nature of legilinguistic translational reality will be modified and therefore will not correspond ideally to the classical explanation scheme applied in linguistics (cf. Bogusławski 1986). Thus, before we apply this scheme, we shall provide its modified structure.

The explanation scheme used in this work has the following structure:

(i) question which is to be answered,
(ii) explanans (at least one general statement and at least one singular statement), and
(iii) explanandum.

The application of the scheme for the purpose of English-Polish legilinguistic translation may be:

Question: Why does the English expression *in the year of our Lord 2011* in sentence S of text T_i of genre G translate as the Polish *w 2011 roku* in the corresponding text T_j

of genre G for the recipients of communicative community C_j?

where:

G – a judgment

T_i – is the source text in English

T_j – is the target text to be produced in Polish

C_j – is the communicative community operating in Polish legal reality

C_{j1} and C_{j2} – are two different communicative communities operating in Polish legal reality

Answering this question we shall in the first place resort to Po 9, and consequently also Po 3 (preservation of the genre), Po 12 (on homosignification and non-divergence), Po 6 (absence of complete homosignification).

General statement: If significator *X*, conveying meaning *M* in translandive text T_i of genre *G* in language L_i, and intended for recipients of community C_i is bound by the relation of the sufficient equivalence with significator *P* with respect to *M* for translative text T_j of genre *G* in language L_j, and intended for recipients of community C_j, then *X* translates as *P* in T_j.

Singular statement 1: The English expression *in the year of our Lord 2011* signifies meaning *M* in text T_i of genre *G* for recipient community C_i.

Singular statement 2: The closest homosignificators of the English expression *in the year of our Lord 2011* in translandive text T_i with respect to *M*, for the corresponding translative text T_j of genre *G* are Y_1 (*w 2011 roku*) for recipient community C_{j1} (communicative community of distant recipients which are to use the translative text in legal communication, e.g. before courts in Poland) and Y_2 (*w roku Pańskim 2011*) for recipient community C_{j2} (communicative community of close recipients interested in the density of religious elements in legal texts in particular languages).

Explanandum: The English expression *in the year of our Lord 2011* in sentence *S* of text T_i of genre *G* translates as the Polish *w 2011 roku* in the corresponding text T_j of genre *G* for the recipients of communicative community C_{j1}.

Let us now resort to the problem of expressing obligation in imperative clauses in statutory instruments in Polish-English translation. In general, imperative clauses express obligation to act.

Question: Why is *jest obowiązany* in imperative clauses translable as *shall* into English?

Answering this question we shall resort to postulate 11 as a general statement (Gs_1). Gs_{2Pl} and Gs_{3Eng} are, in fact, postulates of legilinguistic translatology, or more precisely, they should belong to translational grammars developed for the purposes of Polish-English and English-Polish legal translation. Consequently, our explanation scheme will assume the following shape:

General statement 1: If two heterolingual texts T_i and T_j are sufficiently convergent and homosignificative also with respect to the considered meaning *M*, then they are translationally equivalent and consequently translatable.[15]

General statement 2_{Pl}: The meaning of Conditional Obligation to act imposed on a given actor in an imperative clause in text T_i of text genre *G* being a statutory instrument is expressed in the Polish legal language by the following significators *powinien* (+infinitive), *należy* (+infinitive), *jest obowiązany* (+infinitive) and *jest zobowiązany* (+infinitive) and finally *jest wymagane* (+deverbalized noun) as well as a verb in present tense indicative and future tense indicative.

General statement 3_{Eng}: The meaning of Conditional Obligation to act imposed on a given actor in an imperative clause in text T_i of text genre *G* being a statutory instrument in the English legal language is expressed by the following significators: *shall* (+infinitive) and *must* (+infinitive).

Singular statement 1: Polish *jest obowiązany* (+infinitive) and English *shall* (+infinitive) are sufficiently convergent and homosignifi-

15 Thus, if they are *tr*-convergent and homosignificative under Po 11, then under Po 12 they are not excessively divergent. Furthermore, if they are sufficiently *tr*-convergent, then under Po 10 they are translationally equivalent, and consequently under Postulates 9 and 8 they are translatable.

cative also with respect to the meaning of the Conditional Obligation to act imposed on a given actor in an imperative clause in a statutory instrument.

Singular statement 2: Ergo, Polish *jest obowiązany* (+infinitive) and English *shall* (+infinitive) are translationally equivalent and if significators *powinien* and *shall* are translationally equivalent, then under Po. 2 they are translatable.

Explanandum: Consequently, the Polish *jest obowiązany* is translatable as *shall* into English.

2.9. Concluding remarks

The complexity of the translation process is caused by the fact that it is performed in a multi-dimensional space. In order to translate the text numerous functions are performed by translators to provide a translation product (translatum) of satisfactory quality. Sometimes translators even do not realize how many factors affect their work. Some functions are discharged subconsciously while others are performed consciously. To help make the translator's actions effective, the parametrization of the translation process[16] is presented here. The

16 On norms in translation cf. Levý (1967) who perceives translation as a decision-making process requiring constant choosing of one option out of a number (a set) of alternatives, Popovič (1970b) who states that translation process involves constant choosing between the linguistic and discursive norms and conventions present in the source and target culture, Toury (2001: 53-69) who perceives translation as a norm-governed activity as it is affected by the social and cultural norms binding in the source culture and target culture, where the adherence to "source norms determines translation's adequacy as compared to the source text, subscription to norms originating in the target culture determines its acceptability" (Toury 1995 (2001): 56-57) and who distinguishes three types of norms: (i) the preliminary norm (concerning the choice of the text to be translated, translating via a pivot language or the original, etc.), (ii) the initial norm (translation orientation), and (iii) operational norms (which in turn are divided into the norms relating to the decisions made at the text level, macrostructure of the text; and textual-linguistic norms relating to the deci-

principal purpose is to show the complexity of this process and simultaneously assist in making conscious decisions as far as translation techniques, methods and strategies are concerned.

The application of the parametrization of the translation process is presented in chapter 4 devoted to the calculation of the meanings and chapter 5 on the choice of equivalents for the target text. Finally, the translation algorithm will be presented in chapter 6.

---

sions made at the level of text component parts, microstructure of the text, terminology, etc); Chesterman (1997) who distinguishes product norms (which are used to reflect "the expectations of readers of a translation (of a given type) concerning what a translation (of this type) should be like" (1997: 64) and process norms which relate to the translation process itself and are divided into: (i) the accountability norm (being loyal to the author of the text, the commissioner, the translator and the recipient), (ii) the communication norm (the translation purpose is to optimize communication), and (iii) the relation norm (which states that translation is to establish and maintain "an appropriate relation of relevant similarity [...] between the source text and the target text" (1997: 69)), and Hermans (2002 (2004): 72-90) who states that "the norms and conventions of translation guide and facilitate decision-making" (2002 (2004): 80). He divides norms into weak and strong and more and less durable. Moreover he points out that norms are more or less relevant depending on the communicative situation.

3. Towards Parametrization of Translation

3.1. Introductory remarks on relevant dimensions

The parametrization of the translation process will be achieved by establishing relevant dimensions. The dimensions presented in this work will thus be called *legal translation relevant dimensions* and they will be grouped in five categories of dimensions being:

(i) source-text author,
(ii) translandum, translatum, and text component parts,
(iii) commission and commissioner,
(iv) translator, and
(v) communicative community.

Consequently, each category is composed of a few dimensions. Each dimension is a set of homogenous properties called dimension properties, which indicates that the properties are of the same type and therefore are comparable and simultaneously mutually exclusive – thus the object can take on only one property from each dimension.

Neither the list of categories nor the list of dimensions presented below is exhaustive. In certain instances other types of categories and dimensions may be established as expedient to carry out translation action successfully.

Furthermore it should be stressed once again that the dimensions presented below have been established for the purpose of legal translation. Therefore, some of the dimensions may be applicable solely to legal communication. However, the concept of parametrization of the legal translation process may be adapted to any type of translation.

Properties from each dimension serve the purpose of characterizing the objects existing in the legal communication space. In other words, characterization is the operation of association of properties from specific dimensions to a specific object in legal communication.

In the process of translation objects are compared with regard to their properties; therefore the properties belonging to one dimension must be comparable. If the properties cannot be compared they must belong to different dimensions.

In some cases it is evident that certain properties from given dimensions will presuppose the choice of properties from other dimensions. Thus the property P1 from dimension A may necessarily presuppose the choice of the property P1 from dimension B.

Every dimension should contain the property of *indeterminacy* since at times it may be impossible to decide which property a particular text or its component partakes in. An object will be said to assume this property with respect to a certain dimension if it cannot assume any determined property of this dimension. As stated above, we will deal then with the relation of incommensurability. Consequently, each dimension has determined properties and indetermined properties.

3.2. Source-text (translandum) author

As far as the author of the source text is concerned the following dimensions seem most pertinent in legal translation:

(i) author's capacity (legal qualification) (hereinafter called the authorship),

(ii) author's professional knowledge,

(iii) author's ability to communicate, and

(iv) author's awareness of the art of translation.

These four dimensions will be described in more detail below.

3.2.1. Authorship of the source-text

The *dimension of source-text authorship* reflects the capacity of the author of the original message at the moment of its creation (production). The capacity of the author is his legal qualification, competence, power possessed at the moment of source text production, which affects the importance of the text (e.g. whether the text is binding and for whom, etc.) and as a consequence informs us about the status of the source-text (cf. Newmark 1982 (2008): 21, Kierzkowska 2002: 76-77, Nord 2005 (2006): 47-57).

Consequently, the dimension consists of the following properties:

(i) the author who is a private individual (author as a private individual, who acts as an expert or non-expert, e.g. a suicide),
(ii) the private institutional author (non-governmental body),
(iii) the public institutional author (governmental body),
(iv) the legislator, etc.

The dimension considered here does for instance presuppose the choice of properties from the following dimensions:

(i) the function of the text (whether it is a sample text or a executive text, etc.), and
(ii) the intention of the author of the text (whether the author wishes to inform, to mislead, to be ambiguous, to exercise pressure on the recipient, etc.) so the answer to why the text has been created (cf. on the intention of the text: Newmark 1998 (2007): 12).

3.2.2. Author's professional knowledge

The *dimension of author's knowledge* includes the following sets of properties: lawyer or not-lawyer. If the author is not a lawyer the property of being a non-lawyer may be converted into dimensions with the following properties:

(i) linguist or not-linguist,
(ii) type of profession or education, or
(iii) employment of the author, etc.

This dimension informs the translator about what possible features the source text produced by the author may have, including the considerable extent of specialized terminology and the construction (interpretation) rules, which should be considered in the source text in order to calculate its meaning. The dimension of the author's profession will also affect the determination, e.g. whether the text is written in legal or quasi-legal language.

3.2.3. Author's communicative skills

The *dimension of author's ability to communicate* includes the following set of properties:

(i) ability to communicate clearly and unambiguously, and
(ii) inability to communicate clearly and unambiguously.

The communicative skills of the author affect the source text clarity and comprehensibility. If the author possesses communicative skills the text produced by him will be easy to translate provided that the translator possesses the necessary translation skills. If the author, however, is unable to communicate the message clearly and unambiguously, the translator will in the majority of instances encounter problems with constructing the meaning of the source text and consequently translating it. The principle of translation *rubbish in, rubbish out* meaning that if the quality of the source text is low, the quality of the translation most probably will be low too; or in other words, that one should not expect the translator to produce a target text of a better quality than the source text produced by the author, will then be applicable. It should be mentioned here that it is of no importance whether the communicative skills of the source text author are innate or acquired in the course of, e.g., the education process.

3.2.4. Author's awareness of the art of translation

The *dimension of author's awareness of the art of translation* will include the following set of properties:

(i) aware of the art of translation, and
(ii) unaware of the art of translation.

If the author's communicative skills are meagre, this dimension will be of no importance because the lack of skills will affect the communicativeness of the text no matter whether the author knows the principles of translation or not. However, if the author's communicative skills are considerable and he knows the basics of the art of translation, then if he knows at the moment of text production that the text will be translated into other languages, he will most probably adjust his message in such a way that it is easier to understand for the translation recipient for instance on the level of the so-called system-bound terminology. If the source text author does not know at the moment of text production, that it will be translated into a foreign language, he will most probably adjust the text only to the primary communicative community for which the text is intended.

3.3. Translandum, translatum and their component parts

Source and target text related dimensions refer to linguistic and extra-linguistic features of the text, potentially affecting the process of translation. *Potentially* means that there are situations in which it is enough to associate one property from one dimension to characterize sufficiently the translandum or translatum for the purpose of translation, whereas there are also instances where it will be necessary to associate one property from each dimension to characterize them. Due to the complexity of the translation process it is necessary to set apart at least a few dimensions having properties characterizing the translandum and translatum.

Text properties, grouped in one dimension (i.e. a parameter), may be compared with one another (i.e. are of the same nature, belong together).

Let us now discuss the source text dimensions we propose for the purpose of our typology of source and target text translation relevant environment. The dimensions are applicable to both translandive and translative texts, although both texts may assume different properties from a given dimension. The application of source-text dimensions serves the purpose of calculating the meaning of the source text, whereas target text dimensions are to choose or establish an optimal translative significator. The following dimensions will be discussed below:

(i) communicative situation,
(ii) text delivery form and quality,
(iii) text force/legal effect,
(iv) text purpose/function,

(v) the time of text creation,
(vi) text language variety and variation,
(vii) the lect (language) of the text,
(viii) text legal system,
(ix) the branch of law to which the text refers, and
(x) text genre.

3.3.1. Communicative situation

Communicative situations in the case of the target text may have the following properties:
(i) written text (message) for reading,
(ii) written text (message) for oral delivery and published *in extenso* for reading,
(iii) written (message) text for oral delivery,
(iv) oral text (message) for oral delivery, and
(v) oral text (message) for oral delivery but also recorded for future reading.

Those properties will affect the process of translation significantly as far as the choice of significators is concerned. For instance in the case of written texts intended for oral delivery it will be necessary to avoid direct borrowings, which may not be understood by the recipients-listeners, whereas it will be possible to use such significators in the translation of the same source text intended for reading.

Among the most important dimensions, which are applicable to text component parts and which do not necessarily result from text-related dimensions one may distinguish the following:
(i) the time of text creation (in particular this dimension may contribute to the identification of archaisms),
(ii) text language variety,
(iii) the lect (language) of the text.

Moreover, the moment the lect is identified it may be necessary to identify the sub-lect of the text component part.

Since the properties applicable to the text and its component parts will be the same, the descriptions provided below will apply. It should be stressed here that in some cases other source and target text dimensions may be applied to text component parts as well.

3.3.2. Text delivery form and quality

The *dimension of text delivery form* (also called medium) may be characterized by two main properties, that is to say:
(i) oral text, and
(ii) written text (cf. Nord 2005 (2006): 62-67).

Oral and written texts may have some further sub-properties. The property of being an oral text or a written text may become a dimension having its own set of properties. In other words the property of being an oral text may have many features and thus may be converted into a subdimension with specific properties, e.g. the *dimension of oral text preservation* which in turn will have the following properties:
(i) recorded,
(ii) non-recorded.

Both oral and written texts may be characterized as regards the *dimension of text quality*. Although the dimension of text quality is mentioned here, it will be referred to only marginally. The quality of oral texts is also very important but they are usually interpreted rather than translated. However, some oral texts are recorded in the form of, e.g., minutes and later on translated. Nowadays hand-written texts are seldom encountered, thus the problem of legibility diminishes. However, many legalization clauses on documents are still hand-written. Additionally, many official forms are filled in with handwritten information as well.

Written texts may further be characterized as regards the following dimensions:
(i) the dimension of written text preservation form with the following properties:
 – preserved on an analogue carrier, and
 – preserved on a digital carrier.

(ii) the dimension of written text quality (Newmark 1988 (2007): 16, Dollerup 2007: 112-113) with the following properties:
– low quality,
– average quality, and
– high quality.

(iii) the dimension of written text readability with the following sets of properties:
– handwritten or typed,
– legible and illegible, and finally
– clear or unclear, etc.

3.3.3. Text force and legal effect

The *dimension of the source-text force* reflects the significance of the text and its binding force in a given communicative situation. It will consist of the following pairs of properties:

(i) original or non-original,

(ii) legal document or a copy of a legal document, and

(iii) binding or non-binding text (e.g. a statutory instrument, a bill) (cf. Kierzkowska 2002: 77-76).

The *dimension of the target-text force* will contain the following pairs of properties:

(i) translation functioning as an original or non-original text,

(ii) translation functioning as a legal document or a copy of a legal document, and

(iii) translation functioning as a binding or non-binding text (e.g. a statutory instrument, a bill) (cf. Kierzkowska 2002: 77-78).

The *dimension of the text legal effect* is composed of the following properties:

(i) the source text is binding and its effect is prevailing (the target text only is to inform about the legal effect of the source text),

(ii) the target text is binding and its effect is prevailing (the source text is to inform about the legal effect in the target legal system), and finally

(iii) the source and target text function in plurilingual setting and both will have the same legal effect (Šarčević 2000b).

3.3.4. *Text function*

Having discussed text typologies and functions in chapter one, let us focus on the text function dimension. The target text objective may be the same as the source text purpose or in other words the importance of motive in text production and reception (Nord 2005 (2006): 74-83) may be the same. However, Kierzkowska (2002) maintains after Vermeer that the function of the source text does not need to be the same as the function of the target text. For example any Polish statutory instrument, which has a normative function in the Republic of Poland may be translated into a number of languages. If it is translated into German for the purpose of the German minority or Kashubian for the purpose of the Kashubian minority living in Poland it preserves its normative character. However, if it is translated into other languages it may not be normative but informative only (that is it will just inform the target text recipient about the rights and obligations of Polish citizens).

Due to the rapidly changing and developing communicative technologies and new theories on texts and communications, it is assumed here that the typology of texts should be adjusted to the specific communicative situation and it is the task of the translator to decide which typology suits best his needs in a given real life situation. Therefore, the dimension of the text function will have the following properties:

(i) the source text and target text have the same function, or
(ii) the target text has a different function than the source text.

3.3.5. *Time of text creation*

The *dimension of the time of translandive text creation* (execution) will have the following sets of properties:

(i) valid, partially-valid or non-valid text,
(ii) historical value of the text and current value of the text.

The translator using this dimension must decide which parts of the text are valid, non-valid or of historical value. The aim of the communication will determine which of the text constituent parts will be especially important for the purpose of a given communicative situation (Nord 2005 (2006): 70-74, cf. House 1977).

The *dimension of the time of translative text creation* reflects the importance of the translation with regard to its date of execution in comparison with the source-text execution. This dimension will have the same set of properties as the source-text.

The translator using this dimension may decide to delete non-valid text or parts of the text (the so-called translation by deletion cf. Katan 1999 (2004): 128-138) or translating such a part of text as being of historical value (and for example enabling a greater depth of analysis of the data presented in the text in question) (cf. also Nord 2005 (2006): 70-74 on the relevance of the dimension of time of the source text (i) plot, (ii) creation and (iii) reception and target text (i) creation and (ii) reception).

3.3.6. Language variety

The *dimension of the source-text language variety* mirrors the possibility of the existence of language variety used in different countries.

Although Polish is a one-variety language as far as legal language is concerned[17], there are some languages with more than one variety, e.g. German (used in Austria, Switzerland and Germany), French (used in France, Canada, etc.), Spanish (used in Spain, Argentina, etc.), English (used in the USA, England and Wales, Scotland, Australia, etc.) and Chinese (used in China, Hong-Kong and Taiwan), not to mention other languages including Arabic.

As far as English is concerned one should bear in mind that:

> Only a few centuries ago, the English language consisted of a collection of dialects spoken mainly by monolinguals and only within the shores of a small

17 Some talk about varieties of Polish spoken by Polish minorities in the USA and Australia, and more recently by Poles living in the UK.

> island. Now it includes such typologically distinct varieties as pidgins and creoles, *new* Englishes, and a range of differing standard and non-standard varieties that are spoken on a regular basis in more than 60 different countries around the world (Crystal 1985). English is also, of course, the main language used for communication at an international level. (Cheshire, 1994b: 1)

Cheshire also points out that apart from varieties of English one may differentiate also variations spoken by different speech communities (e.g. urban variation, rural variation, variations depending on the socioeconomic classes to which people belong, native speaker variation, non-native speaker variation, etc.). Thus, not only may the variety of English be troublesome in translation and interpreting, but the difficulty increases with the multitude of variations. The fact that English is the official language in many post-colonial countries where the language in question is enriched by numerous borrowings (often exotics) from other languages in use in a given territory. Moreover, the existence of English with other languages in the same territory may lead to the code-mixing phenomenon as well (Kandiah 1994).

Consequently, this dimension will have the following properties:

(i) one-variety language,
(ii) more-than-one variety language.

In the case of languages, which manifest themselves in more than one variety, the properties will include the language variety to which the source-text may potentially belong. Thus, in case of English[18], which manifests itself in several varieties, this dimension will consist among others of the following properties:

(i) British English,
(ii) American English,
(iii) Indian English,
(iv) Australian English,
(v) Canadian English, etc.

---

18 On differences in High and Low Context Communication orientation in different variants of English and the precision of utterances cf. Katan 1999 (2004): 184-186.

However, in legal communication British English may be further divided and may have the following sub-properties resulting from the legal system used on a given territory:

(i) English in England and Wales,
(ii) English in Scotland, and
(iii) English in Ireland.

Taking into consideration the fact that in the USA there are 55 legal systems (cf. Tokarczyk 1998: 18-19) in force currently one may distinguish:

(i) federal English,
(ii) English used in a given state, and
(iii) English used in a given dependent territory.

The dimension of the source text language variety is congruent with the dimension of the target-text language variety.

In the case of languages which exist in more than one variety, the dimension of the communicative community will determine the language variety which will be applied when formulating the target text.

As already mentioned, apart from varieties, there are also language variations which may affect the effectiveness of language communication. We would like to point out here that the meaning imposed by the variety and variation of the language may pose numerous translation and interpreting problems. Both variety and variation are used by members of a specific communicative community which to some extent may be hermetic from the translator's/interpreter's point of view. For instance,

> In the Southern African context it is pointless to discuss variation in English from the point of view of large-scale social factors such as regional variation, social class variation or variation on a standard-non-standard dimension. We can only discuss variation in terms of communities. By communities is meant those groups who share a common culture, ancestry, race or tribe. (Chishimba 1994: 442)

Furthermore, the type of the community may affect the language choice in the so-called bilingual countries and result in code-switching depending on the communicative situation in which participants are involved (cf. Sahgal 1994, Gonzalez 1994).

The variations may differ from one another in respect of accent, pronunciation (Clarke 1994, Esling 1994, Bayard 1994, Bradley 1994, etc.), style (Chick 1994, Khan 1994), syntax (Mesthrie 1994, Gonzalez 1994), vocabulary (especially borrowings, e.g. Benton 1994, Lowenberg 1994), which in consequence may lead to miscommunication problems. Chick (1994: 446), who analyzed Afrikaans English, states that: "[...] participants misinterpret and misevaluate one another" and the consequences may be very relevant as "[...] repeated miscommunication of this sort generates negative cultural stereotypes" (Chick, 1994: 446).

Lowenberg (1994: 367) gives a few examples illustrating the problem:

> The residents will repair the roofs on a *gotong-royong* basis.
> I have often been criticised by my friends for easily bowing down to apologise, but I will always do so – it is required by both our religion and *adat*.
> A carpenter was jailed for five years and ordered to be given six strokes of the *rotan* by the Session Court today for possession of heroin.

Commenting on the above mentioned examples, he explains the meaning of the italicised terms which are direct borrowings:

> All of the borrowed terms in these sentences refer to institutions unique to Malay-speaking Southeast Asia: *gotong-royong* is a form of communal cooperation, *adat* is a body of traditional law, and the *rotan* is a rattan cane used in officially sanctioned and administered punishments. (Lowenberg 1994: 367)

Lowenberg (1994: 367) also remarks that:

> [...] the ascending status of Bahasa Malaysia is more evident on *lexical-shifts* (Richards 1979: 14), where Malay words replace English words or phrases which are denotatively, but not conotatively, equivalent.

Such words are called banner words (Paine 1981: 14 quoted by Lowenberg 1994: 367) and defined as "[...] single words or phrases [...] that are likely to induce a proposition by inference". Šarčević (2000b) calls such words and phrases in reference to a legal system *system-bound terms*.

3.3.7. Lects

Language is composed of coexistent lects or as Bańczerowski (1996: 16) claims:

> no language manifests itself directly but is mediated by lects. [...] There can be distinguished such lects of a language as: a standard lect (or the so called standard language), a colloquial lect, a dialect, a sociolect, an idiolect.

In reference to languages for special purposes we may encounter in German and Polish studies *Fachlekt* and *Technolect* (*Technolect*) (used by Auburger 1981, F. Grucza 1994, Laurén/Nordmann 1996). In constructing the *dimension of the text lect* among other properties the following should be considered:

(i) specialized lect (technolect or language for special purposes),
(ii) standard lect (or standard language),
(iii) colloquial lect (or colloquial language),
(iv) slang, etc.

In other words, the set of properties will be composed of different lect types.

Within a specialized lect we may distinguish various sub-lects (types of LSPs), e.g. a medical lect, a legal lect (a legi-lect), lect of accounting, etc. It should be stressed here that one of many difficulties connected with legal translation is the fact that it is rarely limited to strictly legal language. Actually most texts in legal communication are formulated in at least two lects. The coexistence of different lects in one text will necessitate the determination of the dominant lect resulting from the text genre and the lects of text component parts (see dimensions applicable to text component parts). For instance, a petition filed by a dissatisfied patient against a hospital will most likely be formulated in legal language (a legal lect or a legi-lect) and the language of medicine (a medical lect), a winding-up petition will be written in a legi-lect and a lect of accounting. Consequently, the property specialized lect in case of some texts will become the *dimension of the specialized lect* with the following exemplary properties:

(i) legi-lect (legal language),
(ii) medical lect (medical language),

(iii) lect of computer science (language of computer science),
(iv) lect of logistics (language of logistics),
(v) lect of telecommunication industry (language of telecommunication industry), etc.

Finally, it should be emphasised here that lects are irrespective of the text genre, as a text of one text genre may be expressed in more than one lect.

There are some target-languages in which the terms are still missing in a given language for special purposes in comparison with the source-language. This feature will affect the process of translation significantly, as the translator will also act as the creator of new lexical items in a given target text.

3.3.8. Legal system

The *dimension of the legal system* has the following sets of properties:
(i) common law system, civil law system, other legal system,
(ii) whether the legal system has been influenced by the Roman legal system to some extent (properties: affected, not affected), and
(iii) to what extent the source language legal system is known to the target text recipients (properties: well known, known to some extent, not known).

It should be stressed here that on numerous occasions the source text legal system determines the meaning of the source text translative units especially in the case of languages having varieties.

It should not be forgotten that:

> [...] for the translator the text is not purely a linguistic phenomenon, but must also be seen in terms of its *communicative* function, as a unit embedded in a given *situation*, and as a part of a broader socio-cultural background. Accepting this as the point of departure, the translator's text analysis should begin by *identifying* the text in terms of culture and situation, as *part of a world-continuum* (Vermeer 1983). (Snell-Hornby 1995 (2007): 69)

It should be emphasised that whether the source-text and target text languages belong to the same legal reality or not is of great importance. If both languages do belong to the same legal reality, the translation on the level of terms is easier as there will be more terms having their significators in the target language. If they belong to different legal realities there will be more legal institutions not having their significators in the target language.

Sapir (1929 in Bassnett 1980 (2004): 21) claims that:

> No two languages are ever sufficiently similar to be considered as representing the same social reality. The worlds in which different societies live are distinct worlds, not merely the same world with different labels attached.

The same refers to legal systems.

3.3.9. Branch of law to which the text refers

The *dimension of the branch of law* is fundamental for calculation of the meaning of the translandive units and establishing an optimal equivalent in the target language. Nowadays there are numerous branches of law. Some of them derive from the Roman law (division into civil law and criminal law, etc.), but new ones have been added to contemporary legal systems as well (international public law, public economic law, competition law, etc.). The most typical branches of law, which may be enumerated here as examples are the following:

(i) civil law,
(ii) civil procedure,
(iii) criminal (penal) law, and
(iv) penal procedure.

Civil law in turn may be divided into:

(i) law of succession,
(ii) law of contracts,
(iii) family law,
(iv) company law,
(v) bankruptcy law, etc.

The dimension of the branch of law will be crucial in determining the meaning of the source text and finding target text significators in the case of the occurrence of legal polysemy in source and target languages respectively.

3.3.10. Text genre

The *dimension of the text genre* is one of the most important dimensions in discerning the meaning of terms used in the source-text. Since there are numerous text genres, the properties listed below serve only exemplary purposes and are not exhaustive in any respect. For instance one may enumerate the following text genres in legal communication:

(i) testaments,
(ii) judgments,
(iii) petitions,
(iv) warrants,
(v) statutory instruments,
(vi) legal reports,
(vii) legal opinions,
(viii) depositions,
(ix) birth, death and marriage certificates,
(x) school certificates,
(xi) university diplomas,
(xii) licences,
(xiii) patents,
(xiv) contracts, etc.

Moreover, each of the properties listed above may be converted into a corresponding dimension having its own set of properties. For instance, the *dimension of being a testament* under Polish law may have the following properties (text sub-genres):

(i) a holograph (hand-written) testament,
(ii) an allograph testament, and
(iii) a testament in a form of a notarial act.

The *dimension of being a specific type of judgment* may in turn have properties such as:

(i) a divorce judgment,
(ii) a financial judgment,
(iii) a final judgment,
(iv) a foreign judgment,
(v) a judgment in the case ABC v. XYZ, etc.

In general, the text genre should remain the same after translation. The situations in which the translator may not reflect the features typical of a given genre of the text in his translation are very rare and will not be analysed here. However, they are related to, e.g. the analysis of texts for comparative linguistics purposes and forensic linguistics purposes (e.g. determining the authorship of the text on the basis of the author's idiolect, etc.). But it may also happen that in the absence of a given genre in a target language, the translator needs to resort to language schemata (patterns) occurring in a hyper- or hypo-genre in respect to the source text genre.

To summarise, dimensions 3.3.1., 3.3.3.-3.3.9. are necessary to ascertain the meaning of the source text translative units and find target text significators, whereas dimension 3.3.2. is useful in assessing the quality of the translation product.

3.4. Commission and commissioner

Vermeer was one of the first scholars to turn the attention of translators to the importance of commission and commissioner in the process of translation. First of all he noted that each translational action is inspired by the commissioner. Moreover, the quality of translation may be affected by the terms settled with the commissioner and information provided by him. Thus commission-related dimensions will mostly serve the purpose of assessing the potential and predictable quality of the translation product and the feasibility of translation due to the imposed conditions.

3.4.1. Commissioner

The commissioner may be a very valuable source of information for the translator (Vermeer 2001). First of all he knows why the text is to be translated and for whom it is translated. Therefore, he can provide information on the communicative community (recipient) for which the translator is to transfer the message. It often happens that the commissioner is the author or knows the author of the text and thus may serve as a communicative link in case any doubts arise in connection with source text interpretation. Moreover, it often happens that the commissioner is an expert in the source text field. In some cases he may even know target language terminology, not having sufficient target language skills to translate the text himself, but at the same time being able to assist the translator in choosing proper significators for the target text.

Having taken these aspects into consideration one may characterize the *commissioner-related dimension* in terms of information provided, that is to say:

(i) absence or in other words lack of information (also called information silence),
(ii) irrelevant and redundant information (also called information noise often resulting from the so-called information flood), and
(iii) sufficient information.

Information silence is the situation in which the translator does not acquire any information needed from the commissioner. Information noise is when he acquires more information than he needs and furthermore some pieces of information are irrelevant or do not help resolve the translator's doubts. Sufficient information is provided by the commissioner insofar as it answers the questions posed by the translator entirely. It should be stressed here that it is the task of the translator to obtain information from the commissioner and to pose pertinent questions. It is the translator who knows the art of translation and who realizes how helpful the commissioner's knowledge may be. The translator cannot expect that the commissioner will be versed in translation techniques and will supply the necessary information on his own initiative. Usually the commissioner, who does not operate as, e.g., a translation agency, has a very stereotypical vision of the translation process and such difficulties that may arise in its performance.

3.4.2. Commission length and duration

The dimension of commission length and duration affects the quality of translation to a considerable extent. In general it has been calculated that, e.g., a simultaneous interpreter should not translate for more than 30 minutes and then should have a break. The AIIC[19] Standards[20] specify that:

> Given the constraints related to quality and health, the normal duration of an interpreter's working day shall not exceed two sessions of between two-and-a-half and three hours each.

If he interprets longer texts without a break, he loses concentration and the risk of making a mistake rises very significantly.

Similar calculations are provided for translators. The European Union has adopted the standard of translating no more than six pages a day for the same reason. Moreover, some scholars indicate that the number of pages which may be translated successfully by a translator per day also depends on the complexity of the text.

Of course there are some individuals who can translate and interpret more and who are exceptions to the rule. But in general the time for translation should be calculated as time per individual page taking into consideration text difficulty margin (cf. Vermeer 2001; Samuelsson-Brown 2004 (2006): 93-113). For the purpose of this paper the properties of this dimension will be the following:

(i) reasonable terms, and
(ii) unreasonable terms.

As far as the time for translation is concerned reasonable terms are on average about six up to eight pages per day, where the page is of 1,800

19 The International Association of Conference Interpreters
20 <http://www.aiic.net/ViewPage.cfm/article122.htm>

characters with spaces. Of course it is possible for a translator to translate 30 pages within three days, if he knows the field very well. But if the commission is very long and requires the translator to work every day for a longer period of time, his ability to concentrate will not suffice to spend such long hours every day (for five or ten days consecutively) and the risk of an increase in the number of mistakes will be much greater.

To summarise, the more unreasonable the terms, in general the lower the quality of translated or interpreted texts.

3.4.3. Remuneration

Another factor affecting the quality of translation is the remuneration per page which the commissioner is willing to pay. In general, the rule is the cheaper the price per page, the less experienced and qualified the translator (cf. Vermeer 2001; Samuelsson-Brown 2004 (2006): 93-113). Again, the properties of this dimension are the following:

(i) reasonable terms, and
(ii) unreasonable terms.

As we live in a financially oriented society, it is scarcely credible that a translator will translate texts free of charge. Moreover, the remuneration must be sufficient to support the translator and his family. The lower the remuneration is, the more pages a day the translator must translate. Of course the remuneration depends on the living conditions in a given country and consequently may vary. The EU rate per page which is established for each member state reflects this interrelationship.

To some extent this dimension is the indicator whether one deals with professional or amateur translators, as amateur translators tend to charge dumping rates per page.[21]

---

21 On the remuneration of translators see the FIT Charter, the Association of Polish Translators [Stowarzyszenie Tłumaczy Polskich], TEPIS [Towarzystwo Tłumaczy Przysięgłych i Specjalistycznych TEPIS] recom-

3.5. Translator

Similarly as in commission-related dimensions, translator-related dimensions are of primary significance in assessing and predicting the quality of the translation product, which may be provided by a given translator. These dimensions reflect the translator's translative potential which influences the quality of translations produced by him.

3.5.1. Translator's educational background

When discussing the qualifications of an ideal legal translator usually it is stated that he should be both a lawyer and linguist (Kierzkowska 2002, 2005). However in reality such a situation is rare. In practice, a good legal translator may be a linguist who has acquired knowledge in the field of law independently, or the reverse. Therefore, the *dimension of translator's education* will include:

(i) lawyer or not-lawyer,
(ii) linguist or not-linguist.

But it cannot be denied that a person who is not versed in law and the legal systems of the source language and target language cannot translate legal texts successfully. Thus the translator's educational background definitely affects the quality of the translations he renders.

In translation studies there have been disputes concerning the learnability of translation skills (cf. Bassnett/Lefevere 1998 (2001): 123) or whether someone must be born a translator. In general, theorists and practitioners agree that the advanced knowledge of two foreign languages is insufficient and some talent or aptitude is necessary to execute the assignment. But education may enhance the inborn linguistic gift and improve the quality of translation products rendered by the translator significantly.

---

mendations as well as AIIC Professional Standards. The remuneration of sworn translators in Poland is regulated to some extent by law.

3.5.2. Translator's qualifications

Although now there are numerous university courses enabling fledgling translators to obtain the necessary education, in the past the situation was quite different. Therefore, many translators who render translation services now are self-taught persons who have learnt their craft by trial and error. In this work, a differentiation between university educated or self-taught translators will not be made. The qualities which will determine whether the translator is an amateur or a professional, will be whether the translator is versed in:

(i) the theory of translation and particularly specialized translation,
(ii) translation procedures, methods and strategies,
(iii) recognizing translation problems.

Therefore, the dimension of the translator's qualifications will have two properties:

(i) being a professional translator or
(ii) being an amateur translator.

3.5.3. Translator's personality

In pertinent literature also some character features are mentioned as having impact on the quality of translations. The most relevant to specialized translation seem whether the translator is:

(i) patient or impatient,
(ii) well-organized or disorganized,
(iii) inquisitive or not inquisitive.

Patience is necessary to spend long hours in front of the computer with the same text. It is especially important in the case of long commissions (translations of, e.g., whole books). Impatient translators quickly get bored and have problems with concentrating on the assignment.

In order to translate long texts translators must be well-organized and methodical. They must be able to plan their work in the longer term and have the self-discipline to work systematically every day.

The task of a legal translator requires an inquisitive mind which does not get discouraged by difficulties connected with calculating the source text meaning and establishing target text equivalents. Sometimes the quest for the meaning and optimal equivalents may be compared to the job of a detective who must collect all the clues in order to solve the puzzle.

3.5.4. Translator's approach to the role of the translator

The translator should be an active mediator in the process of communication (cf. the cultural mediator of Bochner (1981), translation as communication between translator and target audience by Gutt 2000 (2004b): 213-215) who strives to ensure that the message is conveyed to the recipient of the target text in accordance with the commissioner's intentions. In order to be a good translator one should meet the following requirements:

(i) broaden one's knowledge in the field of translation,
(ii) broaden one's knowledge in the field of specialization,
(iii) broaden one's knowledge in the field of linguistics (especially maintaining the advanced level of the source and target languages),
(iv) take part in different workshops, seminars and conferences for translators the aim of which is to increase translator's competences.

All these requirements which have been codified in the Polish Code of Professional Ethics for Sworn Translators (Kierzkowska 2005, 2011) are intended to ensure that the translator will be an active mediator in the communication process

The Polish Code of Professional Ethics will not be discussed here in detail. But it should be stressed that it obliges the translator to extend his knowledge constantly.

The translator is perceived of as a mediator among others by Steiner (1977 (2001)) who states that: "[...] the translator is a bilingual mediating agent between monolingual communication participants in two different language communities." Dollerup (2007: 141) states that: "Another desideratum for the professional translator is to know what precise needs (in a very broad sense) a translation should fulfil with recipients." Alternatively, Hatim (2001a), similarly as Toury

(1995 (2001)), states that translation is performed for the purpose of communication across cultures. The translator is perceived as a communicative link between the message sender and message recipient if they both communicate in different languages. The same view is shared by Olohan (2000), Šarčević (2000b), Jopek-Bosiacka (2006, 2010), Pommer (2008), and others in reference to legal translation. Taft (1981: 73 in Katan 1999 (2004): 12) on the other hand has described the competences (such as knowledge of society [here communicative community], communication skills, technical skills and social skills) of a translator performing the function of a mediator.[22] Those competences are accounted for in our dimensions as well.

The translator should be knowledgeable about the cultural background of the communicative community to which the author of the text and the translation recipients belong. The dimension of the cultural background competence should encompass three planes, that is:

(i) linguistic competence,
(ii) cultural competence, and
(iii) social competence.

Linguistic competence refers to linguistic skills and the desire of the translator to improve his skills in respect of the source and target language. Cultural competence, in turn, refers to the knowledge of culture and cultural norms binding in the source and target environments. Finally, social competence is the ability to adjust one's message to the social situation in which it is to serve.

---

22 "With regard to who the translator is, Hans Vermeer (1978) has described the translator as *bicultural*, and Marry Snell-Hornby (1992) has described him or her as a 'cross-cultural specialist'. Hewson and Martin talk of 'The Translation Operator as a Cultural Operator' (1991: 133-155, 160, 161) and discuss "the identity and motivations of the translation operator". [...] Hatim and Mason (1990: 11) make the same point: 'inevitably we feed our own beliefs, knowledge, attitudes and so on into our processing of texts, so that any translation will, to some extent, reflect the translator's own mental and cultural outlook, despite the best of impartial intentions'. Cultural mediators should therefore be extremely aware of their own cultural identity; and for this reason will need to understand how their own culture influences perception." (Katan 1999 (2004): 14)

With respect to the cultural competence of the translator, he may be:

(iv) mono-cultural,
(v) bi-cultural, or
(vi) poly-cultural (multi-cultural).

A mono-cultural translator is a person who knows only the culture of one language community, whereas a bi-cultural translator knows the source and target language culture, and a poly-cultural translator knows more than two language cultures.

3.5.5. Translator's competence verification

The quality of translations is conditioned by translator's competences and means of their verification (cf. Samuelsson-Brown 2004 (2006): 93-113). The verification process contributes to the enhancement of translator's competences and qualifications. The verification may be performed by different methods among which the following may be distinguished:

(i) examinations,
(ii) professional liability commissions, and
(iii) legal measures available to commissioners.

For instance, in Poland there is a national exam organized by the Ministry of Justice for persons wishing to work as sworn translators and interpreters. The exam is to ensure that unqualified persons cannot become sworn translators.

Moreover, there is the Professional Liability Commission appointed by the Polish Association of Translators, which deals with complaints that the quality of translations rendered by translators has been insufficient. It has the power to penalize sworn translators (the harshest measure is the deprivation of the right to be a sworn translator).

Additionally, dissatisfied commissioners may sue translators and claim damages in civil lawsuits.

3.5.6. Information accessibility at the time of translation rendering

The quality of translation product also depends on the access to information at the time of translation performance. A person interpreting in the courtroom will not have the time or the possibility to consult the Internet or dictionaries in order to find precise equivalents. In such situations he will have to resort to coining occasionalisms (usually descriptive significators), which would not appear if he had access to information sources. Such occasionalisms will serve the purpose of communicating the message for the purpose of a given communicative situation.

Moreover, there are other factors affecting the accessibility of information. For instance, the source and target language combination is a factor which affects the access to easily retrievable information (cf. Samuelsson-Brown 2004 (2006): 62-78). There are language pairs for which there are numerous bilingual dictionaries, including dictionaries of languages for special purposes and such language pairs for which there are no or just few dictionaries (Polish-Estonian, Polish-Chinese). Consulting a bilingual dictionary is the fastest (but not necessarily the most efficient) way to establish sets of available significators for source text units. If there are no bilingual dictionaries or there are dictionaries with insufficient lexicon, translators have to resort to other sources of information (cf. Dollerup 2007: 114-117). Sometimes they have to search for optimal significators via a pivot language (usually English or German), resort to academic course books, statutory instruments, etc. and apply the method of parallel text comparison, which prolong the process of translation. But:

> [...] the higher the degree of specialisation and the more experienced translators are, the less they are likely to relay on bilingual dictionaries alone, but will supplement these with synonym dictionaries and thesauri. (Dollerup 2007: 115)

Another factor, which affects translation process and quality, is the accessibility of publications concerning the legal translation of a given pair of languages. The quantity, quality and diversification of publications on translation problems which are available on the market affect the translator's chances to deepen professional knowledge, which should also include the tricks of the trade. The chance of avoiding making mistakes is also diminished then.

To sum up, the properties of the *dimension of access to information at the time of translation* may include whether the translator has:

(i) access to necessary information or not,
(ii) at his disposal IT tools such as computers, the Internet, terminological databases,
(iii) access to bilingual dictionaries,
(iv) access to publications concerning legal translation,
(v) access to publications concerning legal translation of a given pair of languages, etc.

3.5.7. Translator's information retrieval skills

Nowadays, in the era of globalization and information society it becomes more and more important to be able to retrieve and verify information. Computers and information technology (IT) have pervaded our every day and professional lives (Austermühl 2001). It is hard to imagine that just 10-15 years ago a translator could exist without a computer, just using a typewriter.

The danger connected with the easy access to unlimited pieces of information on the Internet is caused by the fact that some of it is rubbish. Therefore, translators have to be advanced computer and Internet-tool users who possess necessary skills to retrieve reliable information out of the flood of unreliable pieces. Moreover, they must be able to verify the reliability of information in other information sources (cf. Obenaus 1995; Samuelsson-Brown 2004 (2006): 62-78). The dimension of *translator's information retrieval skills* consists in establishing whether the translator is proficient in information retrieval skills or not.

3.6. Communicative communities

The first comprehensive theory of language and communicative community theories was developed by Ludwik Zabrocki (1963). This theory will be adapted to our needs. So firstly, a brief summary of Zabrocki's theory will be presented, and next, its modification to legal translation proposes will be elaborated on.

3.6.1. Zabrocki's theory of communicative communities

According to Zabrocki's theory a communicative community is:

> [...] a group of people, in which there exist objective conditions for exchange of information, regardless of the nature of communication means being employed. Thus, a communicative community may not necessarily have at its disposal a uniform means of communication, and this, in turn, implies, that there may exist various such means within one and the same community. Neither does the concept of a communicative community exclude the possibility of transmitting information by means of gestures. Consequently, the property which establishes a communicative community is the very fact of information transmission, and not the manner, in which this is accomplished. (Bańczerowski 2001: 36-37)

(cf. also Zabrocki 1963: 12-13). On the other hand:

> [...] a language community is a communicative community, which makes use of a uniform means of communication, that is, a common language. Hence, each language community is a communicative community, but not conversely. The latter is the basis for the former. The language community can be viewed as a product of and a kind of superstructure imposed upon the corresponding communicative community. The period of time that the latter lasts is also the time of duration of the former. (Bańczerowski 2001: 37)

Communicative communities are affected by numerous factors such as geographical, political, economic, religious, professional and cultural ones (Zabrocki 1963: 5-37). Nowadays, every person is a member of at least one communicative community, but it actually turns out that we usually belong to many communicative communities (family, friends, colleagues from work, etc.).

Moreover, Zabrocki lists the properties of communicative communities such as (i) active and passive, (ii) durable and indurable, (iii) loose and compact, (iv) primary and secondary, and (v) superordinate and subordinate (Bańczerowski 2001: 38, Zabrocki 1963).

Active communities want to exchange information and they act in such a manner so as to carry out communication processes, whereas in the case of passive communities the need to exchange information is not felt.

Durability of communities is related to the type of bonds between members of a specific community. If the bonds are long-lasting the community will be durable (e.g. a family, hunters' club), but when the bonds are temporary as in the case of people queuing for a bus in England we will have an indurable community (cf. Zabrocki 1963: 13, 20).

> The degree of compactness of a communicative community depends upon the number of the communicative contacts, which in a certain period of time are accomplished. In this respect feudal state communities were more loose than modern state communities. (Bańczerowski 2001: 38)

Primary communicative communities are communities in which native language acquisition takes place, e.g. school, kindergarten and playground communities. Secondary communities are, in turn, those in which we learn another language.

According to Zabrocki (cf. 1963: 12-37), the communicative community which has the political power in a multilingual state forms the superordinate language community.

Communicative communities aim at developing uniform means of communication in the form of a uniform language.

> As a rule that language prevails which represents a communicative community within which the communicative contact is established. In other words, the language which is used by the superordinate communicative community becomes dominant. In light of this assumption, a Swede speaks Swedish within the Swedish communicative community but with Englishmen or the persons of other language communities he will shift to English, since the English communicative community is superordinate with respect to the Swedish one. (Bańczerowski 2001: 39)

What must also be taken into consideration are

(i) integrational (unifying) factors, and
(ii) disintegrational (differentiating) factors (Zabrocki 1963: 16-20).

Integrational factors result in the formation of larger communicative communities out of smaller ones, whereas the disintegrational factors result in the opposite trend, that is to say, the division of one larger community into smaller ones. Right now we face a very strong trend of extralinguistic factors affecting the integration and disintegration of communicative communities. For instance, the Internet, on the one hand acts as a unifying factor by eliminating the disintegrational power of distance between the members of a given communicative community. On the other hand it can also act as a disintegrational factor within a multi-generation communicative community (e.g. a family in which a grandfather is used to sending letters by post, and the grandson to exchanging e-mails). So among the most typical integrational and disintegrational factors such as political, cultural, economic ones we should also enumerate the IT (the Internet, mobile phones, etc.). So it may be assumed that economy and modern information technologies are primary unifying factors in the process of the development of a modern global community using English as a community language all over the world. English acts as a unifying factor due to the fact that multilingualism is uneconomical. However, looking into the past one cannot be certain whether English will remain a *lingua franca* of a global community as it may in the future be replaced by, e.g., Chinese. In accordance with communicative communities theory the language of the optimal superordinate communicative community wins. Thus taking into consideration economic factors it may happen that English will be replaced by another language. This is due to the fact that language communities change over time. However, for the time being a worldwide communicative community seems to use English.

3.6.2. Communicative communities in legal communication

Kierzkowska (2002) distinguishes three types of recipients of legal translation products and suggests the translation strategy applicable to each of the groups. A similar approach is presented by Savory (1958:

26) who, on the other hand distinguishes four types of audience addressed by a translation that is:

> 1. Readers who are ignorant of the original language and are interested only in literary content. [[...]]. 2. Readers who are interested in learning the language of the original and wish to increase their familiarity with it partly through relevant literature in translation. [...]. 3. Readers who once knew the language of the original and have forgotten it. [...] 4. Specialists who are familiar with the original language (in Reiss 2000 (2004): 102).

Again he suggests four types of translation methods, which are adapted to each group respectively. However, it is hard to agree that such generalizations are sufficient for the purpose of translation. First of all it is possible to apply more than one translation method in one translation designed for one type of recipients. Moreover, limiting the scope of recipients to only three or four types also seems too simplistic. For the purpose of this work we will distinguish the properties of communicative communities affecting the process of choosing target text equivalents for source text translative units. However, it should be stressed here that the number of recipients (target text communicative communities) is unlimited, and the groups selected below serve only demonstrative purposes to illustrate the problems connected with the translation of legal texts. Each of the specified communicative communities may take different properties out of the sets described below.

There are three fundamental groups of communicative communities which may be distinguished as objects functioning in the translative space of legal communication that is:

(i) a communicative community to which the author of the translandum (source text) belongs,

(ii) a communicative community to which the translator belongs, and finally

(iii) a communicative community to which the recipients of translatum (target text) belong. [23]

23 Recipients of the target text are called differently in different translation studies and theories e.g. readership (Newmark 1988: 13).

However, when the author of the message speaks the source language and the recipient the target language the situation is even more complicated as the interlingual translation/interpreting has to be employed and this may require translation/interpreting between languages belonging to different legal systems.

The relation between the author and the translator may be as follows:

(i) the author and translator belong to the same communicative community,

(ii) the author and translator belong to different communicative communities, and

(iii) the author and translator partially belong to the same communicative community.

The relation between the translator and the recipient of the target text may *mutatis mutandis* be as follows:

(i) the translator and the recipient belong to the same communicative community,

(ii) the translator and the recipient belong to different communicative communities, and

(iii) the translator and the recipient partially belong to the same communicative community.

Every time the translator fails to belong to the same communicative community as the author the risk of mistranslation occurs. Every time the translator fails to belong to the same communicative community as the target text recipients the risk of producing an incomprehensible text occurs.

As has already been stated, the translator in order to translate the text at some point must become a member of the communicative community to which the source text author and target text recipients belong. However, it may happen that his knowledge is deficient and he will belong to such communicative communities only partially.

Let us now focus on the communicative communities to which the author and the translator belong.

If the translator belongs to the author's communicative community, there is a higher probability that the message (source text) produced by the author will be understood by the translator even if the community is very hermetic. The translator, who is a member of the author's communicative community, is at the same time the intended final recipient and the intermediary recipient/sender. The property of being an intended or non-intended intermediary recipient would be of importance whether the author is aware of the state of translation art or not. Moreover, the properties of expertise and awareness of legal system differences will also affect the message. Expert communicative community members are prone to produce more specialised texts, with a higher concentration of specialised terminology, than the members of a lay communicative community. Furthermore, if the author is aware of the legal system differences and knows that the text will be translated into the target language, he may endeavour to facilitate understanding of source legal system-bound terminology to target legal system recipients.

However if the translator does not belong to the author's communicative community, the properties of the author and of that community would be vital for the understanding of the source text. The more hermetic the communicative community is and the less able to communicate clearly and unambiguously the author is, the more difficult it is for the translator to grasp the whole meaning of the source text. Consequently, the greater the risk of making mistakes when interpreting the source text.

It should be borne in mind, however, that those authors who are aware of the art of translation and legal system differences might facilitate the translator's job to a large extent if at the moment of text production they know that the text will be translated (that is when the translator is an intended intermediary recipient).

In general if the author is unable to adjust his message to the intended recipient needs, it actually is immaterial whether he is aware of the art of translation or not. If the author is an expert he is usually more prone to produce hermetic texts as he will aim at precision in his field of expertise.

To sum up, the communicative community to which the author of the text belongs will affect the process of establishing the intended meaning of the source text. In general, the translator should account for the fact that the translation process is affected by possible relations/interactions between all those groups of communicative communities.

Each communicative community operating in legal reality may be characterized by five sets of properties specified by Zabrocki (1963), but apart from these five sets of properties there are other properties, which are even more pertinent from the translator's point of view, e.g.:

(i) language community,
(ii) education of community members,
(iii) profession of community members,
(iv) nationality of community members, and
(v) presupposed knowledge of community members.

Moreover, each community may have one or a combination of the following four properties:

(i) communicative communities aware of the source language legal system, and
(ii) communicative communities unaware of the source language legal system,
(iii) communicative communities aware of the target language legal system, and
(iv) communicative communities unaware of the target language legal system.

In Kierzkowska's model (2002) the first two properties were described as close and distant recipients, respectively.

In order to characterize communicative communities of the source text the author, translator and translation recipient will use the dimensions with the following sets of properties:

(i) active or passive,
(ii) loose or compact,
(iii) primary, secondary or mixed,
(iv) superordinate, subordinate or independent,
(v) monolingual or multilingual or plurilingual,
(vi) expert, lay or mixed,
(vii) hermetic or non-hermetic, and
(viii) aware and unaware of legal systems.

Each communicative community may assume one property from each set of properties.

The property of being *active* means that the members of a given communicative community are willing to exchange information and therefore are open to communication. *Passive* communicative communities are not interested in exchanging information and thus their willingness to understand the message will be much lower than in the case of active communicative communities.

The property of being *loose* or *compact* refers to the number of contacts, which take place within a given communicative community. Loose communicative communities make contact rarely, whereas compact communicative communities exchange information frequently. Therefore, the knowledge of the compact communicative communities is usually greater than that of loose communicative communities.

Primary communicative communities in translation are communicative communities for which the target language is the native language. Whereas *secondary* communicative communities will be communicative communities for which the target language is a foreign language. *Mixed* communicative communities will be composed of some members for whom the target language is a foreign language and some members for whom the target language is a native language.

The relationship designation of being *superordinate*, *subordinate* or *independent* refers to the relationship between the source language communicative community (the sender of the message formulated in the source language) and target language communicative community (the recipient of the message formulated in the target language). Thus, one may differentiate

(i) a superordinate source language communicative community sending a message to the subordinate target language communicative community,

(ii) a subordinate source language communicative community sending a message to the superordinate target language communicative community, and finally

(iii) independent source language communicative communities sending a message to the independent target language communicative community.

Superordinate communicative communities are communities which due to their status may impose their legal interpretation of the message on the subordinate language communities. It means that the superordinate language community imposes its legal system on the subordinate language community members. It occurs when the law of the superordinate language community is to be applied in the case of disputes between two communities, or to legal relations between communities established by the message sent by one community to the other (e.g. provisions of private and public international law). In other words, if the message (the text which is to be translated) constitutes any legal bonds between the source-language communicative community and target language communicative community, one may identify a subordinate and superordinate communicative community.

The independent communicative communities, in contrast, are communities which simply exchange information, but the exchanged messages do not constitute any legal bonds between the source-language communicative community and target language communicative community. The role of messages is simply informative.

There are also monolingual, multilingual and plurilingual communicative communities. *Monolingual* communicative communities are communities established by people knowing only one language and therefore as a rule having a limited knowledge about the other language legal system. *Multilingual* communicative communities will be communities composed of members who use different mother tongues and the target language is just the language of international communication for them. But it should be stressed that for some members of such a community the target language may be the native language and the language of international communication at the same time. Of course source language communicative communities *per analogiam* may also be monolingual and multilingual. But for the purpose of this work, only target language communicative communities will be considered. However, there are also *plurilingual communicative communities* which are communities operating in legal reality with one legal system but plurilingual legislation enacted due to the co-existence of ethnic minorities in one territory or one legal system being imposed on the nations which are member states of an international organization (e.g. the European Union).

The dimension of being a member of an expert, lay or mixed communicative community refers to the knowledge, experience and education of the communicative community members. *Expert communicative communities* are composed of people knowing at least their own legal system (the legal system of the target or their native language). An expert communicative community will be composed of e.g. lawyers. *Lay communicative communities* are composed of people having a very limited knowledge of the legal system in which they function. They often function in such a system by conforming to traditional, customary modes of behaviour and moral standards rather than complying with legal provisions binding in their country of origin. Therefore they often unconsciously break the law if the law is not in accordance with their common sense and sense of justice (e.g. by not paying the tax on loans from their relatives or friends, etc.). A *mixed communicative community* will be composed of both experts and laypersons. The translation for the purpose of such a community will pose more problems than the translation for homogeneous communicative communities, as divergent or sometimes even opposing/contradictory communicative needs will have to be satisfied by the translated text.

The feature of being *hermetic* or *non-hermetic* refers to the availability of language sources. Each communicative community uses a special language typical of its members. The language is used, developed and understood by the members of a given communicative community and at the same time may be difficult to understand for persons not belonging to this community. The more difficult it is to understand and learn the language of a given communicative community, the more hermetic the language is. Furthermore, the number of publications in and about a given language will also affect the hermetic character of the language in question.

For instance, the language of Gypsies in Poland is very hermetic as there are no dictionaries or course books on it. It is passed from one generation to another and it mainly exists in its oral variant. But there will be other pairs of languages within which one will be hermetic in relation to one another. As already mentioned, the Polish-Estonian pair is very hermetic, as there are very limited possibilities for a Pole to learn Estonian in Poland. There are no Polish-Estonian and Estonian-Polish legal dictionaries, etc. The language of teenagers may be very hermetic to adults, and so on.

The communicative community of lawyers using legal language as means of communication is conservative/hermetic as the language serves the purpose of facilitating communication within their community and constituting a communicational barrier. The purpose of the barrier is not to allow the community to be absorbed by other communities and not to enable any other community to be absorbed by the communicative community of lawyers. Moreover,

> [...] every people or nation identifies itself through the language, in which it has stored its unique historical, spiritual, and material development. History stores in the languages the reflection of an extralingual system, which, in turn, is uniquely mirrored by particular language communities. (Bańczerowski 2001: 40)

Therefore, in the instance of hermetic languages it is very difficult and time-consuming for a translator to establish potential target language significators for the source language translative units. In such cases, the translator will be more prone to resort to descriptive and denotative significators in cases in which he will be unable to find connotative ones.

There are also such communicative communities which are *aware* of the differences in legal systems and such which are *unaware* of the differences in legal systems. Aware communicative communities will expect the translation to convey the approximate meaning and will be open to different types of borrowings stressing the difference between the source language legal system and the target language legal system, whereas unaware communicative communities will tend to associate source language legal system elements with target language legal system elements.

The impact of the properties of selected communicative communities on translation will be discussed in more detail below and in subsequent chapters.

We have distinguished three groups of communicative communities that is (i) the communicative community to which the author of the text belongs (but it should be borne in mind that sometimes the author of the text does not belong to the communicative community of the source-text recipients and therefore there may be one more communicative community then), (ii) the communicative community to which the translator belongs and (iii) the communicative community formed by the recipients of translation. Since the translator is the person calculating the meaning of the source text and its component parts it is necessary first to analyse the relation between the first and second type of communicative communities.

However, it should be borne in mind that in the light of the theory of communicative communities the translator as an intermediary recipient of the source text and an intermediary sender of the target text (cf. F. Grucza's (1981, 1998) translation process model) is always predestined to become a member of the communicative community to which the primary sender (the author of the source text) and the final recipient (the target text recipient) belong. Otherwise, we would have to assume that translation is impossible of performance or futile, due to the fact that (i) if the translator is not a member of the communicative community to which the author of the text belongs, he will not be able to understand the message, and/or (ii) if the translator is not a member of the communicative community to which the target text recipient belongs, he most probably will not be able to produce the target text which will be understandable and comprehensible for such a communicative community.

In general, the author creates the source text for a specific purpose and specific recipients. It is a well-known fact that most authors adjust their messages subconsciously or consciously to the communicative community of message recipients. In case of legal communication we may distinguish the following communication situations:

(i) the author produces a message for a recipient knowing the source language,
(ii) the author produces a message for a recipient not knowing the source language, and finally
(iii) the author produces a message for recipients knowing and not knowing the source language.

The first communicative situation takes place when the author at the time of the message creation does not take into consideration the fact that it may be translated into other languages in the future. He creates the text for a specific audience (communicative community to which he belongs). The primary sender and the intended final recipient constitute the author's communicative community communicating in the source language. The non-intended final recipient is a member of the target language communicative community. And the translator normally belongs to the third communicative community. In that case the important dimensions concerning the author of the source text would be the following: (i) the authorship of the text, (ii) the author's professional knowledge and (iii) his communicative skills. The dimension concerning his current professional up-to-date knowledge would be irrelevant in that case due to the fact that at the moment of text creation the author is not aware that the text will be translated into a foreign language in the future. However, two variants may be distinguished here. The translator may be taken into consideration as the intended intermediary recipient and as a non-intended intermediary recipient. In such a translative system all four author-related dimensions will be applicable.

If the author produces a message for a recipient not knowing the source language, there are two intended recipients of the text, that is to say the translator as an intermediary recipient and target language speaking communicative community.

If the author produces a message for recipients knowing and not knowing the source language, we find three intended recipients of the source text. The first recipient group is composed of recipients belonging to the author's communicative community. The second recipient, who is an intermediary, is the translator, although not always recognized by the author as the intended recipient. And the third recipient is the target language communicative community.

Here are six exemplary types of texts which represent different communicative situations for which the author may assume different properties, which will affect his communication with the text recipients (the communicative community to which he is supposed to belong and for which he creates the message).

(i) A statute

Statutes are prepared by a legislator. In Poland for instancc a lcgislator is a fictious person who in fact at the very beginning is usually composed of a panel of lawyers who at least in theory should specialize in legal drafting. The draft is sometimes prepared in cooperation with specialists in a given field which is to be regulated by the statute. Next, the draft is sent to Parliament for consideration. Every Member of Parliament has a right to suggest some changes in the contents of the draft. Then the bill which is created as a result of the cooperation of lawyers, specialists and MPs must be enacted (accepted by Parliament and the President). When the procedure is completed the bill becomes a statutory instrument. The communicative community to which the author of the statute belongs is extremely active, durable, compact, superordinate, as far as its expertise is concerned it is a mixed community, and finally hermetic. Most of the members of the community are aware of the source language legal system. The aim of the legislation is to inform the citizen about his rights and duties. Each and every citizen should know the law he is supposed to abide by. But in fact even lawyers are unable to keep up-to-date with all the enacted legislation and they have to specialize in a given branch of law. The principles *ignorantia iuris (juris) nocet* and *ignorantia iuris (juris) non excusat* serve the purpose of making the law enforceable and penalizing the citizen breaking the law no matter whether he breaks the law consciously or unconsciously. Concluding, the recipients of the message (a statutory instrument) form two groups: (i) lawyers who belong to the same legal community as the legislator and (ii) common people who do not belong to the same communicative community as the legislator. Both groups are the intended recipients of legislation. However, legislation is directly addressed only to the first group, which is supposed to act on many occasions as an intermediary in communicating it to the second group of recipients.

(ii) A contract in the form of a notarial act (deed)

Such contracts are prepared in Poland by notaries who act as experts and if need be are obliged to explain the meaning of the contract orally to the parties. However, the burden to ask proper questions clarifying unknown contents of the contract is on the parties not on the notary. The notary is only obliged to read out the contract to the interested parties. Therefore the author of the contract (the notary) may belong to a different communicative community than its recipients (the parties obliged to perform it). It happens so because a notary drafting a notarial document belongs to a passive, superordinate, monolingual, expert, hermetic and aware of the source language legal system communicative community.

(iii) A contract for the sale of a vehicle

In Poland one may use a ready to print contract form or the contract may be prepared by the buyer and the seller without the help of a lawyer. Those parties when signing the contract belong to the same communicative community which is active, loose (one time contact not to be continued in the future), monolingual, lay and non-hermetic.

(iv) A holograph testament

It is usually prepared by a layperson (the testator) who wishes to inform his successors about his last will (the distribution of his property after his death). As a rule the testator and the successors belong to the same communicative community. They belong to the communicative community which is active, monolingual, lay and non-hermetic.

(v) A petition

Petitions are addressed at the same time to the court and the defendant/respondent. The petitioner may be the author of the petition or he may resort to the help of a lawyer. If the petitioner is the author of the petition, he most probably will belong to the same communicative community as the defendant/respondent. On the other hand if the lawyer is the author, he most probably will belong to the same communicative community as the court. The petitioner may be expert, lay or mixed and depending on which of those three properties he takes on, he will take on different properties from other dimensions.

(vi) A judgment

A judgment is drafted by the court and although it is addressed to the parties engaging in a dispute before the court, such parties rarely belong to the same communicative community as the court. Therefore the parties not belonging to the same communicative community as the court are entitled to legal representation. Legal representation is usually exercised by lawyers who are supposed to act as intermediaries in court-to-participant in proceedings communication. In other words, legal representatives are supposed to act as translators/interpreters in intralingual communication. The court belongs to the hermetic, superordinate and expert communicative community whereas the participants in proceedings may be expert, lay or mixed. It should be borne in mind that the suggested properties may change in real life situations and are just hypothetical but statistically most probable.

Concluding, at the level of monolingual legal communication the author of the produced message and its recipient may belong to different communicative communities and their communication without the help of a person belonging to both communicative communities able to translate the messages may not be effective. Of course in many situations the intralingual- and interlingual-translation may be necessary only for the benefit of one participant (usually lacking in legal knowledge). Sometimes it even happens that the author of the source text does not produce the text with the intended recipient's knowledge in mind. This often happens in the case of academic course-books in Poland which are written in such a hermetic language that understanding them without the help of the lecturer is extremely difficult. The lecturer in such cases acts as an intralingual translator or interpreter to be exact.

3.7. Concluding remarks

The list of the dimensions presented above is not exhaustive and may be extended to serve the purposes of other translational situations. However, the aim of this work is to show the application of the approach to specific translational situations (legal communication). Some of these dimensions have also been described by Kierzkowska (2002: 74-86) and Šarčević (2000b).

The commissioner- and translator-related dimensions definitely affect the quality of the produced target-text (cf. Hejwowski 2004: 124-149). However, in this work they will not be analysed in detail. The assumption is that the properties of those dimensions are ideal for the purpose of translation. They will be taken into consideration only when discussing some translation problems (mistakes and errors) observed in analysed translations.

4. Calculating Translandive Text Meaning

4.1. Introductory remarks on meaning in translation

As long as we know, there have been different approaches to translation. Initially, the word-for-word translation was considered translation proper. Then, translators started noticing that this method has deficiencies and may result in distortions in the meaning and nearly always results in target texts being difficult to follow. Cicero, was one of the first translators known at present to notice that there is an alternative for word-for-word translation as analysing his translations he admitted that there are some passages *in quibus non verbum pro verbo necesse habui reddere, sed omnium verborum vimque servavi.*[24] Saint Jerome of Stridonium noted that *non verbum e verbo sed sensum exprimere de sensu* (to express not word by word, but sense by sense), which means that the *sense* of the translated message is more important than words. Martin Luther, in turn, opted for conveying the *message* in an understandable way. Therefore his approach to the translation of the Bible, published first in 1522, was revolutionary in a way, as he applied what we call now a target-oriented translation in order to make the text of the Bible comprehensible for everyday Germans[25]. More recent theories of translation put emphasis on the meaning, function and effect.

---

24 "And I did not translate them as an interpreter, but as an orator, keeping the same ideas and the forms, or as one might say, the 'figures' of thought, but in language which conforms to our usage. And in so doing, I did not hold it necessary to render word for word, but I preserved the general style and force of the language." (*De optimoe genere oratum 5.14-15*, English version in Copeland, 1995: 33)

25 "We shouldn't go and ask the Latin text how to speak German, as those fools do, we must ask the housewives and children, the ordinary man in the street and listen to what they say and translate accordingly – then they'll understand

Tytler in his *Essay on the Principles of Translation* of 1790 introduced three laws of translation, that is:

> I. That the Translation should give a complete transcript of the ideas of the original work.
> II. That the style and manner of writing should be of the same character with that of the original.
> III. That the Translation should have all the ease of original composition. (Tytler 2007: 9)

He stated that the *meaning* and the *sense* of the author should be conveyed in the target text but:

> Where the sense of an author is doubtful, and where more than one meaning can be given to the same passage or expression, (which, by the way, is always a defect in composition), the translator is called upon to exercise his judgment, and to select that meaning which is most consonant to the train of thought in the whole passage, or to the author's usual mode of thinking, and of expressing himself. To imitate the obscurity or ambiguity of the original, is a fault; and it is still a greater, to give more than one meaning [...]. (Tytler 2007: 17-18)

The meaning of the source text translative units is divided in translation studies into (i) the referential meaning, (ii) the pragmatic meaning and (iii) the intralingual meaning (cf. Lipiński 2000).

Referential meaning is the relation between the sign (translative unit) and its referent, that is to say the element of reality to which the sign refers, "the words as symbols which refer to objects, events, abstracts, relations" (Nida/Taber 1982 (2004): 56).

Pragmatic meaning is the relation between the sign and its users (the communicative community using a given sign in a given communicative context) (it is also called the connotative meaning and defined as "[...] the words as prompters of reactions of the participants in communication" (Nida/Taber 1982 (2004): 56)). It especially refers to such signs which have their synonyms or quasi-synonyms[26] in a given

---

and see we're talking proper German to them." (from *Sendbrief vom Dolmetschen* translated by Snell-Hornby, in Snell-Hornby 1995: 9)

26 "The ancient addition to English mixture and the Old English relish from synonym joined in the Middle English period to produce word-doubling on an

source text. In such situations the members of a communicative community decide which sign to use or sometimes they even invent or coin new signs for the purpose of communication within the communicative community. Sometimes the signs are invented to make the communication more hermetic and difficult to understand to non-members of a given communicative community[27] or to make the language in which a given community communicates more prestigious[28]. Tiersma (1999: 5) accurately remarks that:

> [...] lawyers [...] tend to quickly revert to ponderous, arcane, and obscure legal language. From the point of view of the public, virtually every feature of legal language in some way impedes clear communication.

Intralingual meaning, on the other hand, is the relation between the signs of a given language. Although in the case of communication for special purposes it plays a marginal role, it may also lead to the interference between the source text features and target text features (e.g. using inappropriate personal pronouns the gender of which agrees with the gender of the source-text noun instead of the target text noun, etc.) (Lipiński 2000: 72-85).

Gutt (2000: 41-53), on the other hand, claims that the translator should aim at reaching *optimal relevance* which is necessary to provide successful communication, and the aim may be reached by using

---

unprecedented scale. With deposits of Celtic and Norse, Latin, and now French, the storehouse of word material was filled to overflowing. And overflow it did, scattering bilingual synonyms in every direction, and establishing a habit that has carried into the present. What may have once been rationalized as necessary translation soon became a fixed style." (Mellinkoff 1963: 120)

27 "For years French had been the language of education (along with Latin for the clergy and the scholarly). The more English became the common currency of all classes of society, the more French became the mark of the noble and the wealthy. And it was precisely these two groups who sent their sons to the law. No others could afford it. No others had the same interest in knowing the intricacies of the land law. Like other medieval arts organized into guilds, the law was a mystery. And there is no reason to believe that the ruling cliques of England were eager to share the legal mysteries with plebeians." (Mellinkoff 1963: 100-101)

28 "There is evidence that the profession was less than enthusiastic over being ordered to talk and write English." (Mellinkoff 1963: 128)

the right contextual information. In general, he perceives translation as the process of overcoming context- and culture-based problems (cf. also Gutt 2004a).

Kielar (1977: 39, 48) also opts for conveying the *relevant meaning* of the source text in the target text. She (1999: 188) states that:

> Gutt's relevance (1991) seems to be the key to the translator's success. [...] The translator is supposed to make some assumptions about what is relevant to his receptors. [...] Such procedures are highly flexible: the principle of relevance is applied to a set of circumstances and it is valid only under such circumstances. With the principle of relevance in mind, the translator takes into account the whole network of complex social and cultural relations which determine the meaning of allegedly corresponding SL and TL textual elements and texts.

Vermeer focuses on the function (or in other words *skopos*) of the text and the modification of the target text in such a way that it does not necessarily convey the meaning but the function intended for the target text. At the same time he stresses that the source text and the target text do not have to have the same function (Vermeer 2001: 232).

F. Grucza (1985, 1986a, 1986b, 1996, 1999) perceives translation not only as a mechanical process of copying the meaning of a source text in the form of a target text but also an act of creation.

De Groot (1988: 409) states that when translating legal texts it is necessary to compare the *meaning* of the source term with the meaning of the target term in another language or legal system in order to check whether they may be treated as equivalents.

Joseph (1995: 17), similarly as F. Grucza (1999: 3), states that it is impossible to convey the whole content of the text due to differing traditional, cultural systemic, political and literary factors.

Pieńkos (1999: 119) claims that translation is not the search for identical meaning but the quest for situational equivalence.

Kierzkowska (2002: 41), similarly as Casagrande (1954: 335)[29] claims that it is impossible to convey the whole content of a legal text in translation due to the fact that each element of a statutory text refers

29 "The emphasis is on the content of the message as such rather than on its aesthetic form, grammatical form or the cultural context, all of which are subsidiary to the practical, matter-of-fact goal."

to a strictly specified reality (legal system), and the conveyance of all primary meanings and associations is in fact impossible of performance. Consequently, many of the stylistic or aesthetic features of source texts, as of secondary importance for target text recipients, are not revealed in the target text. Jumpelt (1961: 18), on the other hand, put emphasis on conveying the information content of the source text in specialized translation similarly as Kade (1968: 75) who perceived translation as the reproduction of the source text content.

Šarčević (2000b) states that when translating authoritative (having legal force, binding) texts if the text of the translation is to have the same function as the source text, it is most important to produce translations which would convey not the same meaning (as it is actually impossible to convey the same meaning), but which would lead to the same *legal effect* (translations which would be interpreted in the same way as far as legal results are concerned as the original).

As we can see from just a few quoted approaches to translation (cf. also Krzeszowski 2012), there has been a shift from conveying words, through the necessity to convey the meaning, function, up to the conveyance of the effect of the source text in the target text.

4.2. Calculating translandive text meaning

Calculating the translandive text meaning is the starting point of each translation enterprise, and the translative meaning is what we achieve at the end of it. The translative meaning is not only affected by the translandive one but also affected by the *skopos* of the translational action and the source text and target text legal effect. Those features will be taken into account when finding optimal equivalents in order to decide which similarities and differences between the source text translative unit and its potential equivalent must be made visible for the communicative community for which the target text is intended. The meaning cannot be ignored in the act of communication because understanding only occurs when the speaker and listener (recipient) attach the same meaning and sense to words and sentences (Bautro

1935: 14). When calculating the translative meaning one must also be aware that:

> legal (and especially political) doctrine may exercise and does exercise a mighty influence upon the legal system by unconsciously and consciously determining the meaning of sign vehicles. Thus, language is an important means of interaction between public opinion and a legal system (Hexner 1941: 51).

The meaning of the source text is calculated on the basis of the meaning of its component parts embedded in the context.

Therefore, each translative unit may have three sets of meaning, that is:

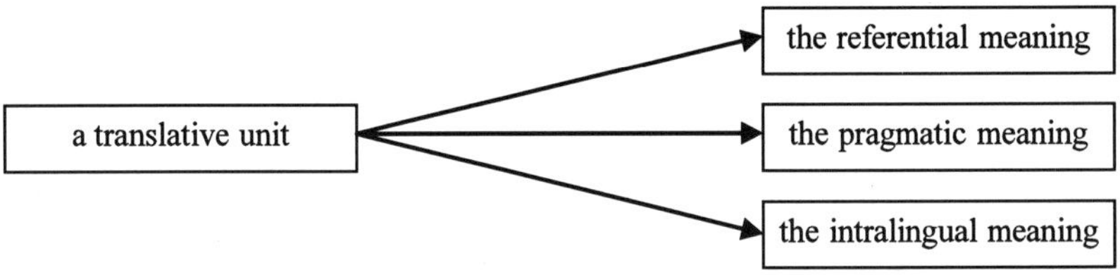

Figure 3. Types of meanings in translation.

As far as the division into referential, pragmatic and intralingual meanings is concerned in the case of translation of texts formulated in languages for special purposes, the most important as a rule is the referential meaning, then pragmatic one (cf. Šarčević 2000b: 66, Sager/Dungworth/McDonald 1980: 70-81; Lerat 1995; Lipiński 2000: 39-53). Nevertheless, it does not mean that in legal translation we may ignore the pragmatic meaning. The intralingual meaning plays a marginal role and it will be taken into consideration only when discussing translative errors resulting from interlingual interference.

All meanings of a given translative unit whether referential or pragmatic constitute the set of potential translative meanings. The task of the translator is to choose the proper meaning out of the set. We may distinguish three typical sets of meanings:

(i) the empty set (the rarest, however possible, cf. subchapter 4.7. on words with undecodable meanings),

(ii) one element set (which is the most comfortable situation for the translator as the choice is unambiguous and not burdened with the risk of a mistake), and

(iii) more than one element set (when the source-text dimensions have to be applied in order to choose the proper meaning).

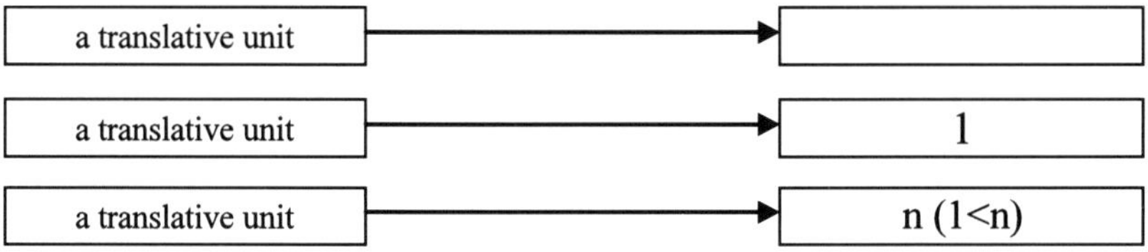

Figure 4. Sets of potential meanings of the translandive text units for situations (i), (ii), and (iii) respectively.

In order to be able to find out the meaning of the text, the translator has to understand it but not over-interpret it (Šarčević 2000b: 87).

There are some text features which enable prediction of the general meaning of the text, of course. One such feature is the genre of the text. For instance, if the text is a statutory instrument, it would impose rights and duties on the actors enumerated in the text. If the text were a testament, it would state the testator's (author's) wishes concerning the distribution of his estate, etc. Therefore, the feature of the text genre, gives the translator a general idea of the meaning of the source text (at least the most probable meaning as there are some divergences and exceptions from the rule, e.g. the testament of Pope John Paul II was a moral testament rather than the disposal of his earthly belongings).

As far as the context is concerned, the macrostructure of the text and the location of the text component part within the macrostructure should be mentioned. To be more explicit, the calculation (in colloquial language: interpretation; or in legal terms: construction) of the meaning of the source text translative units depends on context. Context is a type of monitoring information enabling one to check whether the calculated meaning is optimal in a given communicative situation because:

> [...] the meaning of legal texts is usually dependent on local context, thus raising the question to what extent the actual receivers, i.e., the judiciary, can be

expected to attach the same meaning to each of the parallel texts of a plurilingual instrument. While Vermeer and other contemporary translation theorists regard local context as being synonymous with cultural context (Hönig/Kussmaul 1982: 58; exceptions in Kussmaul 1995: 74), the meaning of legal texts is determined primarily by legal context. When dealing with legal texts, it is always necessary to determine according to which legal system the text, parts thereof, or even individual institutions and concepts are to be interpreted (Šarčević 2000b: 67).

Lawyers apply different methods of construction of legal texts. In general, we may distinguish six main types of construction (cf. Stawecki, Winczorek 2002: 151) that is:

(i) literal,
(ii) grammatical,
(iii) systemic,
(iv) teleological,
(v) comparative,
(vi) expanding, and finally
(vii) restricting.

Lawyers apply the so-called *systemic construction / interpretation* in which the actual meaning of a legal provision is established / calculated on the basis of the provision's location within a given statutory instrument, branch of law and the rules of interpretation adopted in a given legal system or branch of law. There is also the *contextual construction / interpretation* used by lawyers which is a type of systemic construction (also cf. Šarčević 2000b: 62). In general it is assumed that the provision has been located in a given part of a text by the legislator consciously, and therefore the location (here: the context) affects the meaning of a given legal provision (Kaczmarek/Matulewska 2008: 85-86). Not only lawyers but also translators need to heed the context in order to calculate the meaning. Furthermore, context may be especially important in situations in which the author of the source text uses polysemous translative units or cuts descriptive terms leaving only the root of the term for the purpose of language economy. Let us give a few examples.

(45) Polish Code of Commercial Companies and Partnerships
(Dział III *Spółki kapitałowe*)

Art. 19. Złożenie podpisów przez wszystkich członków zarządu pod dokumentem wystawionym przez *spółkę* jest wymagane tylko w przypadku, gdy ustawa tak stanowi.
(Division III *Companies*)
Sec. 19. Signatures of all members of the management board on a document executed by the *company* shall be required only in instances prescribed by the law.

The fact that article 19 is located in Division III titled *Companies* helps solve the problem whether the meaning of the term *spółka* is *a partnership*, *a company* or *a partnership and a company* despite the fact that the Polish legislator uses in this fragment the hypernym *spółka* meaning both *spółka osobowa* (*a partnership*) and *spółka kapitałowa* (*a company/a corporation*).

(46) Polish Code of Civil Procedure.
DZIAŁ V. *Pełnomocnicy procesowi*
Art. 86. Strony i ich organy lub przedstawiciele ustawowi mogą działać przed sądem osobiście lub przez *pełnomocników*.
DIVISION V. *Attorneys ad litem*
Article 86. Parties and their bodies or statutory representatives may act before the court personally or through their *attorneys (ad litem)*.

Similarly, the heading of the part devoted to *attorneys ad litem* informs the translator that the term *pełnomocnik* is in fact *pełnomocnik procesowy*.

There is also *grammatical construction / interpretation* which is used by lawyers when they analyse the words and their grammatical setting to find out the meaning. There is also a *linguistic* or *linguistic and logical construction / interpretation* method based on the semantic, syntactic, stylistic and logical interpretation of the text (also cf. Šarčević 2000b: 62, Kaczmarek/Matulewska 2008: 84-85, 87-88). A *teleological construction / interpretation* method is used when in order to decipher the meaning of the text, its purpose is taken into account (also cf. Šarčević 2000b: 62; Kaczmarek/Matulewska 2008: 86-87). The *comparative construction / interpretation* is based on the comparison of the text the meaning of which has not been established yet with texts the meaning of which have already been established (cf. Kaczmarek/Matulewska 2008: 87). The *restricting and expanding construction* methods are the mixtures of grammatical and teleological construction methods. In the former type of construction the shared meaning established as a result of the application of the two interpretation methods is taken as the proper one, whereas in the latter case the broadest meaning is taken (in other words, the sum of the meanings established by the application of the grammatical and teleological interpretation methods) (cf. Kaczmarek/Matulewska 2008: 88-91).

In general, although translators are not supposed to interpret the text, they are supposed to understand it, and in order to understand the source text, they often have to apply one of the above-mentioned construction (interpretation) methods.

4.3. Calculating meaning of translandive text component parts

In order to calculate the meaning of the source text, the translator must decipher (or *decode* (Bassnett 1980 (2004): 23) or *deconstruct* (Davis 2001 (2004)) the meaning of translandive units, which potentially may affect the process of translation. Moreover, "[...] close reading is required, in any challenging text, of the words both out of and in context. In principle, everything has to be looked up that does not make good sense in its context" (Newmark 1988: 11).

The source-text related dimensions defined in chapter 3 serve the purpose of establishing the meanings of the source text and its component parts.

I will consider the following types of translation units for the purpose of this paper:

(i) technical terms,
(ii) semi-technical terms,
(iii) polysemous and homonymous terms,
(iv) words and expressions with flexible meaning,
(v) euphemisms and metaphors,
(vi) system bound terms, and
(vii) translandive units with undecodable meaning.

The procedure of deciphering the meaning will establish which properties are taken on by the term from particular dimensions. The following dimensions are considered most important to illustrate the process of establishing the translandive meaning:
(xi) the authorship of the source-text,
(xii) the source-text delivery form,
(xiii) the source-text status,
(xiv) the time of source text creation,
(xv) the branch of law to which the text refers,
(xvi) the text genre,
(xvii) the language of the source text,
(xviii) the lect,
(xix) the source-text legal reality, and
(xx) the source text language variety existence.

Statistically, the more potential meanings the translative unit has, the more dimensions have to be accounted for in order to calculate the meaning for the purpose of a translation of a given text. Dimensions help eliminate the meanings which are not applicable (not optimal) in a given communicative situation. But in a majority of situations those ten dimensions relevant for written texts suffice to establish the meaning of the source text.

Finally, it should also be emphasised here that the dimension of the text genre or branch of law may refer to the text as well as its component parts and when establishing the meaning both levels should be taken into consideration as for instance intertextual relations may affect the choice of the property in reference to a specific term used in the text. For instance, a winding-up order may refer to the financial statements and apart from insolvency law it may contain terminology from accounting (in which case the English terms *assets*, *estate* and *claim* would be translated differently into Polish depending on the lect present in the translandive unit in question).

In order to present the application of the procedure, I have chosen some units frequently found in texts formulated in different legal language genres.

4.4. Technical terms

Legal vocabulary is composed of technical terms, semi-technical terms, and everyday vocabulary (Alcaraz/Hughes 2002: 16-18). *Technical terms* are usually defined as terms functioning in a given language for special purposes with a precise meaning. Moreover, such terms preserve their specialized meaning even if they start being used in everyday speech. They are often very formal and have their colloquial language counterparts. According to David/Brierley (1985: 19) each legal system

> [...] has a vocabulary used to express concepts, its rules and arranged into categories, it has techniques for expressing rules and interpreting them, it is linked to a view of the social order itself, which determines the way in which the law is applied and shapes the very function of law in that society.

Among such terms we may enumerate *petitioner* and *plaintiff*. Let us imagine that we deal with a petition submitted by counsel on behalf of their client. The properties of the term in respect to the dimensions listed above would be as follows.

Properties taken by the translative unit: *petitioner*

(i) the author of the source-text: usually a lawyer
(ii) source-text delivery form: written
(iii) source-text status: a document
(iv) the time of source text creation: valid
(v) branch of law to which the text refers: family law
(vi) text genre: petition for divorce
(vii) the language of the source text: English
(viii) lect: legi-lect (of petitions in civil cases)
(ix) source-text legal reality: common law
(x) source text language variety: American English

On the basis of the properties of the term we may state the meaning of the text as:

(47) *petitioner* is the person filing a petition for divorce under common law in the USA.

Properties taken by the translative unit: *plaintiff*

(i) the author of the source-text: usually a lawyer
(ii) source-text delivery form: written
(iii) source-text status: a document
(iv) the time of source text creation: non-valid (created before the Civil Procedure Rules of 1998 came into force in England and Wales)
(v) branch of law to which the text refers: contract law
(vi) text genre: petition for payment
(vii) the language of the source text: English
(viii) lect: legi-lect (of petitions in civil cases)
(ix) source-text legal reality: common law
(x) source text language variety: British English

On the basis of the properties of the term we may state the meaning of the text as:

(48) *plaintiff* was the person filing a petition for payment under common law in Great Britain (at present an archaism replaced by the term claimant at the end of the 90s.).

Let us now analyze the term *rybołówstwo* from the Polish statute on sea-fishing.

Properties taken by the translative unit: *rybołówstwo*:

(i) the author of the source-text: legislator
(ii) source-text delivery form: written
(iii) source-text status: binding
(iv) the time of source text creation: valid
(v) branch of law to which the text refers: fishing law
(vi) text genre: a statutory instrument
(vii) the language of the source text: Polish
(viii) lect: the language of fishery
(ix) source-text legal reality: civil law
(x) source text language variety: no varieties

On the basis of the properties of the term we may state the meaning of the translandive unit. However, in the case of some text genres, especially statutory instruments and contracts, there is a possibility that the author has provided a definition, which is applicable to the source-text under scrutiny. Therefore:

(49) *rybołówstwo* is sea fishing (of fish and other marine organisms).

This definition narrows down the meaning of the term *rybołówstwo* (in comparison with the meaning adopted in a colloquial language) to *sea fishing* only, excluding *fishing in inland waters*.

The meaning of technical terms is usually easiest to decipher due to the well-known interpretation of such terms in given communicative contexts. Much more troublesome are other types of translative units.

System-bound terms constitute a special category of technical terms typical only of a given legal system. System-bound terms "[...] designate concepts and institutions peculiar to the legal reality of a specific system or related systems" (Šarčević, 2000b: 233; on culture-bound lexis cf. Katan 1999 (2004): 150-152).

These terms belong to the category of technical terms described above, but from the translator's point of view they may be troublesome due to difficulties connected with finding target text significators for them. Among such terms we may enumerate the Polish term *sędzia-komisarz*.

Properties taken by the system bound term: *sędzia-komisarz*:

(i) the author of the source-text: legislator
(ii) source-text delivery form: written
(iii) source-text status: binding
(iv) the time of source text creation: valid
(v) branch of law to which the text refers: insolvency law
(vi) text genre: a statutory instrument
(vii) the language of the source text: Polish
(viii) lect: language of insolvency
(ix) source-text legal reality: civil law
(x) source text language variety: no varieties

Analogously the properties of the term help delineate its meaning. In the case of some text genres, especially statutory instruments and contracts, there is a possibility that the author has provided a definition which is applicable to the source-text under scrutiny. Therefore under the Polish Act on Insolvency and Rehabilitation:

(50) *sędzia-komisarz* is a professional judge appointed in insolvency proceedings in order to supervise the course of the proceedings. He supervises the activities of the insolvency practitioner, court supervisor and administrator, having very wide supervisory competences.

Having identified the meaning of the translandive text is a starting point for the search for target text equivalents.

4.5. Semi-technical terms

Semi-technical terms are in turn terms which exist not only in the language of the law but also in other languages for special purposes or a colloquial language and their meaning, which depends on the language in which they are used, may differ to some extent or may be completely different. Such terms will be discussed in more detail below in subchapters 4.5.1, 4.5.2 and 4.5.3.

4.5.1. Polysemous and homonymous terms

Polysemy is "[...] the case of a single word, having two or more related senses" (Matthews, 2005: 285). It is also defined as "[...] the association of two or more related senses with a single linguistic form" (Taylor in Cuyckens/Zawada, 1997: xi). Homonymy, in turn, is "[...] the relation between the words whose forms are the same but whose meanings are different and cannot be connected, e.g. between pen 'writing instrument' and pen 'enclosure'" (Matthews, 2005: 164). As far as legal language is concerned we would like to refer to the approach of Sourioux/Lerat (1975: 94-96) who differentiate between linguistic polysemy and legal polysemy, for instance:

(i) French *amendement* is classified as linguistic polysemy as one meaning relates to law 1. amendment (of a bill), and the second one to a different LSP 2. soil fertilization (agriculture).

(ii) French *action* is classified as legal polysemy as it has different meanings related to different branches of the law: 1. share 2. a civil or criminal judicial proceedings.

We find this differentiation into linguistic and legal polysemy very useful for the purpose of establishing the meaning of source text translative units.

Mellinkoff (1963: 11) also turns attention to the problem of linguistic polysemy. He calls such terms *common words with uncommon meaning* stating that they may be easily misinterpreted.

Linguistic polysemy is especially dangerous for translators who are non-lawyers, as translative units may apparently seem understandable and known to them. This may lead to the situation in which the translator fails to apply the procedure of establishing (calculating) the meaning of the translative unit in question and applies an improper equivalent in the target text.

(51) Potential meanings[30] of the term *assets*:
- (i) property of a deceased person that in the hands of his heir or executor is sufficient to pay his debts and legacies,
- (ii) the entire property of all sorts of an insolvent or bankrupt or of a person, association, corporation, or estate applicable or subject to the payment of his or its debts,
- (iii) a quality, condition, or entity that serves as an advantage, support, resource, or source of strength, wit,
- (iv) an item of value owned, or
- (v) the series of items on a balance sheet representing the book values at a given date of resources, rights, or items of property owned.

Let us now present how the properties from dimensions may help the translator.

(i) the author of the source-text: non-lawyer, accountant
(ii) source-text delivery form: written
(iii) source-text status: binding
(iv) the time of source text creation: valid
(v) branch of law to which the text refers: accounting law

30 Definitions quoted from Webster (2003).

(vi) text genre: financial statements
(vii) the language of the source text: English
(viii) lect: legi-lect
(ix) source-text legal reality: common law
(x) source text language variety: American English

On the basis of the properties of the term we may state the meaning of the translative unit by referring to the language for special purposes, namely accounting. This narrows down the potential choices. Therefore:

(52) *assets* means the series of items on a balance sheet representing the book values at a given date of resources, rights, or items of property owned.

The next translative unit which is to be analysed is the verb: *to represent.*

(53) The potential meanings[31] of the verb *to represent* are as follows:
(i) a: to supply the place, perform the duties, exercise the rights, or receive the share of: take the place of in some respect: fill the place of for some purpose: substitute in some capacity for: act the part of, in the place of, or for (as another person) usually by legal right b: to serve (as in a legislative body) by delegated or deputed authority usually resulting from election,
(ii) to set forth or place before someone (as by statement, account, or discourse): exhibit (a fact) to another mind in language: give one's own impressions and judgment of: state with advocacy or with the design of affecting action or judgment: point out by way of protest or remonstrance,
(iii) to serve as a specimen, example, or instance of,
(iv) a: to form an image or representation of in the mind b (1): to apprehend (an object) by means of an idea (2): to recall in memory (an object of previous experience),
(v) to correspond to in kind,
(vi) to make representations against something: present objections: protest,
(vii) to describe as having a specified character or quality,
(viii) to present a fact, especially by the manifestation to another that a fact or the state of mind exists (often refers to facts attested in contracts),

31 Definitions quoted from Webster (2003), Garner 2004.

(ix) to exhibit dramatically: a: to produce on the stage b: to act the part or role of, personate in acting or on the stage,
(x) to present by means of something standing in the place of: serve as the counterpart or image of: typify,
(xi) to exhibit by delineation, depiction, or portrayal - used especially of a work of art,
(xii) to portray by pictorial, plastic, or musical art: delineate, depict,
(xiii) to serve as a sign or symbol of, or
(xiv) to bring clearly before the mind: cause to be known, felt, or apprehended: present especially by description.

If the translator encounters the term *to represent* in a contract, the dimensions again help to limit the number of meanings to the relevant one only:
(i) the author of the source-text: lawyer or non-lawyer
(ii) source-text delivery form: written
(iii) source-text status: binding
(iv) the time of source text creation: valid
(v) branch of law to which the text refers: contract law
(vi) text genre: a contract
(vii) the language of the source text: English
(viii) lect: legi-lect (the language of contracts)
(ix) source-text legal reality: common law
(x) source text language variety: British English

Thus, on the basis of the properties of the term one may state the meaning of the translative unit by referring to the language for special purposes, namely contract law. This narrows down the potential choices. Therefore:

(54) to *represent* means to present a fact, especially by the manifestation to another that a fact or the state of mind exists (often refers to facts attested in contracts).

The Polish translative unit *kasacja* may also pose some translation problems.

(55) The potential meanings[32] of the noun *kasacja* are as follows:
 (i) final appeal, last resort appeal based on the claim that legal provisions have been broken
 (ii) scrapping (of vehicles)
 (iii) dissolution, liquidation, disbandment, suppression

Analogously to previous examples, when the properties taken by the text which is to be translated are as follows, we may choose the relevant meaning.

(i) the author of the source-text: lawyer or non-lawyer
(ii) source-text delivery form: written
(iii) source-text status: binding
(iv) the time of source text creation: valid
(v) branch of law to which the text refers: legal procedure
(vi) text genre: a writing filed to the court
(vii) the language of the source text: Polish
(viii) lect: legi-lect (the language of court decisions)
(ix) source-text legal reality: civil law
(x) source text language variety: no varieties

Actually, in this case we may establish the meaning of the term by referring to the language for special purposes, namely the language of the law. This narrows down the potential choices. Therefore:

(56) *kasacja* means a sort of petition filed before the Supreme Court to have a previously given decision (judgment) reconsidered and reversed due to non-compliance with legal provisions.

Legal polysemy may be very tricky and troublesome as it may lead to many ambiguities. It sometimes happens that one translative unit is used in different source texts belonging to one branch of law (e.g. civil law) and in each of them the unit has a slightly different meaning depending on the sub-branch of law they refer to (e.g. contracts, succession, etc.). The problem is to decide whether the differences between the meanings are vital in a given communicative situation. Let us consider some examples.

---

32 Source of definitions: *Uniwersalny słownik języka polskiego PWN* (CD-Rom).

The first term under scrutiny is the noun *estate*.

(57) The potential meanings[33] of the term *estate* may be as follows:
- (i) the degree, nature, extent, and quality of interest or ownership that one has in land or other property,
- (ii) property; possessions; capital; fortune,
- (iii) historical esp. in feudal times, any of the three social classes having specific political powers: the first estate was the Lords Spiritual (clergy), the second estate the Lords Temporal (nobility), and the third estate the Commons (bourgeoisie),
- (iv) all the property, real or personal, owned by one, or
- (v) the assets and liabilities of a dead or bankrupt person.

Let us assume that the term to be translated assumes the following properties:
- (i) the author of the source-text: lawyer or non-lawyer
- (ii) source-text delivery form: written
- (iii) source-text status: binding
- (iv) the time of source text creation: valid
- (v) branch of law to which the text refers: law of succession
- (vi) text genre: a testament
- (vii) the language of the source text: English
- (viii) lect: legi-lect (language of succession)
- (ix) source-text legal reality: common law
- (x) source text language variety: British English

On the basis of the properties of the term one may state the meaning of the translandive unit by referring to the language for special purposes, namely the language of succession (a sub-branch of civil law). This narrows down the potential choices. Therefore:

(58) *estate* means the assets and liabilities of a dead person.

The next analysed polysemous noun will be *lease*.

(59) The noun *lease* may mean[34]:

---

33 Definitions quoted from Webster (2003), New World College Dictionary <http://www.yourdictionary.com>, Garner (2004).

(i) the period of time for which such a contract is in force a two-year *lease*,
(ii) the property that is leased, or
(iii) a contract by which one party (landlord, or lessor) gives to another (tenant, or lessee) the use and possession of lands, buildings, property, etc. for a specified time and for fixed payments.

As we can see from the definitions quoted above, the term refers to different referents of the same legal institution.

(i) the author of the source-text: lawyer or non-lawyer
(ii) source-text delivery form: written
(iii) source-text status: binding
(iv) the time of source text creation: valid
(v) branch of law to which the text refers: contract law
(vi) text genre: a contract
(vii) the language of the source text: English
(viii) lect: legi-lect
(ix) source-text legal reality: common law
(x) source text language variety: British English

On the basis of the properties of the term one may state the meaning of the translative unit by referring to the language for special purposes, namely the language of contract law. This, however, does not narrow down the potential choices. The choice may be narrowed down only on the basis of the linguistic conclusion that is the analysis of the context in which the term is used. This often happens when polysemy occurs within the same branch of law. The Polish *term* kurator is worth considering among such terms as it has in fact 27 meanings (Zedler 2010, Matulewska 2009).

(60) The meanings of the term *kurator*:
(i) a person appointed to represent a partially incapacited person [kurator dla osoby ubezwłasnowolnionej częściowo].
(ii) a person appointed to represent a legal person not having bodies authorized to act on its behalf [kurator dla osoby prawnej nieposiadającej organów, które mogą prowadzić jej sprawy].

---

34 Definitions quoted from Webster (2003), New World College Dictionary <http://www.yourdictionary.com>, Garner (2004).

(iii) a person appointed to represent a dead spouse when the surviving spouse wants to annul the marriage in a lawsuit [kurator ustanawiany w razie wytoczenia przez jednego z małżonków powództwa o unieważnienie małżeństwa po śmierci drugiego małżonka].

(iv) a person appointed to represent a child when the child cannot be represented by the parents [kurator do reprezentowania dziecka, w sytuacji gdy nie mogą go reprezentować rodzice].

(v) a person appointed to manage the property of a child in the case of concluding the contract of donation on behalf of the child or when the child is a testamentary successor when those tasks cannot be performed by the child's parents [kurator do zarządu majątkiem dziecka w razie zawarcia umowy darowizny na rzecz dziecka albo dziedziczenia testamentowego przez dziecko, w sytuacji gdy zarządu tym majątkiem nie mogą sprawować rodzice dziecka].

(vi) a person appointed to manage the property of a child in case the wellbeing and the interest of the child may be threatened [kurator do zarządu majątkiem dziecka, w sytuacji, gdy dobro dziecka jest zagrożone].

(vii) a person appointed to represent a spouse deceased in the course of adoption proceedings [kurator w postępowaniu o przysposobienie po śmierci w jego toku jednego z małżonków przysposabiających].

(viii) a person appointed to represent a spouse deceased in the course of proceedings concerning the dissolution of the bonds of adoption [kurator w postępowaniu o rozwiązaniu przysposobienia, gdy w toku postępowania jeden z małżonków zmarł].

(ix) a person appointed to represent a person remaining under guardianship until the guardian is able to exercise his duties [kurator dla ochrony osoby pozostającej pod opieką, do czasu objęcia opieki przez opiekuna].

(x) a person appointed to manage the property of a child in the reform school, etc. [kurator dla zarządu majątkiem dziecka pozostającego pod opieką zakładu wychowawczego, itp.].

(xi) a person appointed to represent a person remaining under guardianship when the guardian is temporarily unable to exercise his duties [kurator dla dziecka pozostającego pod opieką, gdy opiekun doznaje przemijającej przeszkody w sprawowaniu opieki].

(xii) a person appointed to represent a partially incapacited person and to manage such person's estate [kurator dla osoby ubezwłasnowolnionej częściowo do jej reprezentowania i do zarządu jej majątkiem].

(xiii) a person appointed to represent a child sired/conceived but not yet born [kurator ustanawiany dla dziecka poczętego lecz jeszcze nie narodzonego].

(xiv) a person appointed to represent a handicapped person whose responsibilities are set by the family court [kurator dla osoby ułomnej, którego zakres kompetencji ustala sąd opiekuńczy].

(xv) a person appointed to represent an absent person having no representative [kurator dla osoby nieobecnej, niemającej pełnomocnika].

(xvi) a person appointed by the court to represent a given person before the court in litigious and non-litigious proceedings [kurator sądowy (kurator procesowy) ustanawiany do reprezentowania danej osoby przed sądem w postępowaniu nieprocesowym i procesowym].

(xvii) a person appointed to manage a succession estate [kurator spadku].

(xviii) a person appointed to represent a person not having the capacity to act in legal proceedings having no legal representative as well as a person not having anybody representing him if there is a need to perform an act instantaneously/without any delay [kurator dla strony nie mającej zdolności procesowej, która nie ma przedstawiciela ustawowego, jak również dla strony nie mającej organu powołanego do jej reprezentacji w razie konieczności dokonania czynności nie cierpiącej zwłoki].

(xix) a person appointed to represent a person whose place of stay is unknown or for the organization having no bodies or having bodies whose place of stay is unknown [kurator dla strony, której miejsce pobytu nie jest znane lub dla organizacji, która nie ma organów, lub mającej organy, których miejsce pobytu nie jest znane].

(xx) a person appointed to protect the rights of a person in the course of the proceedings concerning incapacitation of that person due to health reasons [kurator dla ochrony w toku postępowania o ubezwłasnowolnienie praw osoby, która ma być ubezwłasnowolniona ze względu na stan zdrowia].

(xxi) a person appointed to represent a debtor whose place of stay is unknown in the case of instigating the execution/enforcement proceedings *ex officio* [kurator dla dłużnika, którego miejsce pobytu nie jest znane w przypadku wszczynania egzekucji z urzędu].

(xxii) a person appointed to represent a debtor having no capacity to act in enforcement/execution proceedings [kurator dla dłużnika nie mającego zdolności procesowej w postępowaniu egzekucyjnym].

(xxiii) a person appointed in the course of execution/enforcement proceedings to enforce a debt after seizing it and in enforcement from financial instruments recorded in the securities account and other proprietary rights in order to properly protect the rights of the creditor or debtor on the motion of the creditor or debtor [kurator w postępowaniu egzekucyjnym w egzekucji z wierzytelności po zajęciu wierzytelności oraz w egzekucji z instrumentów finansowych zapisanych na rachunku papierów wartościowych i innych praw majątkowych dla należytej ochrony praw wierzyciela lub dłużnika na wniosek wierzyciela lub dłużnika].

(xxiv) a person appointed by the court when performing execution/enforcement from the immovable property for the person whose place of stay is unknown in order to serve documents on such a person [kurator ustanowiony przez sąd w egzekucji z nieruchomości dla osoby, której miejsce pobytu nie jest znane w celu dokonania takiej osobie doręczeń].

(xxv) a person appointed in the course of insolvency proceedings [kurator w postępowaniu upadłościowym].
(xxvi) probation officer [kurator sądowy w rozumieniu kodeksu karnego realizujący zadania wychowawczo-resocjalizacyjne].
(xxvii) a person responsible for supervising schools, superintendent of schools [kurator oświaty].

All those definitions refer to *custodians*, *guardians*, *trustees*, *administrators*, *managers*, *probation officers* and *supervisors* of different types. In the case of translation from Polish into English it is necessary to know exactly which type of *kurator* is mentioned in the text in order to find a proper target text significator.
(i) the author of the source-text: lawyer (judge)
(ii) source-text delivery form: written
(iii) source-text status: binding
(iv) the time of source text creation: valid
(v) branch of law to which the text refers: law of succession
(vi) text genre: a court decision
(vii) the language of the source text: Polish
(viii) lect: legi-lect
(ix) source-text legal reality: civil law
(x) source text language variety: no varieties

On the basis of the properties of the term we may state the meaning of the translative unit by referring to the language for special purposes, namely the language of the law of succession. This narrows down the potential choices. Therefore:

(61) *kurator* means a person appointed by the court to take care of a succession estate until the rightful successor will be able to take over his duties.

In some cases only one dimension may suffice to calculate the meaning, e.g. the term *rehabilitation* is used in the following branches of law: *criminal law* (the process of seeking to improve criminal's character), *evidence* (the restoration of a witness's credibility after the witness has been impeached) and *insolvency law* (the process of reorganizing a debtor's financial affairs) (Garner 2004:1311). If it is used in the petition to open insolvency proceedings, the branch of law is insolvency, thus only one meaning is left.

Also, it is sometimes possible to calculate the meaning on the basis of the *text genre dimension* only. The term *execution* may be used in numerous text genres and subgenres, e.g. contracts, testaments, court orders (e.g. to enforce a debt) and judgments (e.g. death penalty judgments), etc. If we deal with a contract, then the meaning of the term refers to the contract execution, which is: *the validation of a written instrument*.

More on the relation between colloquial language and legal language as well as polysemy and other legal language features (i) of Polish legal texts may be found in Zieliński (2002/2008: 143-150, 151-175), Choduń (2007: 160); (ii) of Polish and English legal texts may be found in Jopek-Bosiacka (2006: 16-86), Matulewska (2007: 91-143); and (iii) of English legal texts may be found in Alcaraz/Hughes (2002), Garner (2002), Tiersma (1999: 51-86), Šarčević (2000b: 231-241), Gubby (2004).

4.5.2. Words and expressions with flexible meanings

In theory languages for special purposes should be as precise as possible. However, in practice it often turns out that such a precision is not desirable for many reasons. First of all, if legal norms are not flexible enough, there will be the need to enact statutory instruments providing for any possible event, which may take place in real life. This of course is impossible. Firstly, no one can imagine all the possible life situations. Secondly, the number of legal instruments regulating such a number of events would be too vast to apply them effectively. Therefore, the legislator introduces a number of words with flexible meanings. The interpretation of such terms is left at the discretion of judges or other persons applying and observing the law.

The main problem connected with such translative units is that the precise meaning cannot be calculated. Therefore, as a result of the interpretation procedure, the translator gets only the approximate meaning. Fortunately, although the meanings of translative units may be compared to fuzzy blots, the approximate meaning on numerous occasions is sufficient to serve communicative purposes of translation (Smith 1995: 23). Here are some examples of translative units with flexible meanings:

(62) reasonable

(63) due diligence

(64) lokalny zwyczaj [local custom]

(65) zasady współżycia społecznego [public policy, principles of community life]

(66) władza rodzicielska [parental rights, parental authority]

Although translators are not supposed to interpret legal texts as lawyers do (cf. Šarčević 2000b), they are supposed to have similar competences as lawyers. It is stressed that in order to translate legal texts successfully it is necessary to possess the so-called legal competence which

> [...] presupposes not only in-depth knowledge of legal terminology, but also a thorough understanding of legal reasoning and the ability to solve legal problems, to analyse legal texts, and to foresee how a text will be interpreted and applied [...]. (Šarčević 2000b: 113-114)

More on words and expressions with flexible meaning in Polish legal texts may be found in Zieliński (2002/2008: 176:184, Choduń 2007).

4.5.3. Euphemisms, metaphors and false cognates

Euphemisms, metaphors and false cognates constitute a separate category of troublesome translandive units.

Euphemisms are words

> [...] etc. used in place of one avoided as e.g. offensive, indecent, or alarming. E.g. a word for *girl* used of prostitutes in place of the specific word for *prostitute*. (Matthews 2005: 119)

Metaphors are usually defined as:

> [...] a rhetorical element that generally involves using a specific word to express an abstract concept and which takes the form of elliptical comparison

based on an analogy between two objects, two concepts, or two situations that possess a common characteristics. (Delisle et al. 1999: 157)[35]

False cognates, also called false friends or *faux amis*, on the other hand, are such source text units which due to the similarity with target text units form (no matter whether one takes into consideration the pronunciation or spelling) are associated with target text units they resemble and their meaning which is different.

The calculation of the meaning of metaphors and euphemisms may be especially difficult due to the fact that they are rarely listed in dictionaries, and it is usually necessary to consult a native speaker to decipher their meaning correctly. Furthermore, their surface structure meaning may be extremely misleading[36] and may not alert the translator's vigilance. Some languages are more prone to create euphemisms[37] whereas in others lawyers avoid them (for instance Polish is a language with a very limited number of euphemisms used in law).

---

35 On translation of metaphors cf. Pisarska 1989, Newmark 1988 (2007): 104-113.

36 "A euphemism that tends to amuse non-English-speaking students of legal translation is the solemn announcement following the discovery of a crime (often a murder) that *a man is assisting police with their enquiries*. Of course there are excellent procedural reasons for choosing this form of words, and it would be wrong to sneer at any means used to protect the reputation of the innocent or to uphold the democratic principle of the presumption of innocence. But there is no escaping the linguistic fact that literal renderings of this phrase into other languages would most probably lead the audience to believe that Sherlock Holmes had returned, or that Scotland Yard had fallen on hard times and had to call upon the services of members of the general public to help solve its cases. Once again, the translator would be strongly advised to follow the natural habits of the target audience and go with a version indicating that *police are interrogating a suspect*, or words to that effect." (Alcaraz/Hughes 2002: 12)

37 "Many legal euphemisms originated in a Victorian sensibility. Our digests of the law, for example, include sections under the phrase *disorderly houses* because writers considered *whorehouses* or *brothels* or *bordellos* too indelicate. (The non-legal euphemism is *house of ill fame* or *repute*). Despite its appearance, *criminal conversation* is not a legal doctrine that runs afoul of the First Amendment; the phrase refers to adulterous sex (which, of course, inevitably interferes with *conjugal felicity*). Only recently have we sloughed off the

The calculation of the meaning of metaphors[38], euphemisms and false cognates does not differ from the calculation of the meaning of other translative units. The only difference is that they must be spotted by a translator. Unless they are recognized, the translator may fail to apply the procedure of the meaning calculation.

Calculating the meaning of false cognates: *contract of marriage*
(i) the author of the source-text: legislator
(ii) source-text delivery form: written
(iii) source-text status: binding
(iv) the time of source text creation: valid
(v) branch of law to which the text refers: family law
(vi) text genre: a statutory instrument
(vii) the language of the source text: English
(viii) lect: legi-lect
(ix) source-text legal reality: common law
(x) source text language variety: British or American

The meaning of the translative unit *contract of marriage* despite the one suggested by the surface structure of the syntagma is: *a form of mutual consent required for a matrimonial relationship to exist ac-*

---

overzealous euphemizing about homosexuality, known formerly as *the abominable and detestable crime against nature*.

Although some euphemisms, like the last one, are terribly slanted, others result from an understandable desire to sound objective, by avoiding biased words of the past. *Extramarital*, for example, strikes us as more neutral than *adulterous* (as used in the previous paragraph). And many legal writers are now inclined to use *non-marital children* or *children out of wedlock* instead of *illegitimate children* or, worse yet, *bastards*. Why indeed scar the innocent children with ugly epithets." (Garner 2002: 34)

38 "In fact, there are hundreds of metaphors, buried and unburied, in the language of the law. But this does not mean that the legal translator has a sort of [...] poetic licence in dealing with them. Given the traditional and eminently conservative nature of legal phraseology, it is quite likely that the same or similar figurative usages will be found in many different languages. Whenever this is not the case, perhaps the wisest course is for the translator to choose the plainest possible rendering rather than run the risk of fanciful or highly coloured expressions at odds with the generally formal and even solemn tone of this type of text. (Alcaraz/Hughes 2002: 44)

cording to the law of the place where the consent takes place (Garner 2004: 347). The surface structure of the syntagma, however, may mislead a translator and make him believe that the contract of marriage is a *prenuptial* or *postnuptial agreement*. This meaning, however, is only applied to the translative unit in Canada due to the erroneous literal translation of the statutory French term *contract du marriage* into English (in the course of the adjustment of the legislation language versions to the principle of two official languages in force in Canada).

More on euphemisms and metaphors in (i) Polish legal texts may be found in Zieliński (2002/2008: 189-192) and in English legal texts may be found in Alcaraz/Hughes (2002: 11-14, 44), Garner (2002: 33-34).

4.6. Translandive lingual units with undetermined meaning

Sometimes it happens that the meaning cannot be decoded. It happens when the author of the text does not know the meaning of the sign he uses. Although it may sound absurd, it happens also in legal texts. One of the examples of such a translandive unit the meaning of which is unknown and which is still used is the English legal language is the abbreviation 's.s.' also written 'ss' and 'ss.'. "Lawyers have been using *ss* for nine hundred years and still are not sure what it means" (Mellinkoff 1963: 296).

The abbreviation is used in both American and British English language varieties. It may be found on death certificates, powers of attorney, judgments, etc. It is speculated that it may mean (i) *sections*, (ii) *subscripsi* (signed below), (iii) *sans* (without), (iv) *scilicet* (namely), (v) two gold letters at the ends of the chain of office or collar worn by the Lord Chief Justice of the King's Bench, (vi) a division mark, or (viii) an equivalent of the paragraph mark (cf. Mellinkoff 1963: 86-87, 296, 319-321, Radin 1955: 327, Garner 1995: 825). "Whether *ss* makes sense or not, it continues to decorate affidavits as it has decorated the venue portion of a variety of forms for centuries. Some lawyers believe it is necessary." (Mellinkoff 1963: 320).

Some words are invented for the purpose of copyright protection. Let us quote the fragment of the article titled *Not a Word* from *The New Yorker*[39] which sums up the existence of potential translative units with undecipherable meaning:

> When word leaked out that the recently published second edition of the New Oxford American Dictionary contains a made-up word that starts with the letter "e," an independent investigator set himself the task of sifting through NOAD's thirty-one hundred and twenty-eight "e" entries in search of the phony. [...] Upon being presented with the majority opinion, McKean [the editor-in-chief of the second edition of NOAD] confirmed that "esquivalience" was a fabricated word. She said that Oxford had included it in NOAD's first edition, in 2001, to protect the copyright of the electronic version of the text that accompanied most copies of the book.

Sometimes the translator is unable to decode the meaning due to, for instance, the quality of the source text. In such cases at least in Poland the Code of Sworn Translators and Interpreters suggests that the translator leave the word in the form of a direct borrowing with a suitable comment in brackets informing the translation recipient about the inability to establish the meaning. This principle especially refers to abbreviations.

4.7. Concluding remarks

It should be stressed here that in order to calculate the meaning of the translandive unit the translator must have at his disposal the set of all potential meanings. The calculation of the source text unit meaning is the first step towards a translation process that is finding optimal equivalents in the target language.

---

39 <http://www.newyorker.com/archive/2005/08/29/050829ta_talk_alford>

5. Communicative Communities of Recipients in Legal Communication

5.1. Introductory remarks

This chapter will be devoted to types of communicative communities and their properties affecting the choice of the translation procedure (technique) which should be applied in the translation process.

We may enumerate the following exemplary types of communicative communities taking part in legal communication:

(i) the multi-lingual (international) communicative community,
(ii) the European Union communicative community,
(iii) the common law communicative community,
(iv) the civil law communicative community,
(v) the business-oriented foreign communicative community,
(vi) the legal system ignorant communicative community,
(vii) the business relation bound communicative community.

Of course, it is possible to distinguish many more communicative communities, which embrace recipients of legal texts. However, for the purpose of this work only the most typical ones have been taken into consideration to illustrate the implementation of the presented translation approach.

Having discussed the methods of source text meaning calculation at the textual and component part level, as well as the procedures of establishing significators, the problem of deciding what types of significators are best for specific types of communicative communities should now be addressed. Let us now give short description of selected communicative communities, and next list the dimensions with properties, which may be assumed by them and which determine the type of significator which will be considered sufficiently equivalent (cf. Po 8).

5.2. International communicative community

The *international communicative community* is composed of people belonging to many language communities, for whom the target language is just a means of communication. Thus, we may say that it is a multi-lingual communicative community using a foreign language (often English in order to communicate). As the members of this community are native speakers of different languages and nationals of different countries they are acquainted with different legal systems. Consequently, in the process of communication they may want to learn something about other legal systems and they want to share with others what they know about their own legal system.

The typical international communicative community is the group of people taking part in an international conference or people reading the same international journal devoted to a specific field. Thus, in the case of law this communicative community will take part in international law conferences or will read legal journals such as INSOL (a journal devoted to insolvency matters).

Moreover, we may distinguish two types of community members as far as legal system awareness is concerned:

(i) community members aware of the differences in legal systems, and

(ii) community members not aware of the differences in legal systems.

It should be stressed here that there are many cases in which participants in communication are aware of the differences in legal communities. However, there are certain events in which the members of the community (e.g. conference participants) are not aware of the differences or not all of them are aware of them and consequently they do not realize the potential problems which may arise due to them. The typical situation in which the communicative community is not fully aware of the problems are the international meetings of Euro deputies and other representatives of governments. Such people often deal with a wide range of matters, which are not necessarily within their scope of competence or qualifications. For example doctors must make decisions concerning legal regulations in co-operation with lawyers. Lawyers have limited medical knowledge, whereas doctors limited legal knowledge. Such a communicative community will have to communicate in a way which will enable mutual understanding. This means that some information will be excessive (obvious or even trivial) for one part of the community but necessary for the other part to understand the subject matter and the other way round.

In the case of communicative community members meeting face to face there is always room for questions clarifying unclear messages. However, if we take into consideration the translation process it is much more difficult to work out certain solutions and to make decisions concerning the successful choice of language means. The more we know about the communicative community for which we translate the better chances for a good translation. Since the international communicative community is in fact composed of people coming from different countries, different legal systems and possibly having different expectations and varied command of the language of communication, it is very difficult to provide equivalents, which would be understood in the same way by everyone. It may even be said that the task is impossible of performance and that a certain degree of imprecision and ambiguity will always be present in every translation. Therefore, we should remember that: "While lawyers cannot expect translators to produce parallel texts which are equal in meaning, they do expect them to produce parallel texts which are equal in legal effect" (Šarčević 2000b: 71).

Let us take the command of the language in consideration first. If the author of the text had a sufficient command of the target language, he would not need to resort to the help of a translator to produce the target text. Of course this factor does not refer to the situation in which the author is a commissioner and translator himself but this situation occurs very rarely.

What about legal systems? Lawyers as a rule specialize in a given field/branch of law. So they are specialists in civil law, in civil procedure, administrative law, tax law, etc. If a lawyer is the author of the text, which is to be translated, he may know the terminology used in his field in the target language or not. For example the German-speaking lawyer may write an article for a German legal journal and in such an instance he may help the translator solve some terminological problems. But if the same lawyer prepares the text for an English legal journal he will not be able to help the translator with potential English equivalents. Thus, the burden of responsibility for finding understandable equivalents will rest solely on the translator.

Translation strategies

The international communicative community is by far the most difficult one from the translator's point of view. Not only should a translator on many occasions resort to cultureless equivalents understandable for the majority or preferably all communicative community members, but also should preserve the source-language idiosyncrasies. Definitely, the task does not seem feasible.

The equivalents applied should be general and precise at the same time. They should communicate that the legal institution dealt with is similar to some other institution known to the communicative community members and at the same time it should stress the differences which are important from the communicative point of view.

Moreover, different translation strategies will be applied to the following types of texts:

(i) written text (message) for reading,

(ii) written text (message) for oral delivery and published *in extenso* for reading,

(iii) written (message) text for oral delivery.

Taking into consideration the fact that English is not the best language to use when discussing civil law regimes and the number of countries in which English is the official or one of official languages, one quickly appreciates the unlimited number of translation problems, which may occur when communicating in English. The number of countries where English is an official language (more than 60 countries cf. Cheshire 1994) corresponds to a wide variety of legal regimes and consequently sets of legal terminology, which means one thing to the eye of a lawyer from that country and may mean something slightly or completely different to lawyers from other countries. So how do lawyers all around the world communicate using English? What kind of language tools do they use to convey the message? Can these tools be of any help to translators? Some examples taken from journals for lawyers are considered to find the answer to the posed question.

Here are presented a few strategies applied by the authors of articles published in the INSOL journals. INSOL is a worldwide organization of insolvency practitioners. The journals are designed for lawyers, accountants and other professionals, who take part in the process of insolvency. The first set of examples is taken from INSOL World, a quarterly devoted to insolvency law worldwide.

Firstly, one should define the communicative community to which the readers of INSOL World belong. Readers of the journal form the communicative community composed of people belonging to many language communities, for whom the target language is just a means of communication – so it is a multi-lingual communicative community using English for communication. Moreover it is a community composed of people belonging to common law countries, civil law countries, and other legal regime countries. Finally the readers of INSOL World are mainly insolvency practitioners, accountants and other insolvency-related professionals, etc. That is to say people specializing in a very narrow branch of law and willing to learn about different aspects of insolvency law worldwide. Furthermore, their thorough knowledge of the field results in the fact that they aim at precision when communicating with each other.

Consequently, the communicative community composed of INSOL members/readers will have the following properties:

(i) active,
(ii) compact (the journal is published on a regular basis and sent to INSOL members),
(iii) secondary or primary,
(iv) independent,
(v) multilingual,
(vi) expert,
(vii) hermetic (insolvency law is considered one of the most difficult branches of law among lawyers as it encompasses elements of civil law, trade law, contract law, law of torts, civil procedure, criminal procedure, criminal law, etc.), and
(viii) aware of legal system differences.

So what kind of linguistic tools do they resort to in order to achieve precision in communication? First of all, they use different types of borrowings and internationalisms. However, it should be stressed that direct borrowings (mainly exotics) are always supplied with their closest dynamic equivalents in English. Let us look at a few examples.

In an article devoted to the insolvency law in Belgium the author (Wouters 1/2005: 12) gives dynamic equivalents known worldwide (internationalisms) and exotics in inverted commas, e.g.:

(67) bankruptcy proceedings "*Het faillissement/La Faillité*"

(68) Voluntary Arrangements with the Creditors "*Het gerechtelijk akkoord/Le concordat judiciare*"

which have been listed in Annex A to the Council Regulation (EC) 1346/2000 on insolvency proceedings

Thus (by using internationalisms) the main idea is conveyed to the readers of the text formulated in English, but those who are interested in more in-depth information on the subject-matter are given the original names of institutions, which definitely may help them in their explorations in Belgian bankruptcy law. The exotics given in inverted commas additionally stress that those institutions are similar to a certain extant but not exactly the same as their English equivalents.

A similar technique has been used in the text devoted to French law. This time the author (Didier 4/2005: 34) aiming at precision supplied the original French terms (exotics) in brackets and in inverted commas:

(69) Mediation proceedings ("conciliacion" in French),

(70) The individual voluntary arrangement ("accord amiable"),

(71) Counselling proceedings ("mandate ad hoc"),

(72) A rescue proceedings ("procedure de sauvegarde").

Again, the main idea is conveyed to the readers and the information necessary for more in-depth analysis is also provided.

A similar technique was used by the authors (Stessi/Luiki 4/2005: 38) of the article on Slovak bankruptcy law. This time the authors provided exotics in brackets e.g.:

(73) Bankruptcy proceedings (konkurz)

(74) Restructuring proceedings (restrukturalizacia)

(75) Release from debt of private individuals (oddłużenie fizycznej osoby)

The author of the article on the insolvency law of Nepal used a similar technique, however for different purposes. He provided exotics only for the names of institutions and legal acts, which do not have their dynamic equivalents or possible quasi-dynamic equivalents in English and in brackets he provided their translations, that is to say:

(76) *Mulukin Ain* 1963 (Country Code) (Bharat Raj Upreti 4/2005:22)

In the example below he provided an explanatory note rather than a literal translation or a dynamic equivalent:

(77) *Beema Sameti* (Insurance regulating authority) (Bharat Raj Upreti 4/2005:23)

He used dynamic equivalents or internationalisms for other terms. The technique used is sometimes called generalization. Generalization is the term used in translation studies to refer to the situation in which the translator uses a TL term of a broader meaning than the SL term as an equivalent. This technique is used when precision is less important than conveying the general overall idea of the text. This technique finds application when the recipients of the TL text are informed about something for the first time and their knowledge is not deep enough to flood them with too many details. Here are some examples (Bharat Raj Upreti 4/2005: 22):

(78) Law of liquidation

(79) Law of rescue/restructuring

(80) Personal bankruptcy

(81) Corporate insolvency

Thus the text is made easy to follow for readers. Probably the author assumed that the insolvency law in Nepal is more a piece of curious information rather than information of great importance for the readers of INSOL World and therefore there is no need to go into detail when stressing every single difference between Nepalese institutions of insolvency law and other legal systems.

This strategy seems to be justified to a great extent as there are many more insolvency practitioners dealing with cross-border insolvencies in European countries and thus interested in every potential difference in insolvency law institutions in, e.g., European countries than lawyers dealing with cross-border insolvencies involving Nepalese debtors or creditors.

The next technique, which involves direct borrowings used as equivalents, has been used by the author of the article on Italian insolvency proceedings. When writing about the reform of the Italian Bankruptcy Law the author uses a direct borrowing from Italian *curatore fallimentare*. The direct borrowing used is the term *curator* with the footnote definition explaining its meaning. Thus, in the article we read:

(82) Pursuant to the reform (...) the functions of the curator[40] and the creditors' committee are highly empowered (Serao 3/2006:43)

This type of equivalent is called explanation or definition in translation studies. However rare, it is a very useful tool for achieving precision in the text. It is especially useful in texts for reading.

To summarise, the following types of significators are considered optimal:

(i) exotics accompanied with connotative equivalents,
(ii) exotics with short descriptive equivalents,
(iii) exotics with internationalisms
(iv) exotics with calques,
(v) other types of direct borrowings with short descriptive equivalents,

40 From now on, we will call 'curator' the person appointed by the Court to manage the assets of a wound up company. To a certain extent, this function is similar to the function undertaken, in different jurisdictions, by the 'liquidator' or the 'receiver'.

(vi) internationalisms (mainly from soft-law, e.g. INSOL guidelines in case of INSOL readers and authors),
(vii) modified connotative equivalents, and
(viii) connotative equivalents.

The most frequent techniques are borrowings (exotics, loanwords and calques) supplied with explanatory notes (usually short descriptions or connotative equivalents) as well as internationalisms. Connotative equivalents are used when the degree of similarity between the source text unit and target text connotative significator is great or when the disparity between the semantic fields of two terms is irrelevant in a given communicative situation (the stress is put on similarities rather than differences).

Therefore, the following translative directives may be inferred:

Directive 1
If similarity between the source and target language concepts is important, then connotative equivalents are used.

Directive 2
If similarity between the source and target language concepts is important but there are some differences which may be of interest to some target text recipients, then modified connotative equivalents are used or connotative equivalents supplied with exotics.

Directive 3
If the aim of the target text is to convey a general idea without stressing similarities or differences, but primarily showing the mechanics of some legal institutions, then internationalisms are used.

Directive 4
When the differences between the source and target language concepts are of vital importance, then the following techniques of providing significators are recommended:
(i) exotics accompanied with connotative equivalents,
(ii) exotics with short descriptive equivalents,
(iii) exotics with internationalisms,

(iv) exotics with calques (if the term is composed of more than one word and the sum of meanings of single words reveals the meaning of the term in question), and

(v) other types of direct borrowings with short descriptive equivalents.

Moreover, exotics are usually used only once, when the term is enumerated for the first time. It rarely happens that the author uses an exotic further on in the text.

It should also be stressed that the above directives refer to written texts for reading. In the case of texts for oral delivery exotics would not be recommended especially when the text is to be interpreted simultaneously or consecutively into other languages. If need be, it is possible to use exotics by introducing them with 'the institution which is in Polish called *sędzia-komisarz*' or something to that effect. But still for interpreters not speaking Polish and translating from English as a pivot language (relay), the Polish word may be impossible to reproduce as far as its pronunciation is concerned. Therefore, using exotics and even direct borrowings in texts which are to be delivered orally is a practice fraught with risks from the point of view of communication. Much better are modified connotative significators.

Therefore, in the case of written texts for oral delivery the following directives should be applied:

Directive 5
If similarity between the source and target language concepts is important, then connotative equivalents should be used.

Directive 6
If the aim of the target text is to convey a general idea without stressing similarities or differences, but mostly showing the mechanics of some legal institutions, then internationalisms should be used.

Directive 7
If there is a difference between the source and target language concepts which is important but there are some similarities as well, then modified connotative equivalents should be used.

However, when imagining a different international communicative community, namely the community of readers of crime stories by Grisham, this communicative community will have the following properties:

(i) active or passive,
(ii) compact or loose,
(iii) primary or secondary,
(iv) independent,
(v) monolingual or multilingual,
(vi) mixed,
(vii) non-hermetic if target language legal reality is common law and hermetic if target language legal reality is civil law, and
(viii) most probably composed of members aware and unaware of legal system differences.

This type of a communicative community is probably the most troublesome for every translator, as meeting the needs of members of so diverse a community is very difficult. The readers will be lawyers, professors, accountants but also cooks, housewives, cleaners, teenagers, etc. Therefore, the knowledge of the members differs significantly and it will be almost impossible to satisfy the expectations of readers well acquainted with common law and those who know nothing about common law legal reality.

Consequently, the translators must resort to such significators which will not interrupt the plot, and give less knowledgeable members (as far as common law legal reality is concerned) the possibility of understanding unknown source language concepts. Therefore, translators will have to resort to

(i) connotative significators whenever possible,
(ii) modified connotative significators,
(iii) in exceptional cases borrowings or other neologisms supplied with definitions in footnotes or glossaries at the end of the book, which may be read by interested or more inquisitive members of the target language communicative community.

The latter technique, however, should be avoided if possible as footnote comments and definitions are often considered as translator's failure to solve the problem of conveying the source text message in the target text.

Therefore, the following directives may be inferred for this type of communicative community of recipients:

Directive 8

If the translator translates a literary text with elements of a source language legal system for recipients with varied knowledge and expectations, in order not to interrupt the plot, and make the target text understandable he should use either connotative significators or modified connotative significators or in exceptional cases neologisms with definitions.

5.3. European Union communicative community

The *European Union communicative community* is formed by the members of the European Union language communities. The members of that community are inhabitants/nationals of the European Union member states. Thus, the members of that community are/should be aware of the fact that

(i) the community law exists in parallel with domestic laws,
(ii) some domestic laws have been/are being amended to comply with the community law,
(iii) in some cases the community law prevails,
(iv) in some cases the domestic law may differ from the general guidelines issued by the EU institutions.

The translator on the other hand should be aware of the fact that:

(i) EU law may be found at the EUR-Lex database,
(ii) he is supposed to follow terminology used by the EU including those terminological units which may be found in Eur-Lex as well as in IATE,
(iii) English legal language used by the EU is different from the English used in Great Britain and the USA, etc.,
(iv) all language versions are considered originals,

(v) it is sometimes hard to find out which language version is the original one and which is the translation,
(vi) some translations are made from translations – more errors and mistakes may occur,
(vii) there are special recommendations for EU legislation translators in Poland prepared by UKIE[41],
(viii) mistakes are repeated, and
(ix) there are no dictionaries on the Polish market, which would provide a reliable source of information on the meaning of EU legal terminology.

Finally, it should be stressed here that the new approach to legal translation by Šarčević (2000b) also called legal translation in the mechanism of the law will be applicable to the translation of authenticated texts in plurilingual EU communicative community.

Translation strategies

In order to illustrate the problem of translation for the purpose of the EU communicative community, let us take as an example the readers of Eurofenix (a quarterly devoted to insolvency law in Europe). Firstly, one should define the communicative community to which the readers of Eurofenix belong. Readers of the journal form the communicative community composed of people belonging to many language communities, for whom the target language is just a means of communication – so it is a multi-lingual communicative community. Moreover, it is a community composed of people belonging to common law countries and civil law countries. It is a communicative community composed of people belonging to European Union language communities. Finally the readers, similarly as the INSOL World readers, are mainly insolvency practitioners, accountants and other insolvency-related professionals, etc. That is to say people specialising in insolvency law in the EU Member States, thus they are willing to learn about different aspects of insolvency law within the European Union, especially in the context of cross-border insolvency proceedings.

41 Urząd Komitetu Integracji Europejskiej [Office of the Committee for European Integration].

Consequently, the communicative community composed of Eurofenix members/readers will have the following properties:

(i) active,
(ii) compact (the journal is published on a regular basis and sent to Eurofenix members),
(iii) secondary or primary,
(iv) independent,
(v) multilingual,
(vi) expert,
(vii) hermetic (let us stress again that insolvency law is considered one of the more difficult branches of law among lawyers as it encompasses elements of civil law, trade law, contract law, law of torts, civil procedure, criminal procedure, criminal law, etc.), and
(viii) aware of legal system differences.

They also aim at precision in communication. Thus the techniques used by them will be similar to those described above in the case of INSOL World readers.

Very often exotics supplement other types of equivalents in order to give the more inquisitive recipients of the text the chance to establish precisely the source-text component part meaning if need be, e.g.:

(83) *ad hoc* trustee (*mandataire ad hoc*) hereinafter the author uses *ad hoc* trustee (Toube 4/2007a: 14),

(84) an "acte de défaut de biens" (a certificate of insufficiency of assets) (Toube 4/2007a: 15),

(85) "domicile theory" ("Sitztheorie") (Toube 4/2007b: 15),

(86) "Foundation theory" ("Gründungstheorie") (Toube 4/2007b: 15),

(87) The liquidator (*syndyk*) (Hrycaj 2/2007: 20-21),

(88) The court supervisor (*nadzorca sądowy*) (Hrycaj 2/2007: 20-21),

(89) The receiver (*zarządca*) (Hrycaj 2/2007: 20-21).

Usually thereinafter the authors use English terms.

It should also be borne in mind that using English terms instead of exotics facilitates reading the text. If exotics were used instead of English terms, the target text recipient would have to remember their meaning or would have to refer to the beginning of the text to remind himself of their meaning.

It is also possible to use the exotic accompanied by a definition, e.g. "[...] the term *gage* refers exclusively to security over tangible movables, while *nantissement* refers to a security over intangibles" (Riffard 4/2007: 25).

Thereinafter the author uses the French terms 'gage' and 'nantissement'. In reference to example 5, it should be stressed again that using exotics in the text instead of their target text equivalents might burden the reader with the need to remember their meaning. Therefore, this method is recommendable only in the case of key terms and if there is a limited number of them used in the text.

Moreover, dynamic equivalents are also quite frequent. The following examples of dynamic equivalents accompanied by exotics have been found in the analyzed texts, e.g.:

(90) Bankruptcy (*Konkurs*) (Staehelin 1/2003:10)

(91) Declaration of insolvency (*Insolvenzerklärung*) (Staehelin 1/2003:10)

and not accompanied by exotics, e.g. (Hrycaj 2/2007: 20-21):

(92) Bankruptcy court

(93) Declaration of insolvency

(94) The Bankruptcy and Rehabilitation Law as well as The Law on Bankruptcy and Rehabilitation

(95) The Polish Bankruptcy and Rehabilitation Law

(96) The insolvent estate

(97) Insolvency proceedings

(98) The creditors' committee

(99) Insolvency practitioner

The following calques are used without explanatory notes:

(100) The Minister of Justice

(101) Judge-commissioner

(102) The Chief Justice

(103) Article 170 of, Article 157 section 3, Article 162.2, Article 336,

(104) Execution (Staehelin 1/2003: 10-11)

(105) Seizure of assets (Staehelin 1/2003: 10-11)

(106) To declare bankrupt (Staehelin 1/2003: 10-11)

Sometimes the strategy is the combination of various methods of providing equivalents. For instance, in one of the articles the dynamic equivalent *rescue procedure* is used in the title. In the main body of the text the exotic from French is used: *procédure de sauvegarde*. Finally, the author provides a definition explaining the meaning of the term: the procedure is designed to be halfway between the preventive procedures (*mandate ad hoc*, *conciliation*) and remedial procedures (*redressement judiciare, liquidation judiciare*).

Later on the exotics are used instead of dynamic equivalents or definitions. However, the whole text is devoted to the comparison of institutions (similarities and differences between French and English insolvency institutions).

It is also possible to use generalisation in English and the exotic (domestication in Swedish) (Lofalk 3/2003: 8), e.g.:

(107) old floating charges (*företagshypotek*)

(108) new floating charges (*företagsinteckning*)

Calques supplemented with exotics in brackets are also quite frequently a method of providing equivalents, e.g.:

(109) Special execution (*Spezialexecution*) (Staehelin 1/2003: 10)

(110) General execution (*Generalexecution*) (Staehelin 1/2003: 10)

(111) Principle of universality (*Universalitätsprinzip*) (Staehelin 1/2003: 11)

(112) The principle of territoriality (*Territorialitätprinzip*) (Staehelin 1/2003: 11)

(113) The centre of life relations (*Mittelpunkt der Lebensbeziehungen*) (Staehelin 1/2003: 11)

Sometimes one may find modified dynamic equivalents supplemented with exotics often placed in brackets or simply modified dynamic equivalents, e.g.:

(114) Swiss public policy (*ordre public*) (Staehelin 1/2003: 11)

(115) The German *Bundesgerichtshof* (Staehelin 1/2003: 11)

(116) Swiss bankruptcy law (Staehelin 1/2003: 10-11)

(117) Swiss bankruptcy proceedings (Staehelin 1/2003: 10-11)

(118) Swiss bankruptcies (Staehelin 1/2003: 10-11)

(119) Swiss banking secrecy (Staehelin 1/2003: 10-11)

(120) Swiss debt enforcement law (Staehelin 1/2003: 10-11)

(121) The Swiss Supreme Court (*Bundesgericht*) (Staehelin 1/2003: 11)

To sum up, the following types of significators are considered optimal:

(i) exotics accompanied by connotative equivalents,
(ii) exotics with short descriptive equivalents,
(iii) exotics with EU internationalisms
(iv) exotics with calques,
(v) other types of direct borrowings with short descriptive equivalents,
(vi) internationalisms (mainly from EU legislation),

(vii) modified connotative equivalents, and
(viii) connotative equivalents.

The most frequent techniques are borrowings (exotics, loanwords and calques) supplied with explanatory notes (usually short descriptions or connotative equivalents) as well as EU internationalisms. Exotics include the terms listed in schedules to EU legislation. Analogously, as in the case of an international communicative community, connotative equivalents are used when the degree of similarity between the source text translative unit and target text connotative significator is great or when the disparity between the semantic field of two terms is irrelevant in a given text (the stress is put on similarities rather than differences).

Therefore, the following directives may be inferred:

Directive 9
If similarity between the source and target language concepts is important, then connotative equivalents are used.

Directive 10
If similarity between the source and target language concepts is important but there are some differences which may be of interest to some target text recipients, then modified connotative equivalents are used.

Directive 11
If the aim of the target text is to convey a general idea without stressing similarities or differences, but more frequently showing the mechanics of some legal institutions, then EU internationalisms are used.

Directive 12
When the differences between the source and target language concepts are of vital importance, then the following techniques of providing significators are recommended:
(i) exotics accompanied with connotative equivalents,
(ii) exotics with short descriptive equivalents,
(iii) exotics with EU internationalisms,
(iv) exotics with calques, and

(v) other types of direct borrowings with short descriptive equivalents.

Moreover, when differences are considered vital, exotics are often used in the whole text whereas descriptive and connotative significators are given in brackets only once, when the term is enumerated for the first time.

Again, the above corollaries refer to written texts for reading. In the case of texts for oral delivery exotics would not be recommended. Instead of them translators should use modified connotative significators.

Therefore, in the case of written texts for oral delivery for an EU communicative community the same directives should be applied as in the case of international communicative community.

Directive 13
If similarity between the source and target language concepts is important, then connotative equivalents should be used.

Directive 14
If the aim of the target text is to convey a general idea without stressing similarities or differences but generally showing the mechanics of some legal institutions, then EU internationalisms should be used.

Directive 15
If there is a difference between the source and target language concepts, which is important but there are some similarities as well, then modified connotative equivalents should be used.

What then are the techniques used by the European Union institutions? The European Union in its legislation uses EU internationalisms and gives their definitions in statutory instruments. Apart from definitions, the statutory instrument is supplied with annexes containing exotics in EU member state official languages. Below are three examples from the European Council Regulation (EC) No 1346/2000 on insolvency proceedings, e.g. the definition from the main body of the Regulation (Article 2a) is the following:

(122) 'insolvency proceedings' shall mean the collective proceedings referred to in Article 1(1). These proceedings are listed in Annex A.

Exotics listed in Annex A for Ireland, Poland and the UK:

(123) IRELAND

- Compulsory winding-up by the court
- Bankruptcy
- The administration in bankruptcy of the estate of persons dying insolvent
- Winding-up in bankruptcy of partnerships
- Creditors' voluntary winding-up (with confirmation of a court)
- Arrangements under the control of the court which involve the vesting of all or part of the property of the debtor in the Official Assignee for realisation and distribution
- Company examinership

(124) POLSKA

- Postępowanie upadłościowe
- Postępowanie układowe
- Upadłość obejmująca likwidację
- Upadłość z możliwością zawarcia układu

(125) UNITED KINGDOM

- Winding-up by or subject to the supervision of the court
- Creditors' voluntary winding-up (with confirmation by the court)
- Administration, including appointments made by filing prescribed documents with the court
- Voluntary arrangements under insolvency legislation
- Bankruptcy or sequestration.

Definition from the main body of the Regulation (Article 2c) is as follows:

(126) 'winding-up proceedings' shall mean insolvency proceedings within the meaning of point (a) involving realising the assets of the debtor, including where the proceedings have been closed by a composition or other measure terminating the insolvency, or closed by reason of the insufficiency of the assets. Those proceedings are listed in Annex B.

Exotics listed in Annex B for Ireland, Poland and the UK:

(127) IRELAND
- Compulsory winding-up
- Bankruptcy
- The administration in bankruptcy of the estate of persons dying insolvent
- Winding-up in bankruptcy of partnerships
- Creditors' voluntary winding-up (with confirmation of a court)
- Arrangements under the control of the court which involve the vesting of all or part of the property of the debtor in the Official Assignee for realisation and distribution

(128) POLSKA
- Postępowanie upadłościowe
- Upadłość obejmująca likwidację

(129) UNITED KINGDOM
- Winding-up by or subject to the supervision of the court
- Winding-up through administration, including appointments made by filing prescribed documents with the court
- Creditors' voluntary winding-up (with confirmation by the court)
- Bankruptcy or sequestration.

And finally the definition from the main body of the Regulation (Article 2b):

(130) 'liquidator' shall mean any person or body whose function is to administer or liquidate assets of which the debtor has been divested or to supervise the administration of his affairs. Those persons and bodies are listed in Annex C.

Exotics listed in Annex C for Ireland, Poland and the UK:

(131) IRELAND
- Liquidator
- Official Assignee
- Trustee in bankruptcy
- Provisional Liquidator
- Examiner

(132) POLSKA
- Syndyk

- Nadzorca sądowy
- Zarządca

(133) UNITED KINGDOM
- Liquidator
- Supervisor of a voluntary arrangement
- Administrator
- Official Receiver
- Trustee
- Provisional Liquidator
- Judicial factor.

The examples given above clearly show that in some countries more than one significator may be applied as an equivalent for the source text translative unit. It is so because the definitions provided for such internationalisms are very broad and legal realities differ significantly in the EU member states. In the main body of the Polish version of the statutory instrument in question the translator, however, had to use one term due to language economy. The chosen significators are: *insolvency proceedings* → *postępowanie upadłościowe*, *winding-up proceedings* → *postępowanie likwidacyjne*, *liquidator* → *zarządca*. Two connotative equivalents have been used that is to say*postępowanie upadłościowe* and *zarządca*. But the annexes actually modify the meaning of the terms used significantly, which is especially visible in the case of *zarządca* the meaning of which has been extended by the annex in question to embrace all types of insolvency practitioners who participate in different types of insolvency proceedings in Poland.

Moreover, at present the terminology used by the EU institutions has been gathered in a special database IATE (the EU multilingual term base at <http://iate.europa.eu>) where we can find definitions of terms and reliability of used equivalents provided by EU translators and terminologists.

5.4. Common law communicative community

The *common law communicative community* is the community composed of people living in a common law country and therefore more acquainted with the common law legal system. Most of common law communicative communities may be divided into communities using English language varieties. Therefore, we may enumerate, e.g. the American common law communicative community and the British common law communicative community.

In general the communicative community composed of common law communicative community members/readers will have the following properties:

(i) active or passive,
(ii) compact or loose,
(iii) primary,
(iv) subordinate, superordinate or independent
(v) monolingual or multilingual,
(vi) mixed,
(vii) non-hermetic in contacts with other common law communities and hermetic in contacts with civil law communities, and
(viii) most probably composed of members aware and unaware of legal system differences.

In turn, the British common law communicative community will have the following properties:

(i) active or passive,
(ii) compact,
(iii) primary,
(iv) subordinate, superordinate or independent,
(v) mostly monolingual,
(vi) mixed,
(vii) non-hermetic in contacts with other common law communities and hermetic in contacts with civil law communities, and
(viii) most probably composed of members aware and unaware of legal system differences.

On the other hand, the American common law communicative community will have the following properties:

(i) active or passive,
(ii) compact or loose,
(iii) primary or secondary (due to the co-existence of many language minorities),
(iv) subordinate, superordinate or independent
(v) multilingual,
(vi) mixed,
(vii) non-hermetic in contacts with other common law communities and hermetic in contacts with civil law communities, and
(viii) most probably composed of members aware and unaware of legal system differences.

Therefore, the connotative significators will need to be language variety oriented. The table below contains a juxtaposition of examples of English language variety oriented connotative equivalents for selected Polish bankruptcy terms taken from:

(i) the Insolvency Act 1986 (England and Wales),
(ii) the Irish Bankruptcy Act 1988,
(iii) the US Code Title 11 Bankruptcy, and
(iv) the Australian Bankruptcy Act 1966.

Polish source language translative unit	*British English (England and Wales)*	*Irish*	*American*	*Australian*
masa upadłości	Estate, effects, or bankrupt estate	bankrupt's estate, bankrupt's property, the estate of the bankrupt	(property of) the estate	the property of the bankrupt
upadłość	bankruptcy and insolvency	bankruptcy	bankruptcy	bankruptcy

postępowanie upadłościowe obejmujące likwidację maajątku upa-dłego	proceedings in the winding up, winding up, Bankruptcy proceedings	winding up, bankruptcy (proceedings)	bankruptcy procedure	bank-ruptcy proceed-ings

Table 1. English language variety oriented connotative significators for Polish insolvency terms.

Therefore, the following directives may be inferred:

Directive 16

When translating a civil law or other-legal-system imbedded text for the communicative community expert in common law but not civil law, the translator shall look first for

(i) connotative significators,

(ii) if there are partially suitable connotative significators, it is possible to modify the connotative significator,

(iii) if there is no connotative significator, one may look for the equivalent in English for civil law institution in the Louisiana legislation (e.g. Louisiana Civil Code) or alternatively to some extent also the Scottish legislation,

(iv) Latin-oriented equivalent, and

(v) if methods (iii) and (iv) cannot be applied, the translator should resort to descriptive (explanatory equivalents).

Directive 17

When translating a civil law imbedded text for the communicative community expert in common law and civil law, the translator shall look first for

(i) connotative significator supplied with an exotic in the brackets,

(ii) if there are partially suitable connotative significator, it is possible to modify the connotative significator and supply it with an exotic in the brackets,

(iii) if there is no connotative significator, one may look for the equivalent in English for civil law institution in the Louisiana legislation (e.g. Louisiana Civil Code) or alternatively to some extent also the Scottish legislation,

(iv) Latin-oriented significator,
(v) if procedures (iii) and (vi) cannot be applied, the translator should resort to EU oriented significator,
(vi) or may resort to different types of borrowings.

5.5. Civil law communicative community

The *civil law communicative community* is the community composed of people living in civil law countries and therefore more acquainted with the civil law legal system. Civil law communicative communities are composed of citizens of countries in which Roman law was adopted. Usually the adoption of Roman law took place via the legislation introduced by Napoleon I in the form of the Code Napoleon legislation. The Napoleonic codifications were translated into other languages, e.g. German, English (in the state of Louisiana), etc. Finally, civil law countries are for instance located in continental Europe and some states of the USA. However, it should be borne in mind that civil law may be superseded in the territory of civil law states of the USA by the federal common law legislation binding all states (e.g. federal Bankruptcy Act).

In general the communicative community composed of civil law communicative community members/readers will have the following properties:

(i) active or passive,
(ii) compact or loose,
(iii) primary,
(iv) subordinate, superordinate or independent
(v) monolingual or multilingual,
(vi) mixed,
(vii) non-hermetic in contacts with other common law communities and hermetic in contacts with civil law communities, and
(viii) most probably composed of members aware and unaware of legal system differences.

Consequently, the following directives will hold for translation recipients belonging to civil law communicative community:

Directive 18
When translating a civil law imbedded text for the communicative community expert in civil law, the translator should resort to
(i) connotative significators (often with exotics supplied in brackets),
(ii) if there are partially suitable connotative significators, it is possible to modify the connotative significators and/or supply it with an exotic in the brackets; it would be often enough to modify the connotative significators with the adjective referring to the institution's country of origin,
(iii) if there is no connotative or partially connotative significator, coining a neologism (e.g. in the form of a borrowing),
(iv) using a descriptive equivalent.

Directive 19
When translating a common law imbedded text for the communicative community expert in civil law or other legal system but not common law, the translator should look first for
(iii) connotative significators,
(iv) if there are partially suitable connotative significators, it is possible to modify the connotative significators – it would be often enough to modify the connotative significators with the adjective referring to the institution's country of origin,
(v) if there is no connotative or partially connotative significator, descriptive significators should be used.

Directive 20
When translating a common law or a text imbedded in a legal system other than civil law for the communicative community expert in civil law and knowing this other legal system in question, the translator should look first for
(i) connotative significators (often with exotics supplied in brackets),
(ii) if there are partially suitable connotative significators, it is possible to modify the functional equivalent and/or supply it with

an exotic in the brackets; it would be often enough to modify the connotative significators with the adjective referring to the institution's country of origin,

(iii) if there is no connotative or partially connotative significator, coining a neologism (often with an exotic supplied in brackets),

(iv) using a descriptive significator (often with an exotic supplied in brackets).

The table below contains examples of pairs of potential significators where the target one has been provided with the application of one of the procedures (techniques) listed in the directives 18-20.

A pair with a connotative significator	*A pair with a modified connotative significator*	*A pair with a neologism*	*A pair with a descriptive significator*
Fr. bail commercial → *Pol.* najem lokalu użytkowego *Fr.* huissier de justice → *Pol.* komornik fee tail - *Pol.* ordynacja	*Fr.* bail commercial → *Pol.* najem handlowy, najem dla celów handlowych/przemysłowych *Fr.* huissier de justice → *Pol.* francuski komornik	*Fr.* Bail commercial → *Eng.* commercial lease *Fr.* huissier de justice → *Pl./Eng.* huissier de justice	*Fr.* bail commercial → *Pol.* najem dla celów handlowych/przemysłowych *Fr.* huissier de justice → *Pol.* francuski urzędnik o kompetenacjach woźnego sądowego i komornika *Eng.* blue chips → *Ger.* Aktien von Unternehmen hoher Solidität *Eng.* Dow Jones Index → *Pol.* indeks Dow Jonesa (średnia cena akcji 30 przedsiębiorstw sklasyfikowanych jako tzw. blue-chips na Nowojorskiej Giełdzie Papierów Wartościowych)

			Eng. underlying instrument → *Ger.* das einer Option oder einem Optionsschein zugrunde liegende Finanzinstrument *Eng.* escheat – *Pol.* prawo odzyskania posiadania przez państwo (pana feudalnego)

Table 2. Pairs of significators for recipients belonging to civil law communicative communities (examples among others from Grzybek/Matulewska/Nowak-Korcz 2008; Grzybek/Matulewska 2007).

Sometimes calques are the easiest and most obvious method of providing significators, and in some cases this method may be classified as a neologism as well as a modified connotative significator, e.g.:

(134) *Chi.* A 股份→ *Eng.* A shares

(135) *Chi.* B 股份→ *Eng.* B shares

5.6. Business oriented communicative community

The *business-oriented foreign communicative community* is the communicative community composed of people belonging to many language communities not knowing the target language but operating in the target language legal system and due to their business undertakings which are carried out in the target language legal system, are interested in possible differences between target language legal system and other legal systems. The main problem is that the members of this communicative community may use different mother tongues. Usually, they use one of the conference languages as means of communication.

Consequently, the communicative community composed of business-oriented foreign communicative community members/readers will have the following properties:

(i) active,
(ii) compact or loose,
(iii) secondary or primary,
(iv) subordinate,
(v) multilingual,
(vi) mixed,
(vii) non-hermetic, and
(viii) most probably aware of legal system differences (at least aware of the necessity to comply with legal provisions which differ or change in time).

The communicative community will also aim at precision in communication.

If the target language is Polish, then the members of the community will often resort to translations of Polish legislation in German or English. TEPIS[42] is the Polish organization, which offers translations appropriate to their needs. Thus, the examples given in the table below are taken from the Polish Law Collection (Kierzkowska 1996) published by TEPIS.

Polish term	*TEPIS-rendered significator*
upadłość	bankruptcy
upadły	bankrupt
ogłoszenie upadłości	declaration of bankruptcy
dłużnik	debtor
wierzyciel	creditor
masa upadłości	bankruptcy estate
syndyk	official receiver
sędzia-komisarz	judge-commissioner
postępowanie upadłościowe	bankruptcy proceedings
kurator	trustee in bankruptcy
rada wierzycieli	committee of creditors
likwidator	liquidator

42 Polish Society of Sworn and Specialized Translators TEPIS.

zarządca	administrator
likwidacja masy upadłości	liquidation of the bankruptcy estate
nadzór syndyka	supervision of the official receiver
komornik	court executive officer
izba skarbowa	Treasury Department
zakład ubezpieczeń społecznych	the Social Insurance Institution
majątek upadłego	bankrupt's assets
likwidacja majątku masy upadłości	liquidation of assets of the bankruptcy estate
zgromadzenie wierzycieli	meeting of creditors
zgłoszenie wierzytelności	submission of the statement of debt
lista wierzytelności	list of debts
układ	arrangement
zawarcie układu	making of the arrangement
zatwierdzenie układu	approval of the arrangement
podział funduszów masy upadłości	distribution of funds of the bankruptcy estate
umorzenie postępowania upadłościowego	discontinuance of the bankruptcy proceedings
uchylenie postępowania upadłościowego	quashing of the bankruptcy proceedings
ukończenie postępowania upadłościowego	completion of the bankruptcy proceedings

Table 3. TEPIS-rendered significators for selected terms from the *Regulation by the President of the Republic of Poland of 24 October 1934 Bankruptcy Law* (*Rozporządzenie Prezydenta Rzeczypospolitej z dnia 24 października 1934 r. Prawo upadłościowe*).

For instance the connotative American-law oriented significator for *sędzia-komisarz* would be *bankruptcy judge*. But TEPIS deliberately tries to avoid associations with institutions existing in English speaking countries, therefore a neologism in the form of a calque has been coined to avoid possible misunderstandings.

TEPIS suggests for this type of recipients using, if possible, modified connotative significators (functional equivalents) and neologisms. Are they right? In general, TEPIS's strategy is justified by the purpose of translations rendered for businessmen, who need understandable target texts but at the same time must be aware of differences between the legal system they know from their country of origin, and the legal system of the country of destination where they want to operate. Definitely neologisms may be used, in the absence of connotative significators which may be successfully modified, provided that they are understandable and convey a sufficient degree of the translative meaning.

Taking the above mentioned arguments into account, the following directives for the translation for recipients belonging to the business oriented communicative community may be formulated:

Directive 21
When translating for the business oriented communicative community, connotative significators shall be applied for translandive terms where such connotates are fully equivalent with the translandive term in question.

Directive 22
When translating for the business oriented communicative community, modified connotative significators shall be applied for translandive terms where such connotates are in the relation of near equivalence or partial equivalence with the translandive term in question.

Directive 23
When translating for the business oriented communicative community, in the absence of connotative significators remaining in the relation of full, near and partial equivalence with translandive term in question, a neologism shall be coined.

5.7. Legal system ignorant communicative community

The *ignorant communicative community* is the communicative community composed of people belonging to many language communities not knowing the source language legal system and not operating in the source language legal system permanently. This group of people will be composed of, e.g., tourists who are not interested in getting to know the source language legal system, but who want to know what to do or what not to do in order to, e.g., have an enjoyable holiday abroad. They will not be interested in the legal system as such, but in modes of behaviour they have to adopt to survive in the source legal system environment.

The ignorant communicative community is composed of members/readers who will have the following properties:

(i) passive,
(ii) loose,
(iii) usually primary,
(iv) usually subordinate for a while, but in general independent,
(v) monolingual or multilingual,
(vi) mixed,
(vii) non-hermetic, and
(viii) most probably composed of members unaware of legal system differences.

For such a communicative community most appropriate are (i) succinct descriptive equivalents possibly supplied with exotics as well as (ii) comparisons to well-known institutions existing in their target language legal reality (cf. the directives below).

Directive 24

If the communicative community is ignorant, then

(i) connotative significators should be used for very similar concepts,
(ii) modified connotative significators,
(iii) descriptive significators as well as significators supplied with definitions should be used for non-existent or dissimilar concepts.

Directive 25

It is also possible to use an exotic supplied with a definition in exceptional cases if the translator has sufficient grounds to assume that the ignorant communicative community may need it for communication purposes (e.g. as is done in tour guides where the name of the institution, e.g. a post office is given in a source language to enable a tourist to find it if he wants to buy stamps for postcards).

The table below contains a few examples of equivalents for a legal system ignorant communicative community.

Connotative significators:	*Descriptive significators*	*Significator in the form of a definition*
Eng. insolvency proceedings → *Pol.* postępowanie upadłościowe *Eng.* bankruptcy proceedings → *Pol.* postępowanie upadłościowe *Pol.* sędzia-komisarz → *Eng.* bankruptcy judge	*Pol.* kurator (dla osoby nieobecnej) → *Eng.* guardian for an absent person *Pol.* kurator (dla zmarłego małżonka) → *Eng.* guardian for the deceased spouse *Pol.* kurator (dla dłużnika, którego miejsce pobytu nie jest znane) → *Eng.* guardian for an absent debtor.	*Pol.* sędzia-komisarz → *Eng.* A judge-commissioner is a professional judge appointed in the Polish bankruptcy proceedings in order to supervise the course of the proceedings. He supervises the activities of the insolvency practitioner, court supervisor and administrator.

Table 4. Possible equivalents for legal system ignorant communicative community

5.8. Business relation bound communicative community

The *business relation bound communicative community*, which is called by Kierzkowska (2002) a self-determined recipient, is the community which expects that a specific glossary of significators will be used in contacts between source and target language communicative communities. In such cases the translator does not make decisions concerning significators but applies the imposed terminology.

An example occurring in real life should now be considered. A legal practice having its seat in London was engaged by a German company to investigate Polish insolvency law. It has subsequently been revealed that the German company had bought some shares of a Polish company, which was to be declared bankrupt. Confronted with the bankruptcy of the Polish company, the German investor wished to discover what were his chances of minimising his losses. The legal practice in London delegated three lawyers to conduct the investigation, one from the USA branch, another from the London office and a third from the German office. The lawyer from Germany had studied law in Austria, and therefore knew the civil law legal reality better than his colleagues from Great Britain and the USA. As at that time Poland was not a member of the European Union, the Polish bankruptcy law was to be applied. The legal practice in order to find out the possible outcome of the bankruptcy proceedings carried out in Poland under the Polish law asked a Polish professor specialising in bankruptcy law to write an expert legal opinion on the matter in question. The opinion was written in Polish and then translated into English. The commissioner requested the translator to use Latin terminology wherever possible to create a communicative bond between three lawyers educated in law in three different countries. Therefore, for instance the term *skarga pauliańska* discussed previously was translated into English as *the Actio Pauliana*.

Very often legal offices are self-determined communities in respect of the source text author and target text recipient.

Cameron McKenna may serve as an example here as it is a law firm using its own self-determined glossaries. Here are some examples of key insolvency law terms from the Polish-English Law Dictionary for the employees and translators of Cameron McKenna (<http://www.scribd.com/doc/6157790/Cameron-McKenna-Polish-English-Law-Dictionary>):

postępowanie upadłościowe	bankruptcy procedure
syndyk masy upadłościowej	bankruptcy trustee, receiver in bankruptcy
postępowanie układowe	debt restructuring
postępowanie likwidacyjne	liquidation
likwidacja	winding up
postępowanie układowe z wierzycielami	arrangement with creditors
komornik skarbowy	bankruptcy trustee
sędzia-komisarz	judge appointed

Table 5. Cameron-McKenna Polish-English Law Dictionary Excerpt.

Thus, the following directive may be inferred:

Directive 26
If the text is translated for the purpose of the self-determined communicative community, the terms imposed by the commissioner shall be applied regardless of translation strategy adopted by a translator.

5.9. Concluding remarks

To conclude, the properties that each communicative community extracts from the dimensions described above affects the choice of possible significators for source text translative units. There are methods of modifying and coining significators which are optimal for some communicative communities yet unacceptable for others. Thus, the translator needs to make his choices consciously adapting the significator to the communicative community needs.

The more homogeneous the communicative community is, the easier the translator's choices are. The more heterogenous the communicative community is, the more difficult it is to meet the expectations of all members of the community in question. The list of directives provided here is by no means exhaustive and serves the purpose of illustrating the theory proposed in this work.

This chapter has been devoted to the selection of the method of providing equivalents adjusted to a given communicative community of recipients. The issue of comparing semantic fields specific of given significators in the source and target language will be discussed in the next chapter.

6. In Quest of Sufficient Equivalence

6.1. Introductory remarks

This chapter will be devoted to choosing equivalents to be used in the target text on the basis of previously calculated source-text meaning on the basis of the application of the parametrization for the purpose of legal communication with a selected communicative community in mind.

6.2. Establishing sufficient equivalents

The problem of establishing sufficient equivalence between the translandive unit and a translative one is connected with comparing the properties both units take on from a given set of dimensions which are pertinent for the communicative community recipients and enable the translator to produce the translative text meeting the requirements of the postulates listed in chapter 2.

It should be borne in mind that the dimensions listed in chapter 3 and used in chapters 4 and 5 are not always sufficient to decide whether two terms are sufficiently equivalent or not. In the process of translation, the translator must also take into account essential and accidental characteristics of, e.g., compared terms (cf. Šarčević 2000b: 238-239). The hierarchy of dimensions should reflect what is essential and what is accidental for the recipients. Such essential and accidental characteristics of a translandive unit will be the properties this particular unit assumes. Important characteristics will be considered essential whereas secondary characteristics will be considered accidental. To put it differently, in case of terms this stage is the comparison of meanings of the source text units with their potential equivalents in order to decide whether they are sufficiently translationally convergent or permissibly translationally complementary (which would result in sufficient translational equivalence under Po. 9). Let us give a few examples illustrating the issue of calculation of sufficient equivalents.

In general this chapter will be illustrated with examples from insolvency or bankruptcy law. *Bankruptcy law* is the term used in the United States of America, whereas in Great Britain and the European Union the term is *insolvency law*, in Poland it is *prawo upadłościowe*. The proceedings are *mutadis mutandis* called *bankruptcy proceedings* in the USA, *insolvency proceedings* in the UK and *postępowanie upadłościowe* in Poland. But all those proceedings are further subdivided into various types of insolvency proceedings developed in given territories.

Sometimes when the legal reality is similar it is enough to use the general dimensions elaborated on in chapter 3, e.g.:

	term / *dimension*	*bankruptcy petition*	*wniosek o ogłoszenie upadłości*
1.	the author of the text	petitioner or a person acting on his behalf	petitioner or a person acting on his behalf
2.	text delivery form	written	written
3.	text status	binding	binding
4.	the time of text creation	valid	valid
5.	branch of law to which the text refers to	bankruptcy law	bankruptcy law
6.	text genre	a petition	a petition
7.	the language of the text	English	Polish
8.	text legal reality	common law	civil law
9.	text language variety	American English	not applicable

Table 6. Properties of *bankruptcy petition* and *wniosek o ogłoszenie upadłości* derived on the basis of parallel text comparison for the purpose of English-Polish translation.

Although the terms do not share all their properties, the essential ones are the same (no. 1, 3-6). The secondary feature (no. 2) is also the same. As far as features 8-9 are concerned the source and target units do not need to have the same properties, as they inform the translator about potential differences he may encounter in the process of translation enterprise. Feature 7 informs about the translation direction that is from which and into which language the translation is rendered. Thus, the dimensions allow for calculating the distance between the source and potential target text units. But translation direction may affect the distance as it may happen that when translating from English into Polish a given pair composed of the English translandive unit and its Polish functional equivalent is less distant than in the case of the same terms when translating from Polish into English.

When translating from Polish into English for a recipient community operating in American legal reality the terms given above would be sufficiently equivalent. Let us now compare the results of our analysis with two more terms this time from British legal reality.

	term / *dimension*	*bankruptcy petition*	*bankruptcy petition*	*winding-up petition*	*wniosek o ogłoszenie upadłości*
1.	the author of the text	petitioner or a person acting on his behalf	petitioner or a person acting on his behalf	petitioner or a person acting on his behalf	petitioner or a person acting on his behalf
2.	text delivery form	written	written	written	written
3.	text status	binding	binding	binding	binding
4.	the time of text creation	valid	valid	valid	valid
5.	branch of law to which the text refers to	bankruptcy law	Bankruptcy /insolvency law	Bankruptcy/insolvency law	bankruptcy law
6.	text genre	a petition	a petition	a petition	a petition
7.	the language of the text	English	English	English	Polish
8.	text legal reality	common law (sub-property: federal law of the USA)	common law (sub-property: law of England and Wales)	common law (sub-property: law of England and Wales)	civil law

9.	text language variety	American English	British English	British English	Not applicable

Table 7. Properties of *bankruptcy petitions* and *winding-up petition* and *wniosek o ogłoszenie upadłości* derived on the basis of parallel text comparison for the purpose of English-Polish translation.

As we can see from the juxtaposition presented in the table above when translating from Polish into English for the purpose of British English speaking communicative community the dimensions are not sufficient to decide which term to choose (*bankruptcy petition* or *winding-up petition*) as they assume the same properties. Thus, the need arises to compare more of their essential characteristics, e.g.:

	term / *dimension*	*bankruptcy petition*	*bankruptcy petition*	*winding-up petition*	*wniosek o ogłoszenie upadłości*
10.	type of proceedings	bankruptcy proceedings	insolvency proceedings (sub-type: bankruptcy proceedings)	insolvency proceedings (sub-type: winding-up proceedings)	postępowanie upadłościowe (insolvency proceedings)
11.	personality of a petitioner who has capacity to become insolvent	any type of personality: natural or legal person	natural person	legal person	any type of personality: natural or legal person
12.	aim of proceedings	declaration of insolvency: liquidation, arrangement with creditors, restructuring, etc.	declaration of insolvency liquidation	declaration of insolvency liquidation	declaration of insolvency: liquidation, arrangement with creditors, restructuring, etc.

Table 8. Additional properties of *bankruptcy petitions* and *winding-up petition* and *wniosek o ogłoszenie upadłości* derived on the basis of parallel text comparison for the purpose of English-Polish translation.

The more detailed analysis (see table above) reveals that terms refer to different levels of proceedings concerning insolvency and different types of persons that file the petitions in question. Thus when translating from Polish into American English and the other way round the pair *wniosek o ogłoszenie upadłości* and *bankruptcy petition* are sufficiently equivalent (because they are convergent in reference to dimensions 11 and 12 and sufficiently translationally convergent in reference to dimension 10) as stated above. However, as far as characteristics 10-12 are concerned, the British terms are convergent with the Polish one in respect to hyper-dimensions of

(i) the type of proceedings with the exemplary properties such as divorce proceedings, insolvency proceedings, penal proceedings, etc. (and at the same time translationally complementary in respect to the hypo-dimension of the type of insolvency proceedings which for instance may have the following properties: bankruptcy proceedings, winding-up proceedings, administration, administrative receivership, etc.),
(ii) the capacity to become insolvent with properties: persons capable to become insolvent or persons not capable to become insolvent (and at the same time translationally complementary in respect to the hypo-dimension of the type of persons capable of becoming insolvent with the following properties: (a) legal persons, (b) natural persons, (c) legal and natural persons)
(iii) the aim of the proceedings being in divorce proceedings the dissolution of marriage, in insolvency proceedings the declaration of insolvency, etc. depending on the type of proceedings (and at the same time translationally complementary in respect to the hypo-dimension of the aim of the sub-type of insolvency proceedings with the following properties: liquidation, arrangement with creditors, restructuring).

Therefore, when translating from Polish into British English it may be necessary to use a neologism (*insolvency petition*) based on the EU terminology from the Regulation on insolvency proceedings (insolvency petition being a petition filed in insolvency proceedings) as in respect to dimensions of the type of insolvency proceedings, type of persons capable of becoming insolvent and aim of a given type of insolvency proceedings the terms are translationally complementary.

If the translator is able to determine that the aim of the proceedings in the Polish translandive text is the liquidation, then it may be possible to use both terms referring to British legal reality, that is to say, *bankruptcy and/or winding-up petition* (two terms for one). However, if he is able to decide that the Polish term refers to either a natural or a legal person, than the choice may be limited to just one of two terms (*bankruptcy petition* or *winding-up petition* respectively) – which would be the case of translation by restriction. Such decisions are always based on the contextual information contained in the translandive text or information provided by the commissioner. When translating a British translandive text into Polish, however, it would be necessary to add additional information revealing the aim of proceedings and the status of a person it refers to. Thus we could have the following pairs of sufficient equivalents:

(136) bankruptcy petition – wniosek o ogłoszenie upadłości likwidacyjnej osoby fizycznej, and

(137) winding-up petition – wniosek o ogłoszenie upadłości likwidacyjnej osoby prawnej.

The more the legal systems of the source and target language reality differ, the more dimensions may be required to establish sufficient translational equivalents on the basis of permissible complementarity or sufficient convergence (under Po 9) of the so-called system-bound terms.

The main problem with such terms is that it is frequently necessary to establish the meaning of the whole net of terms in order to compare the meaning of the term in question with the possible target text equivalents and to make a decision about which method of providing equivalents for the target text to choose.

A nominee of a company voluntary arrangement and a supervisor of a company voluntary arrangement are types of insolvency practitioners in England and Wales. In order to find out how to translate them into Polish we need to establish the relations of sufficient translational convergence and permissible translational complementarity between the English terms, their potential functional Polish equivalents (that is to say *syndyk*, *nadzorca sądowy*, *tymczasowy nadzorca sądowy*, *zarządca*, and *kurator*) and the requirements of the recipients of the translative text rendered by the translator.

The terms *a nominee of a company voluntary arrangement and a supervisor of a company voluntary arrangement* take on the following properties from the dimensions described in chapter 3:

(i) the author of the source-text: legislator
(ii) source-text delivery form: written
(iii) source-text status: binding
(iv) the time of source text creation: valid
(v) branch of law to which the text refers: insolvency law
(vi) text genre: a statutory instrument
(vii) the language of the source text: English
(viii) source-text legal reality: common law
(ix) source text language variety: British English (to be precise: England and Wales)

Thus, it turns out that the dimensions are not sufficient even to find the differences between two terms embedded in the English and Welsh legal system. Therefore, the need arises to compare more characteristics of insolvency practitioners functioning in the legal system of England and Wales and then compare them with their Polish counterparts.

Insolvency practitioners in England and Wales may be divided into official receivers and qualified insolvency practitioners, who are sometimes also called officeholders. Official receivers are entitled to carry out all the functions for which qualified insolvency practitioners are responsible. Qualified insolvency practitioners, on the other hand, are divided into two groups. Under section 388(1)(2) of Insolvency Act 1986 the first group of insolvency practitioners deals with corporate insolvency. Corporate insolvency practitioners may act as liquidators, provisional liquidators, administrators, administrative receivers, nominees of a company voluntary arrangement and supervisors of a company voluntary arrangement, whereas personal insolvency practitioners include trustees in bankruptcy, interim receivers, nominees of an individual voluntary arrangement and supervisors of an individual voluntary arrangement (Keay/Walton 2003: 35).

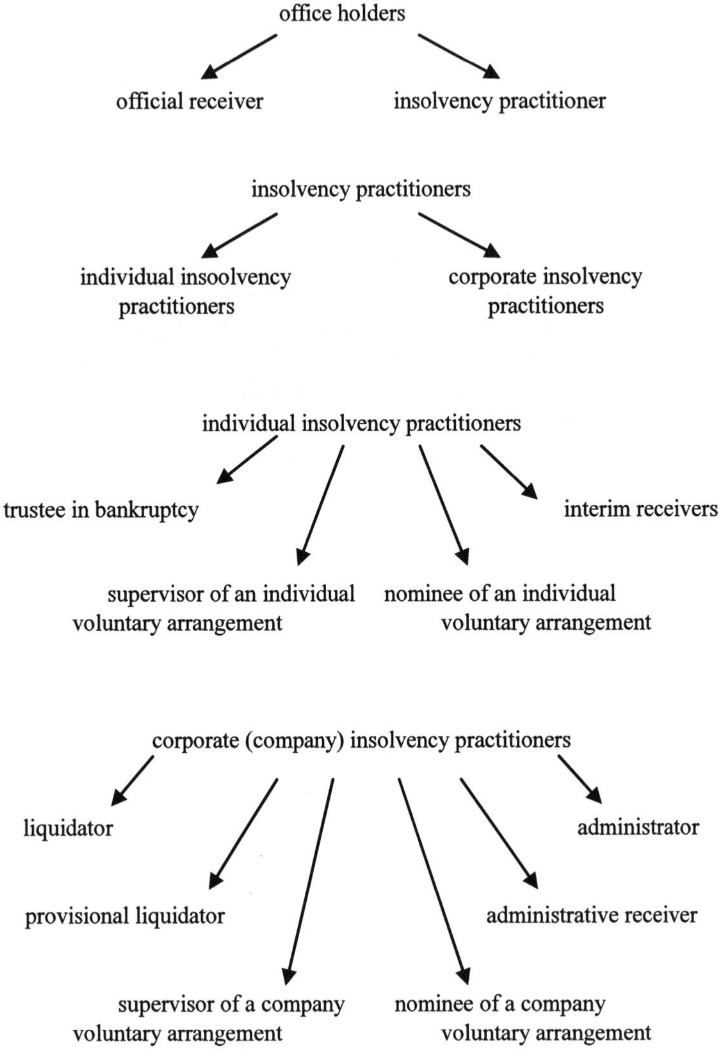

Figure 5. Types of office holders acting in insolvency proceedings in England and Wales.

The information which we can obtain from Figure 5. helps us narrow down the number of potential insolvency practitioners to corporate insolvency practitioners. Let us now focus on types of corporate insolvency practitioners, their responsibilities, competences and types of proceedings in which they are appointed.

Liquidator: In the case of liquidation we may distinguish two principal forms: (i) voluntary winding up, which is initiated by the company in the wake of the resolution adopted by the general meeting and (ii) winding up by the court (also called compulsory winding up). Voluntary winding up may be carried out without the involvement of the court. However, compulsory winding up starts the moment the petition is present at the court. In the case of compulsory winding up the court appoints an official receiver, who acts as a liquidator. Such a liquidator assumes the functions of the company's directors and starts managing the company, collecting, realizing and distributing company's assets. He manages the assets for the benefit of the creditors, who are supposed to receive the distribution after the assets have been realized. The moment the winding up is completed, the company ceases to exist as it is dissolved. Insolvency Act 1986, section 143(1) states that:

> The functions of the liquidator of a company which is being wound up by the court are to secure that the assets of the company are got in, realized and distributed to the company's creditors and, if there is surplus, to the persons entitled to it.

Provisional liquidator: In the case of compulsory winding up, after the presentation of a winding-up petition, the court under section 135 of the Insolvency Act may appoint a provisional liquidator whose powers may be limited by the order appointing him and who carries out functions conferred on him by the court.

Administrator: Under section 8(2) of Insolvency Act 1986 the court may make an administration order in relation to the company which is ailing. The administrator is appointed to manage the affairs, business and property of the company. The administration order is made in order to save all or part of company's undertakings, approve a voluntary arrangement, provide a more advantageous realization of the company's assets than would be effected on a winding up, sanction a compromise under section 425 of the Companies Act. The order as a rule specifies the purpose for which it has been made. Thus, the responsibilities of the administrator may vary depending on the purpose of the order. Until 2002 the administrator could have been appointed only by the court. However, the moment the Enterprise Act 2002 came into force, the administrator may be appointed by a debenture holder, the company or its directors. The powers of the administrator include managing and disposing of company's assets.

Administrative receiver: An administrative receiver is appointed in the case of receivership that is to say a situation in which "[...] a secured creditor enforces the security by appointing a receiver." (Keay/Walton 2003: 42). Under section 29(2) the administrative receiver is:

> [...] (a) a receiver or manager of the whole (or substantially the whole) of company's property appointed by or on behalf of the holders of any debentures of the company secured by a charge which, as created, was a floating charge, or by such a charge and one or more other securities; or (b) a person who would be such a receiver or manager but for the appointment of some other person as the receiver of part of the company's property.

Nominee of a company voluntary arrangement and supervisor of a company voluntary arrangement: A company voluntary arrangement is an insolvency procedure in the course of which a financially troubled company may reach a binding agreement with its creditors about payment of all or some part of its debts over an agreed period of time. The company voluntary arrangement may be proposed by the directors of the company, the administrators of the company, or the liquidator of the company. However neither creditors nor shareholders can propose a company voluntary arrangement. When the company voluntary arrangement is proposed, the insolvency practitioner starts acting as a nominee of a company voluntary arrangement. He is responsible for reporting to court that a meeting of creditors and shareholders should be convened in order to vote for the proposal. In order for the proposal to be approved 75% of the company's creditors must vote for it. The moment the company voluntary arrangement is approved of a nominee of a company voluntary arrangement becomes a supervisor of a company voluntary arrangement.

Having established the meanings of the terms in question we may compare them. The table below contains the juxtaposition of distinguishing features of those types of corporate insolvency practitioners.

dimension / *insolvency practitioner type*	*procedure or stage of the procedure*	*responsibilities*	*appointing institution*
liquidator	liquidation by (a) voluntary winding up and (b) compulsory winding up by the court (see below)	collecting, realizing and distributing company's assets and sometimes managing the company	the company
an official receiver, who acts as a liquidator	compulsory winding up by the court	securing that the assets of the company are got in, realized and distributed to the company's creditors and, if there is surplus, to the persons entitled to it	the court
provisional liquidator	compulsory winding up by the court after the presentation of a winding-up petition	carries out functions conferred on him by the court	the court
administrator	when the administration order is made by the court	managing the affairs, business and property of the company	the court, a debenture holder, the company or its directors
administrative receiver	receivership	managing of the whole (or substantially the whole) of company's property	appointed by or on behalf of the holders of any debentures of the company secured by a charge
nominee of a company voluntary arrangement	after the company voluntary arrangement is proposed	reporting to court that a meeting of creditors and shareholders	the automatic transformation of the previously appointed insol-

		should be convened in order to vote for the proposal	vency practitioner
supervisor of a company voluntary arrangement	from the moment the company voluntary arrangement is approved of	carrying out the tasks in the course of the company voluntary arrangement	the automatic transformation of the nominee of a company voluntary arrangement

Table 9. The comparison of the key features of corporate insolvency practitioners in England and Wales.

Having compared the typical distinguishing characteristics of corporate insolvency practitioners is a starting point for the search for target text equivalents. These types of insolvency practitioners do not occur in Polish insolvency law. However, in order to find equivalents or to coin equivalents for them it is still necessary to calculate their meanings. First of all, it turns out that there is no division into corporate and personal insolvency practitioners in Poland, and all practitioners may act in proceedings concerning the insolvent debtor who is either a natural or a legal person. A more detailed analysis shows that there are fewer types of insolvency proceedings and insolvency practitioners in Poland than in England and Wales and predictably the scopes of responsibilities of English and Polish practitioners vary.

dimension / *Polish insolvency practitioner type*	*procedure or stage of the procedure*	*responsibilities*	*appointing institution*
syndyk	insolvency proceedings (after the declaration of insolvency) aiming at liquidation	collecting, realizing and distributing the insolvent debtor's assets and sometimes managing the company	the court
nadzorca sądowy	insolvency proceedings (after the declaration of insolvency)	supervision of the insolvent debtor's activities, preparing	the court

	aiming at reorganization	accounting reports, making sure that the insolvent debtor's estate is protected against destruction, etc.	
tymczasowy nadzorca sądowy	insolvency proceedings between filing the petition till the declaration of insolvency	supervision of the insolvent debtor's activities, preparing accounting reports, making sure that the insolvent debtor's estate is protected against destruction, etc.	the court
zarządca	insolvency proceedings (after the declaration of insolvency) aiming at reorganization when the insolvent debtor is deprived of the right to manage his estate in whole or in part	managing the affairs, business and property of the insolvent debtor	the court
kurator	any type of insolvency proceedings when the insolvent debtor has no capacity to sue and be sued and has no legal representative appointed for him	representing the insolvent debtor	the court

Table 10. The comparison of the key features of insolvency practitioners in Poland.

Therefore, depending on the needs and requirements of communicative community recipients we may suggest the following pairs of equivalents for selected types of insolvency practitioners and insolvency proceedings revealing the complementarity at the level of the dimension of the aim of insolvency proceedings, type of insolvency proceedings and legal status of the insolvent debtor.

English	*Polish*
(company) insolvency	upadłość osób prawnych
administration	sądowe postępowanie restrukturyzujące/restrukturyzacyjne /reorganizacyjne lub postępowanie układowe
administration order	postanowienie o ustanowieniu zarządu nad majątkiem/przedsiębiorstwem upadłego
administration order appointing more than one administrator and enabling administrators to exercise powers jointly and severally	postanowienie o ustanowieniu zarządu nad majątkiem/przedsiębiorstwem upadłego i powołaniu zarządców ponoszących solidarną odpowiedzialność za wykonywane czynności
administrative receiver	zarządca (całości lub części) majątku działający na rzecz wierzycieli zabezpieczonych
administrative receivership	zarząd na rzecz wierzycieli zabezpieczonych nad majątkiem upadłego
administrator	TLOT: zarządca sądowy, SLOT: administrator sądowy
company (corporate) insolvency	upadłość osób prawnych, upadłość spółek (kapitałowych)
company (corporate) insolvency practitioner	licencjonowany urzędnik (specjalista) ds. upadłości osób prawnych
company voluntary arrangement	postępowanie naprawcze dla przedsiębiorstw posiadających osobowość prawną
compulsory = by the court	sądowy
compulsory winding up	postępowanie upadłościowe sądowe obejmujące likwidację majątku osoby prawnej (spółki kapitałowej)
creditors' voluntary winding up	postępowanie upadłościowe (pozasądowe) obejmujące likwidację majątku osoby prawnej (spółki kapitałowej) prowadzone na wniosek wierzycieli
individual insolvency	upadłość przedsiębiorców będących osobami fizycznymi
individual insolvency practitioner	licencjonowany urzędnik (specjalista) ds. upadłości osób fizycznych
individual voluntary arrangement	postępowanie naprawcze dla przedsiębiorstw prowadzonych przez osoby fizyczne (nieposiadające osobowości prawnej)
insolvency practitioner	licencjonowany specjalista ds. upadłościowych
liquidator	likwidator, ≅ syndyk
members' voluntary winding up	postępowanie upadłościowe (pozasądowe) obejmujące likwidację majątku osoby prawnej (spółki kapitałowej) prowadzone na wniosek organów

	spółki/osoby prawnej
nominee of an CVA (Company Voluntary Arrangement)	tymczasowy kurator/administrator/zarządca i nadzorca postępowania układowego (dla osób prawnych) (przed zatwierdzeniem planu restrukturyzacyjnego)
nominee of an IVA (Individual Voluntary Arrangement)	tymczasowy kurator/administrator/zarządca i nadzorca postępowania układowego (dla osób fizycznych) (przed zatwierdzeniem planu restrukturyzacyjnego)
office-holder	urzędnik lub licencjonowany specjalista ds. upadłościowych
official receiver	urzędnik sądowy ds. upadłości / upadłościowych
personal insolvency	upadłość konsumencka
provisional liquidation	postępowanie upadłościowe z możliwością likwidacji majątku upadłego
provisional liquidator	tymczasowy likwidator, ≅ tymczasowy syndyk
receiver	odbiorca należności, osoba upoważniona do odbioru należności
receiver and manager	zarządca majątku spółki działający na rzecz wierzycieli zabezpieczonych
receivership, administrative receivership	pozasądowy zarząd majątkiem, zarząd, (ale niekiedy może to być sądowy zarząd majątkiem), zarząd majątkiem na wniosek zabezpieczonych wierzycieli
supervisor of an CVA (Company Voluntary Arrangement)	kurator/administrator/zarządca i *nadzorca postępowania układowego* (dla osób prawnych)
supervisor of an IVA (Individual Voluntary Arrangement)	kurator/administrator/zarządca i *nadzorca postępowania układowego* (dla osób fizycznych)
trustee in bankruptcy	likwidator/syndyk powoływany dla osoby fizycznej
voluntary winding up	postępowanie upadłościowe (pozasądowe) obejmujące likwidację majątku osoby prawnej (spółki kapitałowej)
winding up	postępowanie upadłościowe obejmujące likwidację majątku osoby prawnej (spółki kapitałowej)

Table 11. Polish equivalents revealing legal reality differences for selected terminology in the field of insolvency in England and Wales.

Most of the equivalents provided in column 2 are modified functional equivalents or descriptive equivalents informing the recipients about differences in legal realities of the source language and target language units. Slash is used to provide a possible alternative equivalent and brackets are used to include information which may be added for recipients requiring a greater level of precision (needing more detailed information on differences between source and target legal system institutions). Literal translation of the adjectives *voluntary* (lit. *dobrowolny*) and *compulsory* (lit. *przymusowy/obowiązkowy*) constituting a part of some terms into Polish would mislead the recipients and make them believe that in Great Britan there are insolvencies which are declared at the will of the debtor and insolvencies which are obligatorily declared. Therefore, it would be much better to inform the recipients that *voluntary* refers to insolvency proceedings carried out without the active participation of the court (*pozasądowy* lit. *out-of-court*) and *compulsory* refers to insolvency proceedings carried out with the active participation of the court (*sądowy* lit. *in-court*).

6.3. Translation problems

The theory proposed here and its dimensions allow for calculating the distance between the translandive and translative units, which in turn may help avoid the translation problems resulting from insufficient equivalence.

To illustrate the problem of the proper choice of target text equivalents, a few examples of translation mistakes and errors are shown that result from the application of an inappropriate target text significator, that is to say a translative unit which was neither sufficiently translationally convergent nor permissibly translationally complementary. The examples are taken from the *Council Regulation (EC) no 1346/2000 of 29 May 2000 on insolvency proceedings* and its translation into Polish from 2003.

In the Regulation the term *international jurisdiction* (French: *compétence internationale*) was used to refer to the jurisdiction of the courts of an EU Member State which may open insolvency proceedings if the centre of a debtor's main interests is situated within their territory. The term in question takes on the following properties:

(i) the author of the source-text: legislator
(ii) source-text delivery form: written

(iii) source-text status: binding
(iv) the time of source text creation: valid
(v) branch of law to which the text refers: civil law
(vi) text genre: a regulation
(vii) the language of the source text: English
(viii) source-text legal reality: civil law system
(ix) source text language variety: European Union (legal) English

The term was translated into Polish as: *jurysdykcja międzynarodowa* (lit. *international jurisdiction*) instead of *jurysdykcja* (lit. *jurisdiction*) or *jurysdykcja krajowa* (lit. *national jurisdiction*). The translator coined a new term instead of using the existing connotative (functional) equivalent which was introduced into the Polish legal language in 1928 by the members of the Codification Commission of the Republic of Poland (Komisja Kodyfikacyjna Rzeczpospolitej Polskiej 1928: 328-330, volume II). The translator obviously failed to compare essential characteristics of two terms due to the apparent opposition between adjectives constituting their component parts that is to say the English adjective *international* and the Polish adjective *krajowy* (lit. *national*). This ostensible opposition led the translator astray as he failed to adjust the translative text to the requirements of the communicative community of recipients who in the case of the EU legislation are mostly lawyers.

In part 2 of the Regulation the term *cross-border insolvency proceedings* (French: *procédures d'insolvabilité transfrontalières*) is used. It assumes the following properties:

(i) the author of the source-text: legislator
(ii) source-text delivery form: written
(iii) source-text status: binding
(iv) the time of source text creation: valid
(v) branch of law to which the text refers: insolvency law
(vi) text genre: a regulation
(vii) the language of the source text: English
(viii) lect: legi-lect
(ix) source-text legal reality: civil law system
(x) source text language variety: European Union (legal) English

One of the additional features of the term is the fact that it refers to insolvency proceedings carried out against the debtor (called in the Regulation the *undertaking*) whose activities have cross-border effects either because his assets are situated in more than one country or because he has creditors from abroad, etc. The translator has failed to use the existing functional equivalent which is *transgraniczne postepowania w sprawie niewypłacalności* and coined a descriptive equivalent in the following form *postępowania upadłościowe, których skutki mają charakter wykraczający poza granice danego państw*. Again, it is a terminological error resulting from adopting an incorrect translation strategy (a strategy not adjusted to the requirements of recipients) that is to say using a descriptive signifícator instead of the connotative one.

In Article 5(2)(a) of the Regulation the term *mortgage* (French: *hypothéque* and German *Hypothek*) is used. In reference to the EU law it takes on the following properties:

(i) the author of the source-text: legislator
(ii) source-text delivery form: written
(iii) source-text status: binding
(iv) the time of source text creation: valid
(v) branch of law to which the text refers: civil law
(vi) text genre: a regulation
(vii) the language of the source text: English
(viii) source-text legal reality: civil law system
(ix) source text language variety: European Union (legal) English
(x) the object of encumbrance: immovable property

The potential Polish equivalents for *mortgage* (if taking into consideration the meaning of the British-law oriented term) are *zastaw* in case of encumbrances on movable property and *hipoteka* encumbering immovable property. In the context of the Regulation, however, it is *hipoteka*, which also finds confirmation in the French (*hypothèque*) and German (*Hypothek*) language versions of the Regulation. The translator, however, has failed to identify the essential features of the term and supplied a dictionary equivalent: *zastaw hipoteczny*[43]. This

43 Later on there were some attempts made to enact the bill on *zastaw hipoteczny* which was supposed to be a new legal institution in Poland, but they failed.

term does not exist in the Polish legal language and did not exist at the time of rendering the translation, and thus it is a neologism which in fact was coined for the purpose of translating the term *mortgage* used in the English common law system under which *mortgage* may encumber both movable and immovable property. The European Union, however, has limited the semantic field of the term to immovable property, using the term *lien* in reference to encumbrances burdening movable property.

Another translation problem is posed by homonymy and polysemy of words, which has already been discussed in chapter 4. Three such polysemous terms which are used in the Regulation were erroneously translated into Polish that is to say: *assets*, *estate* and *claim*. Let us analyse the properties assumed by them in the Regulation.
The properties of the term *assets* are as follows:
(i) the author of the source-text: legislator
(ii) source-text delivery form: written
(iii) source-text status: binding
(iv) the time of source text creation: valid
(v) branch of law to which the text refers: insolvency law
(vi) text genre: a regulation
(vii) the language of the source text: English
(viii) source-text legal reality: civil law system
(ix) source text language variety: European Union (legal) English
(x) the type of property: part of the estate of the insolvent debtor

The properties of the term *estate* are as follows:
(i) the author of the source-text: legislator
(ii) source-text delivery form: written
(iii) source-text status: binding
(iv) the time of source text creation: valid
(v) branch of law to which the text refers: insolvency law
(vi) text genre: a regulation
(vii) the language of the source text: English
(viii) source-text legal reality: civil law system
(ix) source text language variety: European Union (legal) English
(x) the type of property: entire property of the insolvent debtor

The properties of the term *claim* are as follows:

(i) the author of the source-text: legislator
(ii) source-text delivery form: written
(iii) source-text status: binding
(iv) the time of source text creation: valid
(v) branch of law to which the text refers: insolvency law
(vi) text genre: a regulation
(vii) the language of the source text: English
(viii) source-text legal reality: civil law system
(ix) source text language variety: European Union (legal) English
(x) the type of a right: a demand of a creditor for the payment of a debt owed to him by the insolvent debtor

All three terms assume the same nine properties. But the fifth and last one (which is the essential characteristics) narrow down the semantic field of the terms to insolvency law. In spite of that the term *assets* was translated into Polish as: *aktywa* even though this term assumes the property 'the language of accounting' as far as the dimension of the lect is concerned and the property 'financial law' from the dimension of the branch of law to which the translandive unit refers to. The term which would be sufficiently equivalent in Polish would be *składniki majątku* or *majątek.*

The term *estate*, in turn, was mistaken with the term *real estate*, and translated as *nieruchomość*, despite the fact that in the context of insolvency it is *the (insolvent) debtor's estate* and thus it should be translated as *masa upadłości*. Additionally, the translators should bear in mind that in the case of plurilingual legislation, consulting other language versions may help solve some terminological problems. In that particular case consulting the French or German regulation versions would have helped to avoid this error.

In the Regulation the English term *the claim* was translated into Polish in the following way: *roszczenie* instead of *wierzytelność*. As far as the branch of law is concerned the Polish term *roszczenie* takes on the property 'civil law'. In fact, *wierzytelność* is a type of *roszczenie* (cf. inclusion in Šarčević 2000b: 238-239), which means that the translator unnecessarily supplied the term with a broader meaning (a hypernym). Again the conclusion is that the translator did not know the language of insolvency and failed to supply a proper connotative significator.

Not only have the existing and sufficiently equivalent connotative equivalents not been used for those terms but also the meaning has been changed in all three cases.

6.4. Concluding remarks

The process of establishing sufficient equivalents in practice takes place in the mind of the translator and it is often subconscious. The more aware the translator is of the differences between legal systems, the better his chances are for finding sufficient equivalents.

In order to decide whether the terms are sufficiently equivalent for the purpose of a given translative situation, the translator needs to take into consideration the needs of recipients of the translative text and the degree of similarities and differences between the translandive term and its potential functional equivalent. Such decisions on whether the terms are sufficiently convergent or permissibly translationally complementary for the recipient communicative community are made on the basis of the contextual information revealed in the translandive text and the information provided by the commissioner.

7. Translational Algorithm

Having received the commission from the commissioner and having accepted it, one starts the process of translation.

Translation is the process of calculating the meaning of the source text units and choosing significators for the target text which must be sufficiently equivalent to translandive ones. The aim of translation of texts formulated in a language for special purposes is to communicate the message formulated in the source text to a given group of recipients communicating and understanding target language messages. "In other words a reliable translation is one that expresses the intended meaning and leads to the intended results" (Šarčević 2000b: 88).

In order to achieve this purpose the translator translates the message formulated in the source language into the target language. The aim is realized using different strategies. The strategies consist of different types of steps; alternatively, translation is a series of steps consistent with the adopted translation strategy, which achieves a certain aim.

Choosing significators for the target text is the transfer/conversion of the assumed/calculated meaning of the source text translative units into target text translative units taking place at three levels:

(i) terminological level,
(ii) syntagmal level, and
(iii) grammatical level.

The terminological level refers to the choice of terms. The syntagmal level refers to the choice of (i) word collocations or word combinations (in Polish also in some theories called phraseological units), and (ii) formulaic expressions (fixed syntagmas). The grammatical level refers to the choice of the grammatical structures.

In theory the meaning of the source text is objective; however, in practice the meaning may be ambiguous due to the human factor (the author). Therefore the calculation of the source text meaning usually ends with the assumed meaning resulting from the source text interpretation. The assumed meaning may be correct or incorrect (see fig. 6).

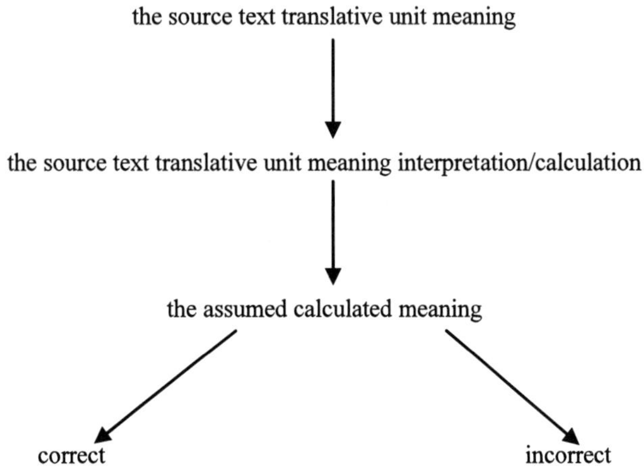

Figure 6. The calculation of the source text meaning

In the case of correctly calculated translative unit meaning, the translator has a chance to find a proper significator in the target text. However, the incorrect meaning results in translative errors. Consequently, the calculation of the source text translative unit meaning is pivotal for the successful calculation of the proper/optimal significator for the target text.

Now the algorithm of translation may be presented starting from the source text meaning calculation and ending with the choice of an optimal significator.

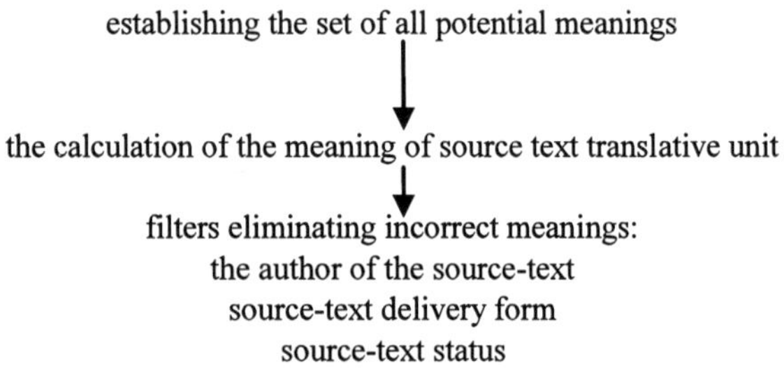

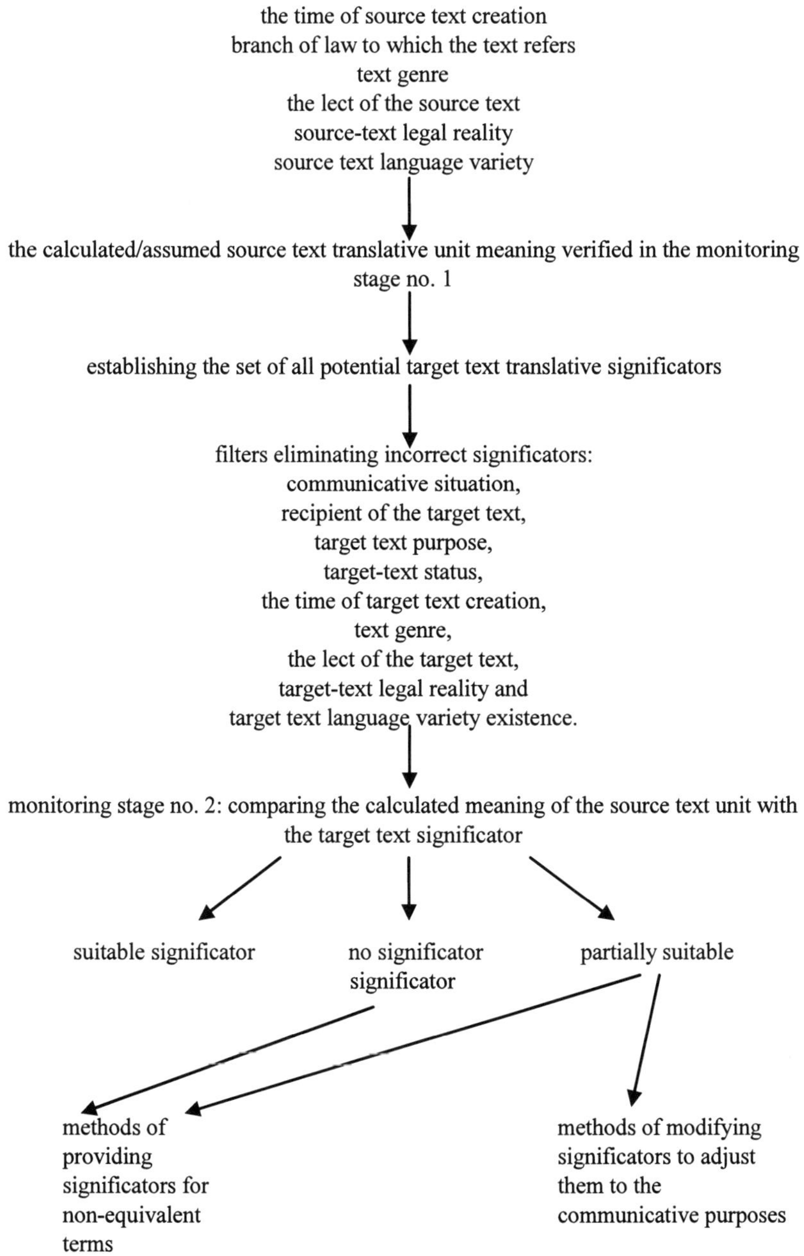

Figure 7. Translation algorithm

Due to the fact that steps 1-3 have already been described, no more examples are given here to illustrate the procedure of the calculation of the source text translative unit meaning. The procedure will be only briefly described in order to make the description of the algorithm complete.

Step 1. Establishing the set of all potential meanings
Each translative unit has a set of its total potential meanings. The moment the set is complete, the translator may start the procedure of eliminating the meanings, which are inappropriate in a given communicative situation.

Step 2. The calculation of the meaning of source text translative unit
The calculation of the meaning of the source text translative unit is performed by the application of filters eliminating incorrect meanings. The dimensions defined in chapter 3 serve the purpose of such filters. In the case of the source text the following dimensions (filters) have been distinguished:

(i) the author of the source-text
(ii) source-text delivery form
(iii) source-text status
(iv) the time of source text creation
(v) branch of law to which the text refers
(vi) text genre
(vii) the lect of the source text
(viii) source-text legal reality
(ix) source text language variety

It should be borne in mind that there are more dimensions that may or even must be used to arrive at a sufficient number of essential and accidental characteristics to determine whether the distance between the translandive unit and a translative one is not too great and the relation of sufficient equivalence holds.

The dimensions may serve the purpose of eliminating inappropriate meanings or choosing potentially appropriate ones.

The dimension of the *author of the source text* helps eliminate the meanings which are inappropriate due to the competences of the author. This dimension also directly affects the dimensions of the text status and language used. It helps furthermore to predict the communicative intention of the author and reduce the potential meanings to those which comply with the source-text communicative purpose.

The *source text delivery form* eliminates the meanings which are typical respectively of oral or written texts only, leaving the forms that may be used in both oral and written texts and those which are typical only of the form in question.

Source text status and *time of creation* help to eliminate meanings which are inappropriate due to the lapse of time (e.g. archaisms) or in other words choose the meaning which is typical of, e.g., the time of source-text creation.

The dimension of the *branch of law* to which the text belongs facilitates the elimination of inappropriate meanings due to the existence of, e.g., legal polysemy within one language.

The dimension of the *text genre* assists the elimination of inappropriate potential meanings which result from, e.g., legal or linguistic polysemy.

The *lect of the source text* eases elimination of inappropriate potential meanings which result from, e.g., linguistic polysemy. Insofar as the language of the source text is concerned it is necessary to follow the following steps:

(i) identify the language lect that is whether we deal with a translative unit formulated in a colloquial language, in legal language or other language for special purposes (LSP). Legal translation is especially challenging because legal texts are rarely formulated solely in a legal language. Usually the translator must deal with at least two LSPs, e.g. a petition filed by a dissatisfied patient suing a hospital will be formulated in legal language and the language of medicine,
(ii) if the language is colloquial one may identify the meaning on the basis of one's general knowledge or general dictionaries,
(iii) if the language is an LSP one must decide which type of LSP is to be dealt with and consult suitable sources to determine the meaning of a translative unit,
(iv) if the language is a quasi-LSP one must calculate/decipher the possible intended meaning.

(138) The set of potential significators for the term *powód* in respect to the dimension of lect
colloquial language: reason, cause
legal language: plaintiff, claimant

(139) The set of potential significators for the term bieg in respect to the dimension of lect
colloquial language: run, running, course
language of sport, run, running, race
language of construction: flight (of stairs)
language of automotive industry: gear
legal language: period, course of time

The dimension of *legal reality* helps eliminate the inappropriate potential meanings which result from the existence of different legal systems that attribute different features to similar concepts.

The *source text language variety* is useful to eliminate the inappropriate potential meanings which result from, e.g., linguistic and legal polysemy within different language varieties.

Step 3. Verification of the calculated meaning of the source text translative unit

As a result of the application of filters described in chapter 2 as dimensions and above, one should obtain the calculated/assumed source text translative unit having one meaning. This meaning should be verified in monitoring stage no. 1 (verification of the meaning in the context in which the translative unit is situated). This unit meaning, in turn, constitutes the basis for the next stage of the translation procedure.

Step 4. Establishing the set of all potential target text translative significators

Establishing the set of all potential target text translative significators on the basis of the calculated/assumed source text translative unit meaning is a very important procedure. In order to generate the set of all potential target text translative significators translators may use the following information sources:

(i) dictionaries (usually bilingual and monolingual),
(ii) encyclopaedias,

(iii) parallel texts,
(iv) course books and other printed materials on the subject matter.
(v) consultations with specialists in a given field,
(vi) consultations with more experienced translators
(vii) the ubiquitous Internet.

Clearly there are also other sources of information which may be used by translators. But the seven indicated above are the most popular and therefore, the author of the work will concentrate on them. The algorithm enables the choice of an optimal significator even if instead of the set of all potential significators for the calculated meaning of the source text translative unit, the translator establishes a set of all potential significators for all potential meanings of the source text translative unit.

Language potential determines the number of potential significators constituting the set. This potential is understood here as the level of terminology development in a given field in a given natural language.

(140) The set of possible significators for the term *zarządca*
- receiver
- administrator
- manager

(141) The set of possible significators for the term *dłużnik*
- debtor
- borrower
- obligor

(142) The set of possible significators for the term wierzyciel
- creditor
- obligee
- lender

(143) The set of possible significators for the term *plan naprawczy*
- rehabilitation plan
- reorganization plan
- reconstruction plan

Step 5. Choosing an optimal target text significator

To choose an optimal target text significator one may apply the following filters eliminating incorrect or less suitable/optimal significators:

(i) communicative situation,
(ii) recipient of the target text,
(iii) target text purpose,
(iv) target-text status,
(v) the time of target text creation,
(vi) text genre,
(vii) the lect of the target text,
(viii) target-text legal reality and
(ix) target text language variety existence

The order of the dimensions enumerated above is actually arbitrary. The problem is that in different communicative situations some of the dimensions would be more important than others. Sometimes it might be sufficient to apply only one dimension as a filter and sometimes all of them will need to be applied simultaneously to render a translation product optimal from the point of view of a given communicative community of recipients.

The dimension of the *communicative situation* principally affects the grammatical level of the translated text. If the translator receives a written text which is to be delivered orally during a conference, he should divide very long sentences into shorter ones in order to make the text understandable. If the sentence is so long and complex that it is necessary for the translator to read it more than once to understand its meaning, it would probably be impossible to understand for the audience listening to the person delivering the text orally. In such cases in order to achieve the communicative aim of translation it is necessary to adjust the text to the communicative situation in which it will function.

The dimension of the *recipient of the target text* determines the so-called translation orientation. But translation orientation is in fact a misleading concept as source-language oriented translation (SLOT) and target-language oriented translation (TLOT) actually rarely exist in their pure forms. In the majority of cases the orientation is a compromise between (i) the translator's knowledge, (ii) assumptions made by him and (iii) available information on the communicative community for which the text is translated. SLOT and TLOT are rarely applied to the whole text. They are usually applied to selected translative units on the terminological level. Moreover the SLOT is applied mostly in the case of translation of system-bound terms, that is, source text translative units, which do not have significators in the target language corresponding sufficiently adequately (the relation of sufficient equivalence does not hold between the translandive unit and any translative unit) to serve communicative purposes. As far as the grammatical level is concerned the SLOT may be extremely rarely applied (usually for the purposes of forensic linguistics). However, it is quite frequently applied by translation adepts and amateur translators, due to the fact that the comparison of parallel texts (which is understood here as the comparison of texts belonging to the same genre but formulated in two languages, namely: the source language and the target language) is very time-consuming. Moreover, access to some text genres is very limited. Currently one may observe a widespread tendency among translators to treat the Internet as the only source of information available on the planet Earth. If something does not exist on the Internet or cannot be obtained from it, it is treated as non-existent. Furthermore, in real-life translative situations translators often work under the pressure of time. If they do not have instant access to parallel texts they fail to consult such information sources and produce SLOT as far as terminological, syntagmal and grammatical levels are concerned. Therefore, although SLOT and TLOT are the myths of translation from the point of view of communicative communities and situations, they are still present in real life translations.

Additionally, the translation orientation is highly dependent on the lexical potential of the target language existing for a given field. If the lexical potential is very limited in a given field, the translators and target language users must resort to different procedures of providing significators for source-text units.

From the point of view of the recipient (that is a communicative community for which the target text is translated), one should adapt the message so that it might be understood by all members of the community, even if the community existence is not permanent but transitory.

The dimension of the *target text recipient* may in some cases directly affect the language variant and language lect, as well as procedures of providing significators for system-bound terms and modification of partial significators. The exemplification of the impact of the communicative community on the choice of significators has been presented in chapters 4-6.

Target text purpose/function determines the array of possible significators. If the function of the text is informative, than the array of significators will be probably wider than in the case of performative function.

Target-text status affects the importance of the translation quality. If the translation is to be considered an original or binding or prevailing language version then the consequences of any errors and mistakes might be much more serious than in other cases. Therefore, significators will have to be much more precise. The level of disparity between the source text translative unit meaning and the meaning of the target text significator must be none or very low.

Languages change constantly. This also applies to languages for special purposes. The *time of target text creation* helps eliminate target text significators, which are archaisms at the moment of translation. For instance when translating a document in which the source text translative unit *powód* is used in 1985, the translator would use the target text significator *plaintiff.* But if the translation were to be rendered in 2005, the translator would use the target text significator *plaintiff* if applying the American English language variety and *claimant* if applying the British English language variety. It is due to the fact that in April 1999 the term *plaintiff* under the *Civil Procedure Rules* has been replaced with the term *claimant* in Great Britain.

Text genre determines the choice of potential significators dependent on the branch of law and the type of document in which the source text translative unit may be found.

(144) The set of potential significators for the term *powód*
- plaintiff
- claimant
- petitioner

As far as the *lect of the target text* (*target text lect*) is concerned it is necessary to follow the following steps:

(i) identify the language lect, that is, whether it is necessary to translate the text into (i) colloquial language, (ii) legal language (legi-lect) or (iii) other language for special purposes (LSP).
(ii) if the language is colloquial one may identify the significators by referring to one's general knowledge or general dictionaries,
(iii) if the language is an LSP it must be decided which type of LSP is to be dealt with and consult suitable sources to choose an optimal significator for a given translative unit,
(iv) if the language is a quasi-LSP one must decide whether to choose a significator from the LSP or colloquial language.

(145) The set of potential significators for the term *adoption*
Colloquial language: *adopcja*
Legal language: *przysposobienie*

(146) The set of potential significators for the term *appeal*
- apelacja
- kasacja
- odwołanie

(147) The set of potential significators for the term *bankruptcy*
colloquial language: *bankructwo*
legal language: *upadłość*

Target-text legal reality importance has been noted by many scholars. Smith (1995: 187) claims that

> [...] finding equivalent and adequate terminology requires translators to recognize differences between the cultures of the legal texts with which they work. Legal culture represents the status and behaviour of a judicial class.

It means that the target text legal reality affects the way in which the target text communicative community perceives significators. Significators are by *analogiam* associated with such elements of the legal reality, which are known to the communicative community members. The wider the knowledge of the communicative community members is of the source language legal reality, the fewer associations with the target legal reality are made.

(148) The set of potential significators for the term *precedens*
- *precedent under common law*
- *precedent under civil law*

To conclude, Smith (1995: 194) optimistically states that:

> Translators can overcome the difficulties that different legal cultures pose by remaining cognizant of fundamental differences in legal systems. [...]. In fact, the clash of legal cultures need not end in a deadly crush. Translators can perform a successful translation if they consider carefully the context of a legal institution – its meaning, tradition, and cultural implications. They also must search diligently for equivalent, adequate terminology, one that clearly conveys a specific legal «style».

Target text language variety existence on the one hand makes the work of a translator more difficult as it usually produces a larger set of potential significators. On the other hand unless we deal with the international communicative community, it makes the choice of an optimal significator much easier as it helps to narrow down the choice to a specific sub-set of significators. Kubacki (2007: 131) accurately remarks that "Terminological diversity may result in applying different terms for one referent." For instance, let us analyse significators for the translative unit *komendant* having the following meaning: *szef/kierownik posterunku policji (commander/head of the police station)*. In the case of language varieties the set of all potential significators will be composed of subsets of potential significators typical of a given language variety, e.g.:

(149) The set of potential English significators for the term *komendant policji*
Australian English sub-set: Deputy Commissioner
Canadian English sub-set: Chief of Police, Commissioner, Chief Constable
British English sub-set: Commissioner
American English sub-set: Chief of Police
Other English variant-oriented significators

(150) The set of possible significators for the term: *upadłość*
- insolvency (EU English)
- insolvency and bankruptcy (British English)
- bankruptcy (American English)

(151) The set of possible significators for the term: *postępowanie upadłościowe*
- insolvency proceedings (EU English)
- insolvency or bankruptcy procedure (British English)
- proceedings in bankruptcy (American English), bankruptcy proceedings

(152) The set of possible significators for the term: *syndyk*
- bankruptcy trustee (American English),
- Official Receiver (British English),
- Liquidator (EU English),
- Trustee in Bankruptcy (used by TEPIS)

Step 6. Monitoring stage

The monitoring stage, which is the comparison of the calculated meaning of the source text unit with the target text significator, is necessary to decide whether the target text significator is optimal from the point of view of a given communicative community.

Step 7. Outcome of the monitoring stage

The result of the procedure may be the following:

(i) one suitable (optimal) significator,
(ii) more than one suitable significator,
(iii) partially suitable significator, and finally
(iv) no significator.

If (i) then the procedure of choosing a significator is completed.

If (ii) then the procedure of choosing a significator is not completed and requires application of the monitoring and control measures to choose the most optimal significator or a combination of significators.

If (iii) then the procedure of choosing a significator is not completed and requires the application of the procedure of modifying the translative unit so it meets the communicative needs of a given communicative community.

If (iv) then the procedure of choosing a significator is not completed and requires the application of one of the procedures of providing significators (equivalents) for the non-equivalent source text translative units in order to create/coin the target text significator, which meets the communicative needs of a given communicative community.

Step 8. Variants of final decision

Step 8a.

The monitoring measures allow for calculating the distance between the translandive unit and suitable equivalents to choose the optimal one (the one which is equivalent to a greater degree or in other words convergent with the translandive unit in the greater number of dimensions than other significators).

Step 8b.

The application of the procedures of modifying the translative unit so that it meets the communicative needs of a given communicative community

Step 8c.

The application of one of the procedures of providing significators (equivalents) for the non-equivalent source text translative units in order to create/coin the target text significator that meets the communicative needs of a given communicative community

To summarise, assumptions and generalizations are unavoidable because no language and no communicative community (composed of more than one person) is homogenous as far as the knowledge of its members and the will to communicate are concerned. Thus, in order to translate the text in an optimal manner one needs to base the choice on at least the following foundations:

(i) adjusting terminological and syntagmal units to the assumed expectations of the determined communicative community,
(ii) adjusting grammatical units to the patterns occurring in the target text of the same genre,
(iii) reflecting the intended function of the text,
(iv) choosing the appropriate macrostructure pattern,
(v) producing a target text having the desired legal effect,
(vi) communicating by avoiding ambiguity.

Although legal translation has never been an easy task, keeping to the procedure may, in our opinion, help increase the quality of target texts.

8. Conclusions

In the first part of the book the state-of-the-art in the field of translative equivalence and legal translation has been outlined. In the second part of the book I have proposed a theory of parametrized legal translation and in the third part shown how this theory may be applied in practice. The aim of the theory outlined is to propose laws (postulates) and dimensions (which are sets of properties of legal reality objects and legal translation relations) used to characterize legal texts and their component parts for the purpose of establishing proper (sufficient) translative equivalents for a selected legal communicative community.

As a result of the application of the communicative community oriented translation approach, based on the application of parameters to the translation process, a translation algorithm has been developed. Moreover, it has been ascertained that the dimensions described by the author help discipline the translator. As a consequence, the translator is more prone to make conscious choices justified by the communicative situation requirements in which the target text is to function. Due to the publication size it has been impossible to describe and examine all dimensions which may affect the process of translation. Therefore, only the most important ones have been inquired into in this work. This research is based on the theoretical foundations described in more detail in chapter 1. Although the impact of certain factors on the translation process and product has been described by many scholars, to my knowledge the factors have not been interpreted and grouped in terms of the corresponding dimensions presented in chapter 3.

This volume has aimed to present in fact a new paradigm of inquiry into theoretical and practical legal linguistic translatology. The theoretical and practical issues elaborated on in the book are illustrated with examples from various languages, tables and graphs. The examples are taken from source texts. As this is a new approach in legal translation studies, the time will show whether it will meet with readers' positive reception.

References

AIIC Standards <http://www.aiic.net/ViewPage.cfm/article122.htm>

Albrecht, Jörn 1973. *Linguistik und Übersetzung*. Tübingen: Romanistische Arbeitshefte 4.

Alcaraz Varó, Enrique / Hughes, Brian 2002. *Legal Translation Explained*. Manchester: S. Jerome Publishing.

Auburger, Leopold 1981. *Funktionale Sprachvarianten. Metalinguistische Untersuchungen zu einer allgemeinen Theorie*. Wiesbaden: Steiner.

Austermühl, Frank 2001. *Electronic Tools for Translators*. Manchester: St. Jerome Publishing.

Baker, Mona (ed.) 2007. *Routledge Encyclopedia of Translation Studies*. Shanghai: Shanghai Foreign Education Press.

Baker, Mona 1992. *In Other Words: A Coursebook on Translation*. London and New York: Routledge.

Bańczerowski, Jerzy / Grzelak, Szymon 2012. Translational quandaries and suggestions. *Folia Orientalia*, no. 49, 41-55.

Bańczerowski, Jerzy / Matulewska, Aleksandra (eds) 2009. *Comparative Legilinguistics*. Warszawa/Poznań: Sowa Druk, vol. 1/2009.

Bańczerowski, Jerzy / Matulewska, Aleksandra (eds) 2010a. *Comparative Legilinguistics*. Poznań: Zakład Graficzny AMU, vol. 2/2010.

Bańczerowski, Jerzy / Matulewska, Aleksandra (eds) 2010b. *Comparative Legilinguistics (Legilingwistyka Porównawcza)*. Poznań: Zakład Graficzny AMU, tom 3/2010.

Bańczerowski, Jerzy / Matulewska, Aleksandra (eds) 2010c. *Comparative Legilinguistics*. Poznań: Zakład Graficzny AMU, vol. 4/2010.

Bańczerowski, Jerzy / Matulewska, Aleksandra (eds) 2011. *Comparative Legilinguistics*. Poznań: Zakład Graficzny AMU, vol. 5/2010.

Bańczerowski, Jerzy / Matulewska, Aleksandra 2012. Towards the Foundations of Legilinguistic Translatology. In Grzegorczyk, Paweł / Knoppek, Krzysztof / Walasik, Marcin (eds) *Proces cywilny. Nauka – Kodyfikacja – Praktyka. Księga jubileuszowa dedykowana Profesorowi Feliksowi Zedlerowi*. Warszawa: Wolters Kluwer Polska, 1225-1261.

Bańczerowski, Jerzy 1996. A Formal Approach to a General Theory of Language. In Sackmann, Robin (ed.) *Theoretical Linguistics and Grammatical Description. Papers in honour of Hans-Heinrich Lieb. Current Issues in Linguistic Theory 138*. Amsterdam/Philadelphia: John Benjamins, 13-30.

Bańczerowski, Jerzy 2001. The Linguistic Legacy of Ludwik Zabrocki. In Stanisław Puppel (ed.) *The Ludwik Zabrocki Memorial Lecture*. Poznań: Adam Mickiewicz University, 9-49.

Bartels, Hans-Joachim 1982. *Methode und Gegenstand intersystemarer Rechtsvergleichung*. Tübingen: J.C.B. Mohr.

Bassnett, Susan / Lefevere, André 1998. *Constructing Cultures. Essays on Literary Translation*. Clevedon: Multilingual Matters Ltd.

Bassnett, Susan / Lefevere, André 2001. *Constructing Cultures. Essays on Literary Translation*. Shanghai: Shanghai Foreign Education Press.

Bassnett, Susan 1980. *Translation Studies* (First Edition). UK: Methuen & Co. Ltd.

Bassnett, Susan 2004. *Translation Studies* (Third Edition). Shanghai: Shanghai Foreign Education Press.

Bautro, Eugenjusz 1935. *Idea lingwistyki i semantyki prawniczej*. Lwów: Dom Książki Polskiej.

Bayard, Donn 1994. Social Constraints on the Phonology of New Zealand English. In Cheshire, Jenny (ed.) *English around the World. Sociolinguistic Perspectives*. Cambridge: Cambridge University Press, 169-186.

Benton, Richard A. 1994. Maor English: a New Zealand myth? In Cheshire, Jenny (ed.) *English around the World. Sociolinguistic Perspectives*. Cambridge: Cambridge University Press, 187-199.

Bhatia, Vijay K. / Candlin, Christopher N. / Evangelisti Allori, Paola (eds) 2008. *Language, Culture and the Law. Linguistics Insights*, vol. 64. Bern: Peter Lang.

Bhatia, Vijay K. / Candlin, Christopher N. / Gotti, Maurizio (eds) 2003. *Legal Discourse in Multilingual and Multicultural Contexts. Linguistics Insights*, vol. 6. Bern: Peter Lang.

Bhatia, Vijay K. / Candlin, Christopher N. / Gotti, Maurizio (eds) 2010. *The Discourses of Dispute Resolution. Linguistics Insights*, vol. 123. Bern: Peter Lang.

Bhatia, Vijay K. / Engberg, Jan / Gotti, Maurizio / Heller, Dorothee (eds) 2005. *Vagueness in Normative Texts. Linguistics Insights,* vol. 23. Bern: Peter Lang.

Biel, Łucja 2007. Współpraca unijna w sprawach karnych. Podstawowe terminy w praktyce translacyjnej. *Lingua legis*, vol. 15, 3-9.

Blomqvist, L. 2006. One Little Word... In Wagner, Anne / Cacciaguidi-Fahy, Sophie (eds) *Legal Language and the Search for Clarity: Practice and Tools*. Bern: Peter Lang, 303-27.

Bochner, Stephan 1981. *The Mediating Person: Bridges between Cultures*. Cambridge: Schenkman.

Bogusławski, Andrzej 1986. O pojęciu wyjaśniania i wyjaśnianiu w lingwistyce. *Biuletyn Polskiego Towarzystwa Językoznawczego*. XL, 45-51.

Borkowski, Tomasz 2011. *Polsko-angielski słownik terminów prawnych Polterm z definicjami*. Warszawa: Wydawnictwo Translegis.

Bradley, David 1994. '/æ/ and /a:/ in Australian English.' In Cheshire, Jenny (ed.) *English around the World. Sociolinguistic Perspectives*. Cambridge: Cambridge University Press, 227-234.

Broeck, Raymond van den 1980. Towards a Text-Type-Oriented Theory of Translation. In Poulsen, Sven-Olaf / Wilss, Wolfram (eds) *Angewandte Übersetzungswissenschaft. Internationales übersetzungswissenschaftliches Kolloquium an der Wirtschaftsuniversität Aarhus/Dänemark, 19-21 Juni 1980*. Aarhus, 82-96.

Bruni, Leonardo 1987. On the Correct Way to Translate. In Griffiths, Gordon / Hankins, James / Thompson, David (trans. and eds) *The Humanism of Leonardo Bruni: Selected Texts*. Binghamton, NY: Center for Medieval and Early Renaissance Studies, 216-229.

Bruni, Leonardo 1992. The Right Way to Translate. In Lefevere, André (ed.) *Translation/History/Culture. A Sourcebook*. London/New York: Routledge, 81-86.

Bryant, Margaret 1962. *English in the Law Courts: The Part that Articles, Prepositions, and Conjunctions Play in Legal Decisions*. New York: Frederick Ungar.

Bühler, Karl 1928. The Origin of Language. *Psychological Bulletin 25*: 169-70.

Bühler, Karl 1934. *Sprachtheorie. Die Darstellungsfunktion der Sprache*. Jena: Gustav Fischer.

Bühler, Karl 1965. *Sprachtheorie*. Stuttgart: G. Fischer.

Bukowski, Piotr / Heydel, Magdalena 2009. *Współczesne teorie przekładu. Antologia.* Kraków: Wydawnictwo Znak.

Cao, Deborah 2007. *Translating Law*. Clevedon: Multilingual Matters Ltd.

Cao, Deborah 2008. *Translating Law*. Shanghai: Shanghai Foreign Education Press.

Casagrande, Joseph B. 1954. The Ends of Translation. *International Journal of American Linguistics 20*, 335-340.

Catford, John 1965. *A Linguistic Theory of Translation. An Essay in Applied Linguistics*. London: Oxford University Press.

Cheshire, Jenny (ed.) 1994. *English around the World. Sociolinguistic Perspectives*. Cambridge: Cambridge University Press.

Cheshire, Jenny 1994. Introduction: Sociolinguistics and English around the World. In Cheshire, Jenny (ed.) *English around the World. Sociolinguistic Perspectives*. Cambridge: Cambridge University Press, 1-11.

Cheshire, Jenny 1994. The UK and the USA. In Cheshire, Jenny (ed.) *English around the World. Sociolinguistic Perspectives*. Cambridge: Cambridge University Press, 13-36.

Chesterman, Andrew / Wagner, Emma 2002. *Can Theory Help Translators? A Dialogue Between the Ivory Tower and the Wordface*. Manchester: St. Jerome Publishing.

Chesterman, Andrew 1997. *Mems of Translation. The Spread of Ideas in Translation Theory*. Amsterdam and Philadelphia: John Benjamins.

Chick, J. Keith 1994. Sources of Consequences of Miscommunication in Africaans English – South African English Encounters. In Cheshire, Jenny (ed.) *English around the World. Sociolinguistic Perspectives*. Cambridge: Cambridge University Press, 446-461.

Chishimba, Maurice M. 1994. Southern Africa. In Cheshire, Jenny (ed.) *English around the World. Sociolinguistic Perspectives*. Cambridge: Cambridge University Press, 435-445.

Choduń, Agnieszka 2006a. Leksyka tekstów aktów prawnych. *Ruch Prawniczy, Ekonomiczny i Socjologiczny*, 4/2006, 19-30.

Choduń, Agnieszka 2006b. Norma językowa a dyrektywy redagowania tekstów aktów prawnych. In Czepita Stanisław (ed.) *Konwencjonalne i formalne aspekty prawa*. Szczecin: Wydawnictwo Naukowe Uniwersytetu Szczecińskiego, 47-53.

Choduń, Agnieszka 2007. *Słownictwo tekstów aktów prawnych w zasobie leksykalnym współczesnej polszczyzny*. Warszawa: Wydawnictwo TRIO.

Clarke, Sandra 1994. Phonological Variation and Recent Language Change in St John's English. In Cheshire, Jenny (ed.) *English around the World. Sociolinguistic Perspectives*. Cambridge: Cambridge University Press, 108-122.

Copeland, Rita 1995. *Rhetoric, Hermeneutics and Translation in the Middle Ages*. Cambridge: Cambridge University Press.

Cornu, Gérard 1990. *Linguistique juridique*. Paris: Montchrestien.

Crystal, David 1985. How Many Millions? The Statistics of English Today. *English Today*, 1, 7-11.

Cuyckens, Hubert / Zawada, Britta (eds) 2001. *Polysemy in Cognitive Linguistics: Selected Papers from the International Cognitive Linguistics Conference*. Amsterdam: John Benjamin's Publishing Company.

David, René / Brierley, John 1985. *Major Legal Systems in the World Today*. London: Stevens.

Davis, Kathleen 2001. *Deconstruction and Translation*. Manchester: St. Jerome Publishing.

Davis, Kathleen 2004. *Deconstruction and Translation*. Shanghai: Shanghai Foreign Education Press.

De Groot, Gérard-Réne 1988. Problems of Legal Translation From the Point of View of a Comparative Lawyer. In *XIth World Congress of FIT Proceedings: Translation – OurFuture*. Maastricht: Euroterm, 407–421.

De Groot, Gérard-Réne 1991. Recht, Rechtsprache und Rechtsystem. *Terminologie et Traduction*, 3, 279-316.

Delisle Jean (et al., ed.) 1999. *Translation Terminology*. Amsterdam/Philadephia: John Benjamins.

Dollerup, Cay 2006. *Basics of Translation Studies*. (First Edition: Romania). Iasi: Institutul European.

Dollerup, Cay 2006/2007. *Basics of Translation Studies*. Shanghai: Shanghai Foreign Education Press.

Dzierżanowska, Halina 1990. *Przekład tekstów nieliterackich*. Warszawa: Państwowe Wydawnictwo Naukowe PWN.

Esling, John H. 1994. Sociophonetic Variation in Vancouver. In Cheshire, Jenny (ed.) *English around the World. Sociolinguistic Perspectives*. Cambridge: Cambridge University Press, 123-133.

Fedorov, Andrei V. 1953. *Vvedenie v teoriu perevoda* [*Introduction to the Theory of Translation*]. Moscow: Vysshaya shkola.

Fisiak, Jacek 1961a. *An Early Middle English Reader*. Łódź: Uniwersytet Łódzki.

Galdia, Marcus 2009. *Legal Linguistics*. Frankfurt am Main: Peter Lang.

Garner Bryan A. 1995. *A Dictionary of Modern Legal Usage*. Oxford: Oxford University Press.

Garner, Brian (ed.) 2004. *Black's Law Dictionary*. Eighth Edition. United States of America: Thomson West.

Garner, Bryan A. 2002. *The Elements of Legal Style*. Oxford/New York: Oxford University Press.

Gémar, Jean-Claude 1987. La Traduction Juridique: Art ou Technique d'Interprétation? *Revue générale de droit*, 18, 495-514.
Gémar, Jean-Claude 1995. *Traduire ou l'art d'interpréter*, vol. I & II. SaintNicolas: Presses de l'Université du Québec.
Gémar, Jean-Claude 2006. What Legal Translation is and is not – Within or Outside the EU. In Pozzo, B. / Jacometti, V. (eds) *Multilingualism and the Harmonisation of European Law*. Kluwer Law International, 69-77.
Giannoni, Davide Simone / Frade, Celina (eds) 2010. *Researching Language and the Law. Linguistics Insights*, vol. 121. Bern: Peter Lang.
Gizbert-Studnicki, Tomasz 1972. Język prawny a język prawniczy. *Zeszyty Naukowe UJ, Prace Prawnicze*, issue 55. Kraków, 219-233.
Gizbert-Studnicki, Tomasz 1978. Język prawny a język etniczny. *Wieloznaczność leksykalna w interpretacji prawniczej*. Kraków, 156-159.
Gizbert-Studnicki, Tomasz 1979. Czy istnieje język prawny? *Państwo i Prawo*, issue 3, 49-60.
Gizbert-Studnicki, Tomasz 1986. Język prawny z perspektywy socjolingwistycznej. *Zeszyty Naukowe UJ, Prace z Nauk Politycznych*, issue 26. Kraków, 1-139.
Goddard, Christopher 2009. Where Legal Cultures Meet: Translating Confrontation into Coexistence. *Investigationes Linguisticae* XVII, 168-205.
Gonzalez, Andrew B. 1994. Stylistic Shifts in English of the Philippine Print Media. In Cheshire, Jenny (ed.) *English around the World. Sociolinguistic Perspectives*. Cambridge: Cambridge University Press, 333-363.
Gortych, Karolina 2009. Translacyjne problemy wyrażania modalności deontycznej w tekstach aktów normatywnych w języku polskim, angielskim i greckim. In Mróz, Anna / Niewiadomski, Adam / Pawelec, Monika (eds) *Prawo i Język*, Warszawa: Zakład graficzny Uniwersytetu Warszawskiego.
Gotti, Maurizio / Williams, Christopher (eds) 2010. *Legal Discourse Across Languages and Cultures. Linguistics Insights*, vol. 117. Bern: Peter Lang.
Goźdź-Roszkowski, Stanisław 1999. The Language of Law as Sublanguage. In Tomaszczyk, Jerzy (ed.) *Aspects of Legal Language and Legal Translation*. Łódź: Wydawnictwo Uniwersytetu Łódzkiego, 7-16.
Groffier, Ethel / Reed, David 1990. *La lexicographie juridique*. Cowansville (Québec): Yvon Blais.
Grucza Franciszek 1998. Wyodrębnienie się, stan aktualny i perspektywy świata translacji oraz translatoryki. *Lingua legis*, no. 6, 2-12.
Grucza, Franciszek 1981. Zagadnienia translatoryki. In Grucza, Franciszek (ed.) *Glottodydaktyka a translatoryka*. Warszawa: Wydawnictwa Uniwersytetu Warszawskiego, 9-29.
Grucza, Franciszek 1985. Lingwistyka, lingwistyka stosowana, glottodydaktyka, translatoryka. In Grucza, Franciszek (ed.) *Lingwistyka, glottodydaktyka, translatoryka*. Warszawa: Wydawnictwa Uniwersytetu Warszawskiego, 19-44.
Grucza, Franciszek 1986a. *Problemy translatoryki i dydaktyki translatorycznej*. Warszawa: Wydawnictwa Uniwersytetu Warszawskiego.

Grucza, Franciszek 1986b. Tłumaczenie, teoria tłumaczeń, translatoryka. In Grucza, Franciszek (ed.) *Problemy translatoryki i dydaktyki translatorycznej*. Warszawa: Wydawnictwa Uniwersytetu Warszawskiego, 9-27.

Grucza, Franciszek 1994. O językach specjalistycznych (= technolektach) jako pewnych składnikach rzeczywistych języków ludzkich. In Grucza, Franciszek / Kozłowska, Zofia (eds.) *Języki specjalistyczne*. Warszawa, 7-27.

Grucza, Franciszek 1996. Wyodrębnienie się, stan aktualny i perspektywy świata translacji oraz translatoryki. In Snopek, Jerzy (ed.) *Tłumaczenie-rzemiosło i sztuka*. Warszawa: Węgierski Instytut Kultury, 10-45.

Grucza, Franciszek 1999. Translacja a kreatywność. *Lingua Legis*, no. 7, 2-4.

Grucza, Franciszek 2007. *Lingwistyka stosowana. Historia – Zagadnienia – Osiągnięcia*. Warszawa: Euro Edukacja.

Grucza, Sambor 2004/2007. *Od lingwistyki tekstu do lingwistyki tekstu specjalistycznego*. Warszawa: Wydawnictwo Euro-Edukacja.

Grucza, Sambor 2007. Zwischen Fachtext und Nicht-Fachtext: ihre Grenzbereiche. In Grucza, Franciszek / Olpińska, Magdalena / Schwenk, Hans-Jörg (eds.) *Germanistische Wahrnehmungen der Multimedialität, Multilingualität und Multikulturalität. Materialien der Jahrestagung des Verbandes Polnischer Germanisten (Opole, 11.-13. Mai 2007)*. Warszawa: Wydawnictwo Euro-Edukacja, 151-160.

Grucza, Sambor 2008. *Lingwistyka języków specjalistycznych*. Warszawa: Wydawnictwo Euro-Edukacja.

Grzybek, Joanna 2009 a. Polysemy, homonymy and other sources of ambiguity in the language of Chinese contracts. *Comparative Legilinguistics: International Journal for Legal Communication*, vol. 1/2009. Warszawa: Wydawnictwo Sowa, 207-215.

Grzybek, Joanna 2009 b. Understanding Chinese and Polish terminology of securities. *Investigationes Linguisticae*, Vol. XVII, 152-167.

Grzybek, Joanna 2010. Lexical features of Chinese lingua legis, In Jacoby, M. (ed.) *China past and present. New Polish papers in Chinese studies*. Warszawa: Warsaw University Press, 103-114.

Gubby, Helen 2004. *English Legal Terminology*. The Hague: Boom Juridische Uitgevers.

Gutt, Ernst-August 1991. *Translation and Relevance: Cognition and Context*. Oxford, Basil Blackwell.

Gutt, Ernst-August 2000. *Translation and Relevance. Cognition and Context*. Manchester: St. Jerome Publishing.

Gutt, Ernst-August 2004a. *Dystans kulturowy a przekład*. Kraków: Universitas.

Gutt, Ernst-August 2004b. *Translation and Relevance. Cognition and Context*. Shanghai: Shanghai Foreign Education Press.

Hatim, Basil / Mason, Ian 1990. *Discourse and the Translator*. Harlow, Essex: Longman.

Hatim, Basil / Mason, Ian 2001. *Discourse and the Translator*. Shanghai: Shanghai Foreign Education Press.

Hatim, Basil / Munday, Jeremy 2004. *Translation. An Advanced Resource Book*. Abingdon: Routledge.

Hatim, Basil / Munday, Jeremy 2010. *Translation. An Advanced Resource Book*. Shanghai: Shanghai Foreign Education Press.

Hatim, Basil 1997. *Communication across Cultures. Translation Theory and Contrastive Text Linguistics*. Exeter: University of Exeter Press.

Hatim, Basil 2001a. *Communication across Cultures. Translation Theory and Contrastive Text Linguistics*. Shanghai: Shanghai Foreign Education Press.

Hatim, Basil 2001b. *Teaching and Researching Translation*. Harlow: Longman Pearson Education.

Haugen, E. 1950. The Analysis of Linguistic Borrowing. *Language* no. 26, 210-231.

Hegenbarth, Rainer 1982. *Juristische Hermeneutik und linguistische Pragmatik*. Königstein/Ts.: Athenäum.

Hejwowski, Krzysztof 2004. *Kognitywno-komunikacyjna teoria przekładu*. Warszawa: Państwowe Wydawnictwo Naukowe.

Hermans, Theo (ed.) 2002. *Translation in Systems. Descriptive and System-oriented Approaches Explained*. Manchester: St. Jerome Publishing.

Hermans, Theo 2004. *Translation in Systems. Descriptive and System-oriented Approaches Explained*. Shanghai: Shanghai Foreign Education Press.

Hewson, Lance / Jacky Martin 1991. *Redefining Translation: The Variational Approach*. London: Routledge.

Hexner, Ervin 1941. *Studies in Legal Terminology*. Chapel Hill: The University of North Carolina Press.

Hickey, Leo (ed.) 1998. *The Pragmatics of Translation*. Clevedon: Multilingual Matters Ltd.

Hickey, Leo (ed.) 2001. *The Pragmatics of Translation*. Shanghai: Shanghai Foreign Education Press.

Hönig, Hans G. 1991. Holmes 'Mapping Theory' and the Landscape of Mental Translation Process. In Kitty, M. (ed.) *Proceedings from the First James S. Holmes Symposium on Translation Studies*. Amsterdam: Rodopi, 77-89.

Hönig, Hans G. / Kussmaul, Paul 1982. *Strategie der Übersetzung. Ein Lehr- und Arbeitsbuch*. Tübingen: Narr.

Houbert, Frederic 2010. Caught in the web of the law le traducteur juridique face à la métaphore. *Comparative Legilinguistics* vol. 2/2010, 167-182.

House, Juliane 1977. *A Model for Translation Quality Assessment*. Tübingen: Gunter Narr Verlag.

House, Juliane 1998. Politeness in Translation. In Hickey, Leo (ed.) *The Pragmatics of Translation*. Clevedon: Multilingual Matters Ltd.

Huet, Pierre-Daniel (Petrus Danielus Huetius) 1683/1992 (reprinted and translated) De optimo genere interpretandi. In Lefevere, André (ed.) *Translation/History/ Culture. A Sourcebook*. London/New York: Routledge, 86-102.

Jadacka, Hanna 2002. *Poradnik językowy dla prawników*. Warszawa: Wydawnictwo Naukowe Semper.

Jäger, Gert 1965. Invariante und Entsprechungstypen bei der Translation. *Fremdsprachen 3*, 1965, 241-249.

Jäger, Gert 1973. Invarianz und Transferierbarkeit. In Neubert, Albrecht / Kade Otto (eds) *Neue Beiträge zu Fragen der Übersetzungswissenschaft*. Leipzig/Frankfurt/M, 47-59.

Jäger, Gert 1975. *Translation und Translationslinguistik*. Linguistische Studien. Halle: VEB Niemeyer.

Jakobson, Roman (1959) 2009. O językoznawczych aspektach przekładu. In Bukowski, Piotr / Heydel, Magdalena (eds) *Współczesne teorie przekładu. Antologia*. Kraków: Wydawnictwo Znak, 43-49.

Jakobson, Roman 1959/1966. On Linguistic Aspects of Translation. In Brower, Reuben A. (ed.) *On Translation*. New York: Oxford University Press, 232-239.

Jopek-Bosiacka, Anna 2006. *Przekład prawny i sądowy*. Warszawa: PWN.

Jopek-Bosiacka, Anna 2010. *Legal Communication: A Cross-Cultural Perspective*. Warsaw: Warsaw University Press.

Jori, Mario 1994. Legal Performative. In Asher, R. E. / Simpson, J. M. Y. (eds) *The Encyclopedia of Language and Linguistics,* vol. 4. Oxford: Pergamon Press, 2092-2097.

Joseph, John E. 1995. Indeterminacy, Translation and the Law. In Morris, M. (ed.) *Translation and the Law*. Amsterdam/Philadelphia: John Benjamins, 15-35

Jumpelt, Rudolf Walter 1961. Die Übersetzung naturwissenchaftlicher und technischer Literatur [Translating natural science and technical texts]. Berlin: Langenscheidt. In The epilogue: *On the objectivability of translation*, 184-187, translated into English in Chesterman, Andrew (ed.) 1989. *Readings on Translation Theory*. Helsinki: Oy Finn Lectura, 33-36.

Kaczmarek, Karolina / Matulewska, Aleksandra 2008. Wykładnia normy prawnej a metodologia przekładu. *Rocznik Przekładoznawczy* 3/4, 2007/2008, 79-92.

Kaczmarek, Karolina 2009. A "tilalmat" és "engedélyt" kifejező eszközök jogi szakszövegben a deontikus modalitás tükrében. In Bárdosi, Vilmos (ed.) *Quo vadis philologia temporum nostrorum?* Korunk civilizációjának nyelvi képe. Budapest: Tinta Könyvkiadó.

Kaczmarek, Karolina 2010. Az utasítás kifejezőeszközei a jogi szakszövegben a deontikus modalitás tükrében. In *Filológia.hu*. A Magyar Tudományos Akadémia Modern Filológiai Társaságának online folyóirata.

Kaczmarek, Karolina 2011. A jogi és a nyelvi normáról a magyar és a lengyel nyelvben. *Languages and Cultures in Research and Education*. Kraków: Uniwersytet Jagielloński, 111-120.

Kade, Otto 1968. *Zufall und Gesetzmäßigkeit in der Übersetzung*. Beihefte zur Zeitschrift Fremdsprachen I. Leipzig: VEB Verlag Enzyklopädie.

Kandiah, Thiru 1994. South Asia. In Cheshire, Jenny (ed.) *English around the World. Sociolinguistic Perspectives*. Cambridge: Cambridge University Press, 271-287.

Katan, David 1999. *Translating Cultures. An Introduction for Translators, Interpreters and Mediators*. Manchester: St. Jerome Publishing.

Katan, David 2004. *Translating Cultures. An Introduction for Translators, Interpreters and Mediators*. Shanghai: Shanghai Foreign Education Press.

Keay, Andrew / Walton, Peter 2003. *Insolvency Law: Corporate and Personal*. London: Pearson Education Limited.

Kelsen, Hans 1979. *Allgemeine Theorie der Normen*. In Ringhofer, K. / Walter, R. (eds). Wien: Manz.
Kennedy, Chris / Bolitho, Rod 1991. *English for Specific Purposes*. London and Basingstoke: Macmillan Press LTD.
Kerby, Jean 1979. Problèmes particuliers à la traduction juridique au Canada. *La Revue de l'Université de Moncton*, 12, 2-3, 14-18.
Khan, Farhat 1994. Final Consonant Cluster Simplification in a Variety of Indian Emglish. In Cheshire, Jenny (ed.) *English around the World. Sociolinguistic Perspectives*. Cambridge: Cambridge University Press, 288-298.
Kielar, Barbara Zofia / Lewandowska, Ewa 1999. Towards Better Communication: Cultural and Terminological Aspects of Polish Translations of English Texts Relating to Copyright Law. In Tomaszczyk, Jerzy (ed.) *Aspects of Legal Language and Legal Translation*. Łódź: Wydawnictwo Uniwersytetu Łódzkiego, 171-182.
Kielar, Barbara Zofia / Miler, Joanna 1993. Through the Looking Glass of Translation – the Verb Phrases of the Statutory Clauses in Kodeks Handlowy and Their English Renditions. In Miler, Joanna (ed.) *International Forum of Legal Translation 1992. Proceedings*. Warsaw: Wydawnictwo TEPIS, 41-53.
Kielar, Barbara Zofia 1973. *Angielskie ekwiwalenty polskich terminów prawnoustrojowych*. Warszawa: Państwowe Wydawnictwo Naukowe.
Kielar, Barbara Zofia 1977. *Language of the Law in the Aspect of Translation*. Warszawa: Wydawnictwo Uniwersytetu Warszawskiego.
Kielar, Barbara Zofia 1979. Styl a język prawny. *Państwo i Prawo*, z. 3, 134-135.
Kielar, Barbara Zofia 1988. *Tłumaczenie i koncepcje translatoryczne*. Wrocław: Zakład Narodowy imienia Ossolińskich Wydawnictwo Polskiej Akademii Nauk.
Kielar, Barbara Zofia 1996. Na manowcach tłumaczenia tekstu prawnego: prawdopodobieństwo wywołania szoku kulturowego. In Grucza, Franciszek / Chomicz-Jung, Krystyna (eds) *Problemy komunikacji interkulturowej. Jedna Europa – wiele języków i wiele kultur*. Warszawa: Wydawnictwo Uniwersytetu Warszawskiego, 135-141.
Kielar, Barbara Zofia 1999. Translating Statutory Texts: in Search of Meaning and Relevance. In Tomaszczyk, Jerzy (ed.) *Aspects of Legal Language and Legal Translation*. Łódź: Wydawnictwo Uniwersytetu Łódzkiego, 183-190.
Kielar, Barbara Zofia 2003. *Zarys translatoryki*. Warszawa: Zakład Graficzny Uniwersytetu Warszawskiego.
Kierzkowska, Danuta (ed.) 1994. *Polish Universities and Schools : Polterm glossary no. 5*. Warsaw: Wydawnictwo TEPIS.
Kierzkowska, Danuta (ed.) 1996. *Polish Law Collection*. Warsaw: Wydawnictwo TEPIS.
Kierzkowska, Danuta (ed.) 2005. *Kodeks Tłumacza Przysięgłego z komentarzem*. Warszawa: Wydawnictwo TEPIS.
Kierzkowska, Danuta (ed.) 2011. *Kodeks Tłumacza Przysięgłego z komentarzem*. Warszawa: Wydawnictwo Translegis.
Kierzkowska, Danuta (ed.) 2011. *Kodeks Tłumacza Przysięgłego z komentarzem*. Warszawa: Wydawnictwo Translegis.

Kierzkowska, Danuta 1993. POLTERM Polish System of Unified Terminology. In Miler, Joanna (ed.) *International Forum of Legal Translation 1992. Proceedings*. Warsaw: Wydawnictwo TEPIS, 81-85.
Kierzkowska, Danuta 1997. On the Practice of Legal and Specialised Translation. In Kierzkowska, Danuta / Rybińska Zofia (eds) *On the Practice of Legal and Specialised Translation*. Warsaw: Wydawnictwo TEPIS, 5-9.
Kierzkowska, Danuta 2002. *Tłumaczenie prawnicze*. Warszawa: Wydawnictwo TEPIS.
Kierzkowska, Danuta (ed.) 1991. *Kodeks tłumacza sądowego*. Warsaw: Wydawnictwo TEPIS.
Kjaer, Anne Lise 2007. Legal Translation in the European Union. A Research Field in Need of a New Approach. In Kredens, Krzysztof / Goźdź-Roszkowski, Stanisław (eds) *Language and the Law: International Outlooks*. Frankfurt am Main: Peter Lang, 69-95.
Klaudy, Kinga 2003. *Languages in Translation. Lectures on the Theory, Teaching and Practice of Translation*. Budapest: Scholastica.
Koller, Werner 1972. *Grundprobleme der Übersetzungstheorie*. Bern: Franke.
Koller, Werner 1979. *Einführung in die Übersetzungswissenschaft*. Heidelberg: Quelle & Meyer.
Kopczyński, Andrzej / Kizeweter, Magdalena (eds) 2009. *Jakość i ocena tłumaczenia*. Warszawa: Wydawnictwo Academica.
Kopczyński, Andrzej 1980. *Conference Interpreting. Some Linguistic and Communicative Problems*. Poznań: Wydawnictwo Naukowe Uniwersytetu im. Adama Mickiewicza.
Kozłowska, Zofia 2002. O błędach językowych w tekstach polskich przekładów. In Kopczyński, Andrzej / Zaliwska-Okrutna, Urszula (eds) *Język rodzimy a język obcy. Komunikacja, przekład, dydaktyka*. Warszawa: Wydawnictwo Uniwersytetu Warszawskiego, 137-149.
Krings, Hans Peter 1986. *Was in den Köpfen von Übersetzern vorgeht. Eine empirische Untersuchung der Struktur des Übersetzungs Prozesses an fortgeschrittenen Französischlernern*. Tübingen: Narr.
Krzeszowski, Tomasz Paweł 2012. *Meaning and Translation. Part 1: Meaning*. Frankfurt am Main: Peter Lang.
Kubacki, Artur Dariusz 2007. Problemy tłumaczenia niemieckojęzycznych dokumentów samochodowych. In Piotrowska Maria (ed.) *Współczesne kierunki analiz przekładowych*. Kraków: Tertium, 121-132.
Kubacki, Artur Dariusz 2008. Odpowiedzialność zawodowa tłumaczy przysięgłych. In Nowak, Piotr / Nowakowski, Paweł (eds) *Język, Komunikacja, Informacja*. vol. 3. Poznań: Wydawnictwo SORUS, 149-161.
Kunz, Keneva 1995. Where the Devil Meets his Grandmother: Iceland and the European Community Legislation. In Marshall, Morris (ed.) *Translation and the Law*. Amsterdam/Philadelphia: John Benjamins, 86-91.
Kussmaul [Kußmaul], Paul 1995. *Training the Translator*. Amsterdam/ Philadelphia: John Benjamins.
Kussmaul [Kußmaul], Paul 1984. Wie genau soll eine Übersetzung sein? Wie können wir Studierenden bei ihren semantischen Entscheidungen helfen? In Wilss,

Wolfram / Thome, Gisela (eds) *Die Theorie des Übersetzens und ihr Aufschlußwert für die Übersetzungs- und Dolmetschdidaktik*, 52-60.
Laurén, Christer / Nordmann, Marianne 1996. *Wissenschaftliche Technolekte*. Tübingen: Narr.
Lefevere, André (ed.) 1992a. *Translation/History/Culture. A Sourcebook*. London/New York: Routledge.
Lefevere, André 2004a. *Translation/History/Culture. A Sourcebook*. Shanghai: Shanghai Foreign Education Press.
Lehto, Leena 1985. Methodological Aspect of Legal Translation. In Tommola, J. / Battarbee, K. (eds) *Papers from the Conference of Departments of English in Finland*. Turku: University of Turku, 147-176.
Lerat, Pierre 1995. *Les langues spécialisées, coll. "Linguistique nouvelle"*. Paris: PUF.
Levý, Jiri 1967. Translation as a Decision Process. In *To Honour Roman Jakobson, Essays on the Occasion of his 70th Birthday,* vol. II. The Hague: Mouton, 1171-1182.
Levý, Jiri 1969. *Die literarische Übersetzung*. Theorie einer Kungstgattung. Frankfurt am Main/Bonn: Athenäum Verlag.
Lipiński, Krzysztof 2000. *Vademecum tłumacza*. Kraków: IDEA.
Lizisowa, Maria Teresa 1986. Z badań nad terminologią prawną. *Rocznik Naukowo-Dydaktyczny WSP Kraków, Prace Językoznawcze*, no. 5, 5-20.
Lizisowa, Maria Teresa 1995. *Podstawowe terminy prawne w statutach staropolskich na tle słowiańskim. Studium semantyczne*. Kraków: Wydawnictwo Naukowe WSP.
Lörscher, Wolfgang 1991. *Translation Performance, Translation Process, and Translation Strategies. A Psycholinguistic Investigation*. Tübingen: Narr.
Lowenberg, Peter H. 1994. Variation in Malaysian English: the pragmatics of languages in contact. In Cheshire, Jenny (ed.) *English around the World. Sociolinguistic Perspectives*. Cambridge: Cambridge University Press, 364-375.
Lukszyn, Jerzy 2009. W kwestii definicji pojęcia „tekst specjalistyczny". *Komunikacja Specjalistyczna 1/2009*, 7-13.
Luther, Martin 1530/1960. *Sendbrief vom Dolmetschen*. Kähler, Ernst (ed.) Reclams Universal-Bibliothek 1578, Stuttgart: Reclam.
Lyons, John 1977. *Semantics*. Vol. 1 and 2, Cambridge: Cambridge University Press.
Maley, Yon 1994. The Language of the Law. In Gibbons, John (ed.) *Language and the Law*. New York: Longman, 11-50.
Malinowska, Ewa (ed.) 2004a. *Język Prawo Społeczeństwo*. Opole: Wydawnictwo Uniwersytetu Opolskiego.
Malinowska, Ewa 1999. Język w urzędach. In Pisarek, Walery (ed.) *Polszczyzna 2000. Orędzie o stanie języka na przełomie tysiącleci*. Kraków: Ośrodek Badań Prsoznawczych. Uniwersystet Jagielloński, 50-74.
Malinowska, Ewa 2004b. Wzorce wypowiedzi urzędowych a ich realizacja. In Malinowska, Ewa (ed.) *Język Prawo Społeczeństwo*. Opole: Wydawnictwo Uniwersytetu Opolskiego, 143-150.
Malinowski, Andrzej 2006. *Polski język prawny*. Warszawa: LexisNexis.
Matthews, Peter 2005. *The Concise Oxford Dictionary of Linguistics*. Oxford: Oxford University Press.

Mattila, Heikki 2006. *Comparative Legal Linguistics*. England: Ashgate.
Matulewska, Aleksandra (ed.) 2011c. *Comparative Legilinguistics*, vol. 8/2011. Poznań: Zakład Graficzny AMU.
Matulewska, Aleksandra (ed.) 2011a. *Comparative Legilinguistics (Legilingwistyka Porównawcza)*, vol. 6/2011. Poznań: Zakład Graficzny AMU.
Matulewska, Aleksandra (ed.) 2011b. *Comparative Legilinguistics*, vol. 7/2011. Poznań: Zakład Graficzny AMU.
Matulewska, Aleksandra (ed.) 2012a. *Comparative Legilinguistics (Legilingwistyka Porównawcza)*, vol. 9/2012. Poznań: Zakład Graficzny AMU.
Matulewska, Aleksandra (ed.) 2012c. *Comparative Legilinguistics*, vol. 10/2012. Poznań: Zakład Graficzny AMU.
Matulewska, Aleksandra 2007. Judgments in Polish-English and English-Polish Translation. *Lingua Legis* no. 15, 23-32.
Matulewska, Aleksandra 2007. *Lingua Legis in Translation*. Peter Lang.
Matulewska, Aleksandra 2009. Problemy przekładu terminologii wieloznacznej występującej w polskich tekstach aktów normatywnych. In Mróz, Anna / Niewiadomski, Adam / Monika Pawelec (eds) *Prawo i Język*. Warszawa: Zakład graficzny Uniwersytetu Warszawskiego, 85-94.
Mellinkoff, David 1963. *The Language of the Law*. Boston/Toronto: Little, Brown and Company.
Mesthrie, Rajend 1994. Syntactic variation in South African Indian English: the relative clause. In Cheshire, Jenny (ed.) *English around the World. Sociolinguistic Perspectives*. Cambridge: Cambridge University Press, 462-473.
Möhn, Dieter / Pelka, Roland 1984. *Fachsprachen, Eine Einführung*. Tübingen: Niemeyer.
Neubert, Albrecht / Kade, Otto (eds) 1973. *Neue Beiträge zu Fragen der Übersetzungswissenschaft*, Leipzig/Frankfurt/M.
Neubert, Albrecht 1968b. Pragmatische Aspekte der Übersetzung. In *Beihefte zur Zeitschrift Fremdsprachen II: Grundfragen der Übersetzungswissenschaft*. Leipzig: Enzyklopädie, 21-33.
Neubert, Albrecht 1973. Invarianz und Pragmatik. In Neubert, Albrecht / Kade, Otto (eds) *Neue Beiträge zu Grundfragen der Übersetzungswissenschaft*, Leipzig: Athenäum, 13-25.
Neubert, Albrecht 1996. Textlinguistics of Translation: The Textual Approach to Translation. In Gaddis, Rose Marilyn (ed.) *Translation Horizons Beyond the Boundaries of Translation Spectrum. Translation Perspectives IX*. Binghamton: Center for Research in Translation, 87-105.
Newmark, Peter 1982. *Approaches to Translation*. Oxford: Pergamon Press Ltd.
Newmark, Peter 1988. *A Textbook of Translation*. UK: Prentice Hall International Ltd.
Newmark, Peter 1991. *About Translation*. Clevedon: Multilingual Matters Ltd.
Newmark, Peter 2006. *About Translation*. Beijing: Foreign Language Teaching and Research Press.
Newmark, Peter 2007. *A Textbook of Translation*. Shanghai: Shanghai Foreign Education Press.

Newmark, Peter 2008. *Approaches to Translation*. Shanghai: Shanghai Foreign Education Press.

Nida, Eugene / Taber, Charles R. 1982. *The Theory and Practice of Translation*. Leiden: E. J. Brill.

Nida, Eugene 1964. *Toward a Science of Translating. With Special Reference to Principles and Procedures Involved in Bible Translating*. Leiden: Brill.

Nida, Eugene 2004a. Principles of Correspondence. In Venuti, Lawrence (ed.) *The Translation Studies Reader*. London and New York: Routledge, 127-139.

Nida, Eugene 2004b. *Towards a Science of Translating*. Shanghai: Shanghai Foreign Education Press.

Nord, Christiane 2005. *Text Analysis in Translation. Theory, Methodology, and Didactic Application of a Model for translation-Oriented Text Analysis*. Amsterdam: Editions Rodopi B. V.

Nord, Christiane 2006. *Text Analysis in Translation. Theory, Methodology, and Didactic Application of a Model for translation-Oriented Text Analysis*. Second Edition. Beijing: Foreign Language Teaching and Research Press.

Nowak, Joanna 2009. Modalność deontyczna w konstytucjach hiszpańskojęzycznych oraz w konstytucji Polski. In Mróz, Anna / Niewiadomski, Adam / Pawelec, Monika (eds) *Prawo i Język*. Warszawa: Wydawnictwo Uniwersytetu Warszawskiego, 171-187.

Obenaus, Gerhard 1995. The Legal Translator as Information Broker. In Marshall, Morris (ed.) *Translation and the Law*. Amsterdam/Philadelphia: John Benjamins, 247-259.

Olohan, Maeve (ed.) 2000. *Intercultural Faultiness. Research Models in Translation Studies I: Textual and Cognitive Aspects*. Manchester: St. Jerome Publishing.

Paine, Robert 1981. When saying is doing. In Paine, Robert (ed.) *Politically Speaking*. Philadelphia: Institute for the Study of Human Issues, 9-22.

Patryas, Wojciech 1997. *Definiowanie pojęć prawnych*. Poznań: Wydawnictwo Naukowe UAM.

Pieńkos, Jerzy 1999. *Podstawy juryslingwistyki. Język w prawie – prawo w języku*. Warszawa: Oficyna Prawnicza Muza S.A.

Pieńkos, Jerzy 2003. *Podstawy przeładoznawstwa. Od teorii do praktyki*. Kraków: Zakamycze.

Piotrowska, Maria 2007. *Proces decyzyjny tłumacza*. Kraków: Wydawnictwo Naukowe Akademii Pedagogicznej.

Pisarska, Alicja / Tomaszkiewicz, Teresa 1996. *Współczesne tendencje przekładoznawcze*. Poznań: Wydawnictwo Naukowe UAM.

Pisarska, Alicja 1989. *Creativity of Translators. The Translation of Metaphorical Expressions in Non-literary Texts*. Poznań: Wydawnictwo Naukowe UAM.

Pommer, Sieglinde E. 2008. No creativity in legal translation? *Babel. Revue internationale de la traduction*, 54 (4), 355-368.

Popovič, Anton 1970b. The Concept 'Shift of Expression' in Translation Analysis. In Holmes, James S. (ed.) *The Nature of Translation. Essays on the Theory and Practice of Literary Translation*. The Hague and Paris/Bratislava: Mouton/Slovak Academy of Sciences, 78-87.

Popovič, Anton 1976. *A Dictionary for the Analysis of Literary Translation*. Edmonton, Alberta: Department of Comparative Literature, University of Alberta.
Popovič, Anton 1977. Translation as communication. In Popovič, Anton / Déneš, Imrich (eds) *Translation as Comparison*. Nitra.
Radin, Max 1955. *Law Dictionary*. New York: Oceana Publications.
Rayar, Louise 1992. Translating Law: Method or Madness? In Miler, Joanna (ed.) *International Forum of Legal Translation 1992. Proceedings*. Warszawa: Wydawnictwo TEPIS, 62-71.
Rayar, Louise 1993. Translating Law: Method or Madness? *International Forum of Legal Translation 1992. Proceedings*. Warsaw: Wydawnictwo TEPIS, 62-71.
Rayar, Louise 1999a. Legal Translation: An Academic Specialism. In Tomaszczyk, Jerzy (ed.) *Aspects of Legal Language and Legal Translation*. Łódź: Wydawnictwo Uniwersytetu Łódzkiego, 129-136.
Rayar, Louise 1999b. The Quality of Source Texts. In Tomaszczyk, Jerzy (ed.) *Aspects of Legal Language and Legal Translation*. Łódź: Wydawnictwo Uniwersytetu Łódzkiego, 157-170.
Reiss, Katherina / Snell-Hornby, Mary / Kadric, Mira (eds) 1995. *Grundfragen der Übersetzungswissenschaft. Wiener Vorlesungen*. Wien: WUV-Universitätsverlag.
Reiss, Katherina 1976. *Texttyp und Űbersetzungsmethode. Der operative Text*. Kronberg: Scriptor.
Reiss, Katherina 2000. *Translation Criticism. The Potentials and Limitations*. Manchester: St. Jerome Publishing.
Reiss, Katherina 2004. *Translation Criticism. The Potentials and Limitations*. Shanghai: Shanghai Foreign Education Press.
Reiss, Katherina / Vermeer, Hans, J. 1984. *Grundlegung einer allgemeinen Translationstheorie*. Tübingen: Max Niemeyer.
Richards, Jack C. 1979. Rhetorical and Communicative styles in the new varieties of English. *Language learning* 29(1), 1-25.
Robinson, Pauline 1991. *ESP Today: A Practitioner's Guide*. Hertfordshire: Prentice Hall.
Rodell, Frederick 1939. *Woe Unto You, Lawyers!* New York: Reynal & Hitchcock.
Roganova, Zoja E. 1971. *Perevod s russkogo yazyka na nemeckii* [*Russian- German Translation*]. Moscow: Vysshaya shkola.
Sager, Juan / David Dungworth / Peter McDonals 1980. *English Special Languages*. Wiesbaden: Oscar Brandstetter.
Sager, Juan 1990. A Practical Course in Terminology Processing. Amsterdam and Philadelphia: John Benjamins.
Sahgal, Anju 1994. Patterns of Language Use in a Bilingual Setting in India. In Cheshire, Jenny (ed.) *English around the World. Sociolinguistic Perspectives*. Cambridge: Cambridge University Press, 299-307.
Samuelsson-Brown, Geoffrey 2004. Fourth revised edition. *A Practical Guide for Translators*. Clevedon: Multilingual Matters Ltd.
Samuelsson-Brown, Geoffrey 2006. *A Practical Guide for Translators*. Fourth revised edition. Beijing: Foreign Language Teaching and Research Press.

Sandrini, Peter 2009. The Parameters of Multilingual Legal Communication in a Globalized World. *Comparative Legilinguistics*, vol. 1/2009, 34-48.
Sapir, Edward 1929. The Status of Linguistics as a Science. *Language No. 5.*
Šaračević, Susan 1997. *New Approach to Legal Translation.* The Hague: Kluwer Law International.
Šarčević, Susan 1988a. Bilingual and Multilingual Legal Dictionaries: New Standards for the Future. *Revue générale de droit* 19, 4, 961-978.
Šarčević, Susan 1988c. Translation of legislation – with special emphasis on languages of limited diffusion. In Nekeman, Paul (ed.) *Translation, our future, XIth World Congress of FIT.* Maastricht: Euroterm, 455-462.
Šarčević, Susan 1989. Conceptual Dictionaries for Translation in the Field of Law. *International Journal of Lexicography* 2, 4, 277-293.
Šarčević, Susan 2000a. Legal Translation and Translation Theory: A Receiver-Oriented Approach. <http://www.tradulex.org/Actes2000/sarcevic.pdf> (02.05.2010)
Šarčević, Susan 2000b. *New Approach to Legal Translation.* The Hague: Kluwer Law International.
Šarčević, Susan 1988b. The Challenge of Legal Lexicography: Implications for Bilingual and Multilingual Dictionaries. In Snell-Hornby, Mary (ed.) *ZüriLEX '86 Proceedings*, Tübingen: Francke, 307-314.
Savory, Theodore H. 1958. *The Art of Translation.* Philadelphia: DuFour.
Schleiermacher, Friedrich 1813/1838. *Über die verschiedenen Methoden des Übersetzens. Friedrich Schleiermacher's sämmtliche Werke.* Berlin: Reimer. III/2: 207–245.
Schleiermacher, Friedrich 1992. *On the Different Methods of Translating.* In Lefevere, André (ed.) *Translation/History/Culture. A Sourcebook.* London/New York: Routledge, 141-166.
Schroth, Peter W. 1986. Legal Translation. *American Journal of Comparative Law* 1986, 47-65.
Sczaniecki, Michał 1985. *Powszechna historia państwa i prawa.* Warszawa: Państwowe Wydawnictwo Naukowe.
Smith, Sylvia A. 1995. Culture Clash: Anglo-American Case Law and German Civil Law in Translation. In Marshall, Morris (ed.) *Translation and the Law.* American Translators Association Scholarly Monograph Series, vol. VIII, 1995. Amsterdam/Philadelphia: John Benjamins, 181-197.
Snell-Hornby, Mary 1995. *Translation Studies. An Integrated Approach.* Amsterdam: John Benjamins.
Snell-Hornby, Mary 1992. The Professional Translator of Tomorrow: Language Specialist or All-Round Expert? In Dollerup, Cay / Loddegaard, Anne (eds) *Teaching Translation and Interpreting: Training, Talent and Experience.* Amsterdam/Philadelphia: John Benjamins, 9-22.
Snell-Hornby, Mary 2007. *Translation Studies. An Integrated Approach.* Shanghai: Shanghai Foreign Education Press.
Solan, Lawrence 1984. *The Language of Judges.* Chicago and London: The University of Chicago Press.

Sourioux, Jean-Louis / Lerat, Pierre 1975. Le langage du droit. Paris: Presses universitaires de France.

Sperber, Dan / Wilson, Deirdre 1986. *Relevance: Communication and Cognition.* Oxford: Blackwell.

Stawecki, Tomasz / Winczorek, Piotr 2002. *Wstęp do prawoznawstwa*. Warszawa: C.H. Beck.

Steiner, George 1977. *After Babel. Aspects of Language and Translation*. Oxford: Oxford University Press.

Steiner, George 2001. *After Babel. Aspects of Language and Translation*. Shanghai: Shanghai Foreign Education Press.

Tabakowska, Elżbieta 1993. *Cognitive Linguistics and Poetics of Translation*. Tübingen: Gunter Narr Verlag.

Tabakowska, Elżbieta 1999. *O przekładzie na przykładzie*. Kraków: Wydawnictwo Znak.

Tabakowska, Elżbieta 2001. *Językoznawstwo kognitywne a poetyka przekładu*. Kraków: Universitas.

Tabakowska, Elżbieta 2009. *Tłumacząc się z tłumaczenia*. Kraków: Wydawnictwo Znak.

Taft, Ronald 1981. The Role and Personality of the Mediator. In Bochner, Stephen (ed.) *The Mediating Person: Bridges between Cultures*. Cambridge: Schenkman, 53-88.

Taylor, John R. 1995. *Linguistic categorization: Prototypes in linguistic theory*. 2nd ed. Oxford: Clarendon Press.

Tessuto, Girolamo 2008. Legal Concepts and Terminography: Analysis and Application. In Bhatia, Vijay K. / Candlin, Christopher N. / Allori, Paola Evangelisti (eds) *Language, Culture and the Law: The Formulation of legal Concepts across Systems and Cultures.* Bern: Peter Lang, 283-302.

Tiersma, Peter M. 1999. *Legal Language*. Chicago/London: The University of Chicago Press.

Tokarczyk, Roman 1998. *Prawo amerykańskie*. Kraków: Zakamycze.

Toury, Gideon 1980. *In Search of a Theory of Translation*. Tel Aviv: The Porter Institute for Poetics and Semiotics, Tel Aviv University.

Toury, Gideon 1995. *Descriptive Translation Studies and Beyond*. Amsterdam: John Benjamins.

Toury, Gideon 2001. *Descriptive Translation Studies and Beyond*. Shanghai: Shanghai Foreign Education Press.

Tryuk, Małgorzata 2006. *Przekład ustny środowiskowy*. Warszawa: Wydawnictwo Naukowe PWN.

Tryuk, Małgorzata 2007. *Przekład ustny konferencyjny*. Warszawa: Wydawnictwo Naukowe PWN.

Tytler, Alexander Fraser 2007. *Essay on Principles of Translation*. Beijing: Foreign Language Teaching and Research Press.

Vermeer, Hans J. 1978. Ein Rahmen für eine Allgemeine Translationstheorie. *Lebende Sprachen* 3, 99-102.

Vermeer, Hans J. 1983. *Aufsätze zur Translationstheorie*. Heidelberg: Mimeo.

Vermeer, Hans J. 1986. Übersetzen als kultureller Transfer. In Snell-Hornby, Mary (ed.) *Übersetzungswissenschaft – eine Neuorientierung*. Tübingen: Francke, 30-53.

Vermeer, Hans J. 2001, Skopos and Commission in Translational Action. In Venuti, Lawrence / Baker, Mona (eds) *The Translation Studies Reader*. London/New York: Routlege, 221-232.

Vinay, Jean-Paul / Darbelnet, Jean 1966. *Stylistique comparée du français et de l'anglais*. Paris: Didier.

Wagner, Anne / Cacciaguidi-Fahy, Sophie (eds) 2006. *Legal Language and the Search for Clarity. Linguistics Insights*, vol. 37. Bern: Peter Lang.

Weber, Harmut 1982. Language for Specific Purposes, Text Typology, and Text Analysis: Aspects of a Pragmatic-Functional Approach. In Hoedt / Lundquist / Picht / Qvistgaard (eds) *Proceedings of the 3rd European Symposium on LSP, Pragmatics and LSP*. Copenhagen, 219-234.

Weston, Martin 1991. *An English Reader's Guide to the French Legal System*. New York/Oxford: Berg.

Wille, Lucyna 2002. *Uniwersalistyczne implikacje teorii przekładu*. Rzeszów: Wydawnictwo Uniwersytetu Rzeszowskiego.

Williams, Christopher 2005/2007, *Tradition and Change in Legal English. Linguistics Insights*, vol. 20. Bern: Peter Lang.

Williams, Jenny / Chesterman, Andrew 2002. *The Map. A Beginner's Guide to Doing Research in Translation Studies*. Manchester: St. Jerome Publishing.

Williams, Jenny / Chesterman, Andrew 2007. *The Map. A Beginner's Guide to Doing Research in Translation Studies*. Shanghai: Shanghai Foreign Education Press.

Wilss, Wolfram 1977a. *The Science of Translation. Problems and Methods*. Tübingen: Gunter Narr Verlag.

Wilss, Wolfram 1980. Semiotik und Übersetzungswissenschaft. In Wilss, Wolfram (ed.) *Semiotik und Übersetzen*. Tübingen: Narr, 9-22.

Wilss, Wolfram 2001. *The Science of Translation. Problems and Methods*. Shanghai: Shanghai Foreign Education Press.

Wilss, Wolfram, 1977b. *Übersetzungswissenschaft. Probleme und Methoden*. Stuttgart: Ernst Klett.

Witczak(-Plisiecka), Iwona 1999. Selected Issues Concerning the Legal Performative and the Language of legislation. In Tomaszczyk, Jerzy (ed.) *Aspects of Legal Language and Legal Translation*. Łódź: Wydawnictwo Uniwersytetu Łódzkiego, 23-30.

Witczak-Plisiecka, Iwona 2009. Legal Speech Acts in a Cognitive Linguistic Perspective – Focus on Modality. *Comparative Legilinguistics*. vol. 1/2009, 159-175.

Wojtasiewicz, Olgierd 1957. *Wstęp do teorii tłumaczenia*. Wrocław/Warszawa: Zakład im. Ossolińskich – Wydawnictwo Polskiej Akademii Nauk.

Wojtasiewicz, Olgierd 2005. *Wstęp do teorii tłumaczenia*. Warszawa: Wydawnictwo TEPIS.

Wróblewski, Bronisław 1948. *Język prawny i prawniczy*. Kraków: Polska Akademia Umiejętności.

Wróblewski, Jerzy 1956. Wykładnia prawa a terminologia prawna. *Państwo i Prawo*, vol. 5-6, 843-865.

Wróblewski, Jerzy 1984. Zagadnienia terminologii nauk prawnych. *Nauka Polska*, no. 3, 75-86.

Wróblewski, Jerzy 1987. Zagadnienia polskiej terminologii prawnej i prawniczej. *Studia Prawno-Ekonomiczne*, vol. 39, 14-34.

Wronkowska, Sławomira / Zieliński, Maciej 1993. *Problemy i zasady redagowania tekstów prawnych*. Warszawa: Urząd Rady Ministrów.

Wronkowska, Sławomira / Zieliński, Maciej 1997. *Zasady techniki prawodawczej*. Warszawa: Wydawnictwo Sejmowe.

Yankova, Diana 2004. *Statutory Provisions in English and Bulgarian*. Sofia: Tip-Top Press.

Zabrocki, Ludwik 1963. *Wspólnoty komunikatywne w genezie i rozwoju języka niemieckiego. Część I. Prehistoria języka niemieckiego*. Wrocław/Warszawa/Kraków: Zakład Narodowy imienia Ossolińskich Wydawnictwo Polskiej Akademii Nauk.

Zedler, Feliks 2010. Wybrane zagadnienia z zakresu prawa i postępowania cywilnego w aspekcie translatologicznym z języka polskiego na angielski. *Comparative Legilinguistics* vol. 3/2010, 91-98.

Zieliński, Maciej 1999. Języki prawne i prawnicze. In Pisarek, Walery (ed.) *Polszczyzna 2000. Orędzie o stanie języka na przełomie tysiącleci*. Kraków: Ośrodek Badań Prasoznawczych. Uniwersystet Jagielloński, 75-96.

Zieliński, Maciej 2002/2008. *Wykładnia prawa. Zasady. Reguły. Wskazówki*. Warszawa: Wydawnictwo Prawnicze LexisNexis.

Ziembiński, Zenon 1960. Przepis prawny a norma prawna. *Ruch Prawniczy Ekonomiczny i Socjologiczny*. 1/1960.

Source materials:

Bharat, Raj Upreti 2005. The New Insolvency Law in Nepal. In *INSOL WORLD 4/2005*, 22-23.

Didier, Isabelle 2005. France: The Company Rescue Proceedings Act. *INSOL World 4/2005*, 34-35.

Hrycaj, Anna 2007. All you need to know about becoming an Insolvency Practitioner in Europe: Poland. *Eurofenix*, issue 28, 2/2007, 20-21.

Lofalk, Guy 2003. The far-reaching reforms of Swedish insolvency legislation. *Eurofenix*, 3/2003, 8-11.

Lowitzsch, Jens (ed.) 2007. *The Insolvency Law of Central and Eastern Europe*. Vol. 2/2007, INSOL Europe.

Pellier, Vincent / Théron, Christophe 2007. Why did the French invent the rescue procedure? *Eurofenix*, issue 28, 2/2007, 18-19.

Recovery. The Association of Business Recovery Professionals. Autumn, 3/2004

Riffard, Jean-François 2007. Reform of the French securities law: A revolution in half-tone? *Eurofenix* 4/2007, 24-25.

Serao, Francesco 2006. The Curator and the Creditors' Committee in the Reformed Italian Bankruptcy Law. *INSOL World*, Third Quarter 2006, 43.

Staehelin, Daniel 2003. Switzerland and EU-regulated insolvency cases. *Eurofenix*, 1/2003, 10-12.

Stessi, Michaela / Luiki Paul 2005. New Developments in Slovak Bankruptcy Law. *INSOL World* 4/2005, 38.

Szpunar, Maciej 2005. The present situation of private law in Poland. *The European Legal Forum* 6-2005, IPR VERLAG, I-257-I-320.

Toube, Felicity 2007a. European Insolvency News. News from France. *Eurofenix* 4/2007, 14-15.

Toube, Felicity 2007b. European Insolvency News. News from Germany. *Eurofenix* 4/2007, 15.

Wesses, Bob 2006. *International Insolvency Law*. Deventer: Wolters Kluwer Business.

Wouters, Nora 2005. Cross-Border Insolvency Proceedings in Belgium. *INSOL World*, First Quarter 2005, 12-13.

Statutory Instruments:

Council Regulation (EC) no 1346/2000 of 29 May 2000 on insolvency proceedings (Official Journal of the European Communities, L 1 60/1 of 30 June 2000).

Règlement (CE) N° 1346/2000 du Conseil du 29 mai 2000 relatif aux procédures d'insolvabilité (Journal officiel des Communautés européennes L 1 60/1 du 30 juin 2000).

Rozporządzenie prezesa rady ministrów z dnia 20 czerwca 2002r. w sprawie zasad techniki prawodawczej (Dz.U. z dnia 5 lipca 2002r.).

Rozporządzenie Prezydenta Rzeczypospolitej z dnia 24 października 1934 r. Prawo upadłościowe [Regulation by the President of the Republic of Poland of 24 October 1934 Bankruptcy Law].

Rozporządzenie Rady (WE) nr 1346/2000 z dnia 29 maja 2000 r. w sprawie postępowania upadłościowego (two Polish translation versions of 2004 and 2008).

The British Insolvency Act 1986 <http://www.insolvency.gov.uk/insolvencyprofessionandlegislation/legislation/uk/insolvencyact.pdf>.

The Commonwealth of Australia Bankruptcy Act 1966 <http://www.comlaw.gov.au/comlaw/Legislation/ActCompilation1.nsf/0/622FC7A1613FDCD4CA2571A0001CF2EB/$file/Bankruptcy1966Vol1_WD02_Version1.pdf>.

The European Council Regulation (EC) No 1346/2000 on insolvency proceedings.

The Irish Bankruptcy Act 1988 <http://www.irishstatutebook.ie/1988/en/act/pub/0027/>.

The translation of Rozporządzenie Prezydenta Rzeczypospolitej z dnia 24 października 1934 r. Prawo upadłościowe (Regulation by the President of the Republic of Poland of 24 October 1934 Bankruptcy Law) into English rendered by TEPIS (Kierzkowska 1996, 271-307).

The US Code Title 11 Bankruptcy <http://www.law.cornell.edu/uscode/search/display.html?terms=receiver&url=/uscode/html/uscode11/>.

Ustawa z dnia 28 lutego 2003. Prawo upadłościowe i naprawcze.

Verordnung (EG) Nr. 1346/2000 des Rates vom 29. Mai 2000 über Insolvenzverfahren.

Dictionaries and encyclopaedias:
Bar, Ludwik 1986. *Słownik prawniczy polsko-angielski*. Warszawa: Ossolineum.
Black's Law Dictionary. 1979. Fifth Edition. United States of America: St Paul Minn. West Publishing Co.
Collin, Peter H. / Bartnicki, K. 2001. *Słownik prawa*. Warszawa: Peter Collin Publishing & Wydawnictwo Wilga.
Delisle, Jean (et al., eds) 1999. *Translation Terminology*. Amsterdam/Philadephia: John Benjamins.
Garner, Bryan A. (ed.) 2004. *Black's Law Dictionary*. Eighth Edition. United States of America: Thomson West.
Gordon, Jacek 2008. *Słownik terminologii prawniczej i gospodarczej polsko-angielski, angielsko-polski*. Warszawa: Poltext.
Jaślan, J. / Jaślan, H. 1991. *Słownik terminologii prawniczej i ekonomicznej angielsko-polski*. Warszawa: Wiedza Powszechna.
Łozińska-Małkiewicz, Ewa / Małkiewicz, Joanna 1997. *Polsko-angielski słownik terminologii prawniczej*. Toruń: Wydawnictwo Ewa.
Łozińska-Małkiewicz, Ewa / Małkiewicz, Joanna 2005. *Polsko-angielski słownik terminologii prawniczej*. Toruń: Wydawnictwo Ewa.
Matthews, P. H. 2005. *The Concise Oxford Dictionary of Linguistics*. Oxford: Oxford University Press.
Myrczek, Ewa 2006. *Dictionary of Law Terms*. Warszawa: Wydawnictwo C. H. Beck.
Ożga, Ewa 1998. *Słownik terminologii prawniczej angielsko-polski. Część 2*. Bydgoszcz: Oficyna Wydawnicza Branta.
Ożga, Ewa 2006. *The Great Dictionary of Law and Economics*. Warszawa: C. H. Beck.
Pieńkos, Jerzy 2002. *Polsko-angielski słownik prawniczy*. Kraków: Zakamycze.
Uniwersalny Słownik Języka Polskiego PWN. Wersja 3.0.
Webster's Third New International Dictionary, Unabridged CD-Rom (2003).

Index of key terms

Index of authors

Linguistic Insights

Studies in Language and Communication

This series aims to promote specialist language studies in the fields of linguistic theory and applied linguistics, by publishing volumes that focus on specific aspects of language use in one or several languages and provide valuable insights into language and communication research. A cross-disciplinary approach is favoured and most European languages are accepted.

The series includes two types of books:

- **Monographs** – featuring in-depth studies on special aspects of language theory, language analysis or language teaching.
- **Collected papers** – assembling papers from workshops, conferences or symposia.

Each volume of the series is subjected to a double peer-reviewing process.

Vol. 1 Maurizio Gotti & Marina Dossena (eds)
Modality in Specialized Texts. Selected Papers of the 1st CERLIS Conference.
421 pages. 2001. ISBN 3-906767-10-8 · US-ISBN 0-8204-5340-4

Vol. 2 Giuseppina Cortese & Philip Riley (eds)
Domain-specific English. Textual Practices across Communities and Classrooms.
420 pages. 2002. ISBN 3-906768-98-8 · US-ISBN 0-8204-5884-8

Vol. 3 Maurizio Gotti, Dorothee Heller & Marina Dossena (eds)
Conflict and Negotiation in Specialized Texts. Selected Papers of the 2nd CERLIS Conference.
470 pages. 2002. ISBN 3-906769-12-7 · US-ISBN 0-8204-5887-2

Vol. 4 Maurizio Gotti, Marina Dossena, Richard Dury, Roberta Facchinetti & Maria Lima
Variation in Central Modals. A Repertoire of Forms and Types of Usage in Middle English and Early Modern English.
364 pages. 2002. ISBN 3-906769-84-4 · US-ISBN 0-8204-5898-8

Editorial address:

Prof. Maurizio Gotti Università di Bergamo, Facoltà di Lingue e Letterature Straniere,
Via Salvecchio 19, 24129 Bergamo, Italy
Fax: 0039 035 2052789, E-Mail: m.gotti@unibg.it

Vol. 5 Stefania Nuccorini (ed.)
Phrases and Phraseology. Data and Descriptions.
187 pages. 2002. ISBN 3-906770-08-7 · US-ISBN 0-8204-5933-X

Vol. 6 Vijay Bhatia, Christopher N. Candlin & Maurizio Gotti (eds)
Legal Discourse in Multilingual and Multicultural Contexts.
Arbitration Texts in Europe.
385 pages. 2003. ISBN 3-906770-85-0 · US-ISBN 0-8204-6254-3

Vol. 7 Marina Dossena & Charles Jones (eds)
Insights into Late Modern English. 2nd edition.
378 pages. 2003, 2007.
ISBN 978-3-03911-257-9 · US-ISBN 978-0-8204-8927-8

Vol. 8 Maurizio Gotti
Specialized Discourse. Linguistic Features and Changing Conventions.
351 pages. 2003, 2005.
ISBN 3-03910-606-6 · US-ISBN 0-8204-7000-7

Vol. 9 Alan Partington, John Morley & Louann Haarman (eds)
Corpora and Discourse.
420 pages. 2004. ISBN 3-03910-026-2 · US-ISBN 0-8204-6262-4

Vol. 10 Martina Möllering
The Acquisition of German Modal Particles. A Corpus-Based Approach.
290 pages. 2004. ISBN 3-03910-043-2 · US-ISBN 0-8204-6273-X

Vol. 11 David Hart (ed.)
English Modality in Context. Diachronic Perspectives.
261 pages. 2003. ISBN 3-03910-046-7 · US-ISBN 0-8204-6852-5

Vol. 12 Wendy Swanson
Modes of Co-reference as an Indicator of Genre.
430 pages. 2003. ISBN 3-03910-052-1 · US-ISBN 0-8204-6855-X

Vol. 13 Gina Poncini
Discursive Strategies in Multicultural Business Meetings.
2nd edition. 338 pages. 2004, 2007.
ISBN 978-3-03911-296-8 · US-ISBN 978-0-8204-8937-7

Vol. 14 Christopher N. Candlin & Maurizio Gotti (eds)
Intercultural Aspects of Specialized Communication.
2nd edition. 369 pages. 2004, 2007.
ISBN 978-3-03911-258-6 · US-ISBN 978-0-8204-8926-1

Vol. 15 Gabriella Del Lungo Camiciotti & Elena Tognini Bonelli (eds)
Academic Discourse. New Insights into Evaluation.
234 pages. 2004. ISBN 3-03910-353-9 · US-ISBN 0-8204-7016-3

Vol. 16 Marina Dossena & Roger Lass (eds)
Methods and Data in English Historical Dialectology.
405 pages. 2004. ISBN 3-03910-362-8 · US-ISBN 0-8204-7018-X

Vol. 17 Judy Noguchi
The Science Review Article. An Opportune Genre in
the Construction of Science.
274 pages. 2006. ISBN 3-03910-426-8 · US-ISBN 0-8204-7034-1

Vol. 18 Giuseppina Cortese & Anna Duszak (eds)
Identity, Community, Discourse. English in Intercultural Settings.
495 pages. 2005. ISBN 3-03910-632-5 · US-ISBN 0-8204-7163-1

Vol. 19 Anna Trosborg & Poul Erik Flyvholm Jørgensen (eds)
Business Discourse. Texts and Contexts.
250 pages. 2005. ISBN 3-03910-606-6 · US-ISBN 0-8204-7000-7

Vol. 20 Christopher Williams
Tradition and Change in Legal English. Verbal Constructions in Prescriptive Texts.
2nd revised edition. 216 pages. 2005, 2007. ISBN 978-3-03911-444-3.

Vol. 21 Katarzyna Dziubalska-Kolaczyk & Joanna Przedlacka (eds)
English Pronunciation Models: A Changing Scene.
2nd edition. 476 pages. 2005, 2008. ISBN 978-3-03911-682-9.

Vol. 22 Christián Abello-Contesse, Rubén Chacón-Beltrán, M. Dolores López-Jiménez & M. Mar Torreblanca-López (eds)
Age in L2 Acquisition and Teaching.
214 pages. 2006. ISBN 3-03910-668-6 · US-ISBN 0-8204-7174-7

Vol. 23 Vijay K. Bhatia, Maurizio Gotti, Jan Engberg & Dorothee Heller (eds)
Vagueness in Normative Texts.
474 pages. 2005. ISBN 3-03910-653-8 · US-ISBN 0-8204-7169-0

Vol. 24 Paul Gillaerts & Maurizio Gotti (eds)
Genre Variation in Business Letters. 2nd printing.
407 pages. 2008. ISBN 978-3-03911-681-2.

Vol. 25 Ana María Hornero, María José Luzón & Silvia Murillo (eds)
Corpus Linguistics. Applications for the Study of English.
2nd printing. 526 pages. 2006, 2008. ISBN 978-3-03911-726-0

Vol. 26 J. Lachlan Mackenzie & María de los Ángeles Gómez-González (eds)
Studies in Functional Discourse Grammar.
259 pages. 2005. ISBN 3-03910-696-1 · US-ISBN 0-8204-7558-0

Vol. 27 Debbie G. E. Ho
Classroom Talk. Exploring the Sociocultural Structure of Formal ESL Learning.
2nd edition. 254 pages. 2006, 2007. ISBN 978-3-03911-434-4

Vol. 28 Javier Pérez-Guerra, Dolores González-Álvarez, Jorge L. Bueno-Alonso & Esperanza Rama-Martínez (eds)
'Of Varying Language and Opposing Creed'. New Insights into Late Modern English.
455 pages. 2007. ISBN 978-3-03910-788-9

Vol. 29 Francesca Bargiela-Chiappini & Maurizio Gotti (eds)
Asian Business Discourse(s).
350 pages. 2005. ISBN 3-03910-804-2 · US-ISBN 0-8204-7574-2

Vol. 30 Nicholas Brownlees (ed.)
News Discourse in Early Modern Britain. Selected Papers of CHINED 2004.
300 pages. 2006. ISBN 3-03910-805-0 · US-ISBN 0-8204-8025-8

Vol. 31 Roberta Facchinetti & Matti Rissanen (eds)
Corpus-based Studies of Diachronic English.
300 pages. 2006. ISBN 3-03910-851-4 · US-ISBN 0-8204-8040-1

Vol. 32 Marina Dossena & Susan M. Fitzmaurice (eds)
Business and Official Correspondence. Historical Investigations.
209 pages. 2006. ISBN 3-03910-880-8 · US-ISBN 0-8204-8352-4

Vol. 33 Giuliana Garzone & Srikant Sarangi (eds)
Discourse, Ideology and Specialized Communication.
494 pages. 2007. ISBN 978-3-03910-888-6

Vol. 34 Giuliana Garzone & Cornelia Ilie (eds)
The Use of English in Institutional and Business Settings.
An Intercultural Perspective.
372 pages. 2007. ISBN 978-3-03910-889-3

Vol. 35 Vijay K. Bhatia & Maurizio Gotti (eds)
Explorations in Specialized Genres.
316 pages. 2006. ISBN 3-03910-995-2 · US-ISBN 0-8204-8372-9

Vol. 36 Heribert Picht (ed.)
Modern Approaches to Terminological Theories and Applications.
432 pages. 2006. ISBN 3-03911-156-6 · US-ISBN 0-8204-8380-X

Vol. 37 Anne Wagner & Sophie Cacciaguidi-Fahy (eds)
Legal Language and the Search for Clarity / Le langage juridique et la quête de clarté.
Practice and Tools / Pratiques et instruments.
487 pages. 2006. ISBN 3-03911-169-8 · US-ISBN 0-8204-8388-5

Vol. 38 Juan Carlos Palmer-Silveira, Miguel F. Ruiz-Garrido &
Inmaculada Fortanet-Gómez (eds)
Intercultural and International Business Communication.
Theory, Research and Teaching.
2nd edition. 343 pages. 2006, 2008. ISBN 978-3-03911-680-5

Vol. 39 Christiane Dalton-Puffer, Dieter Kastovsky, Nikolaus Ritt &
Herbert Schendl (eds)
Syntax, Style and Grammatical Norms. English from 1500–2000.
250 pages. 2006. ISBN 3-03911-181-7 · US-ISBN 0-8204-8394-X

Vol. 40 Marina Dossena & Irma Taavitsainen (eds)
Diachronic Perspectives on Domain-Specific English.
280 pages. 2006. ISBN 3-03910-176-0 · US-ISBN 0-8204-8391-5

Vol. 41 John Flowerdew & Maurizio Gotti (eds)
Studies in Specialized Discourse.
293 pages. 2006. ISBN 3-03911-178-7

Vol. 42 Ken Hyland & Marina Bondi (eds)
Academic Discourse Across Disciplines.
320 pages. 2006. ISBN 3-03911-183-3 · US-ISBN 0-8204-8396-6

Vol. 43 Paul Gillaerts & Philip Shaw (eds)
The Map and the Landscape. Norms and Practices in Genre.
256 pages. 2006. ISBN 3-03911-182-5 · US-ISBN 0-8204-8395-4

Vol. 44 Maurizio Gotti & Davide Giannoni (eds)
New Trends in Specialized Discourse Analysis.
301 pages. 2006. ISBN 3-03911-184-1 · US-ISBN 0-8204-8381-8

Vol. 45 Maurizio Gotti & Françoise Salager-Meyer (eds)
Advances in Medical Discourse Analysis. Oral and Written Contexts.
492 pages. 2006. ISBN 3-03911-185-X · US-ISBN 0-8204-8382-6

Vol. 46 Maurizio Gotti & Susan Šarcević (eds)
Insights into Specialized Translation.
396 pages. 2006. ISBN 3-03911-186-8 · US-ISBN 0-8204-8383-4

Vol. 47 Khurshid Ahmad & Margaret Rogers (eds)
Evidence-based LSP. Translation, Text and Terminology.
584 pages. 2007. ISBN 978-3-03911-187-9

Vol. 48 Hao Sun & Dániel Z. Kádár (eds)
It's the Dragon's Turn. Chinese Institutional Discourses.
262 pages. 2008. ISBN 978-3-03911-175-6

Vol. 49 Cristina Suárez-Gómez
Relativization in Early English (950-1250). the Position of Relative Clauses.
149 pages. 2006. ISBN 3-03911-203-1 · US-ISBN 0-8204-8904-2

Vol. 50 Maria Vittoria Calvi & Luisa Chierichetti (eds)
Nuevas tendencias en el discurso de especialidad.
319 pages. 2006. ISBN 978-3-03911-261-6

Vol. 51 Mari Carmen Campoy & María José Luzón (eds)
Spoken Corpora in Applied Linguistics.
274 pages. 2008. ISBN 978-3-03911-275-3

Vol. 52 Konrad Ehlich & Dorothee Heller (Hrsg.)
Die Wissenschaft und ihre Sprachen.
323 pages. 2006. ISBN 978-3-03911-272-2

Vol. 53 Jingyu Zhang
The Semantic Salience Hierarchy Model. The L2 Acquisition of Psych Predicates
273 pages. 2007. ISBN 978-3-03911-300-2

Vol. 54 Norman Fairclough, Giuseppina Cortese & Patrizia Ardizzone (eds)
Discourse and Contemporary Social Change.
555 pages. 2007. ISBN 978-3-03911-276-0

Vol. 55 Jan Engberg, Marianne Grove Ditlevsen, Peter Kastberg & Martin Stegu (eds)
New Directions in LSP Teaching.
331 pages. 2007. ISBN 978-3-03911-433-7

Vol. 56 Dorothee Heller & Konrad Ehlich (Hrsg.)
Studien zur Rechtskommunikation.
322 pages. 2007. ISBN 978-3-03911-436-8

Vol. 57 Teruhiro Ishiguro & Kang-kwong Luke (eds)
Grammar in Cross-Linguistic Perspective.
The Syntax, Semantics, and Pragmatics of Japanese and Chinese.
304 pages. 2012. ISBN 978-3-03911-445-0

Vol. 58 Carmen Frehner
Email – SMS – MMS
294 pages. 2008. ISBN 978-3-03911-451-1

Vol. 59 Isabel Balteiro
The Directionality of Conversion in English. A Dia-Synchronic Study.
276 pages. 2007. ISBN 978-3-03911-241-8

Vol. 60 Maria Milagros Del Saz Rubio
English Discourse Markers of Reformulation.
237 pages. 2007. ISBN 978-3-03911-196-1

Vol. 61 Sally Burgess & Pedro Martín-Martín (eds)
English as an Additional Language in Research Publication and Communication.
259 pages. 2008. ISBN 978-3-03911-462-7

Vol. 62 Sandrine Onillon
Pratiques et représentations de l'écrit.
458 pages. 2008. ISBN 978-3-03911-464-1

Vol. 63 Hugo Bowles & Paul Seedhouse (eds)
Conversation Analysis and Language for Specific Purposes.
2nd edition. 337 pages. 2007, 2009. ISBN 978-3-0343-0045-2

Vol. 64 Vijay K. Bhatia, Christopher N. Candlin & Paola Evangelisti Allori (eds)
Language, Culture and the Law.
The Formulation of Legal Concepts across Systems and Cultures.
342 pages. 2008. ISBN 978-3-03911-470-2

Vol. 65 Jonathan Culpeper & Dániel Z. Kádár (eds)
Historical (Im)politeness.
300 pages. 2010. ISBN 978-3-03911-496-2

Vol. 66 Linda Lombardo (ed.)
Using Corpora to Learn about Language and Discourse.
237 pages. 2009. ISBN 978-3-03911-522-8

Vol. 67 Natsumi Wakamoto
Extroversion/Introversion in Foreign Language Learning.
Interactions with Learner Strategy Use.
159 pages. 2009. ISBN 978-3-03911-596-9

Vol. 68 Eva Alcón-Soler (ed.)
Learning How to Request in an Instructed Language Learning Context.
260 pages. 2008. ISBN 978-3-03911-601-0

Vol. 69 Domenico Pezzini
The Translation of Religious Texts in the Middle Ages.
428 pages. 2008. ISBN 978-3-03911-600-3

Vol. 70 Tomoko Tode
Effects of Frequency in Classroom Second Language Learning.
Quasi-experiment and stimulated-recall analysis.
195 pages. 2008. ISBN 978-3-03911-602-7

Vol. 71 Egor Tsedryk
Fusion symétrique et alternances ditransitives.
211 pages. 2009. ISBN 978-3-03911-609-6

Vol. 72 Cynthia J. Kellett Bidoli & Elana Ochse (eds)
English in International Deaf Communication.
444 pages. 2008. ISBN 978-3-03911-610-2

Vol. 73 Joan C. Beal, Carmela Nocera & Massimo Sturiale (eds)
Perspectives on Prescriptivism.
269 pages. 2008. ISBN 978-3-03911-632-4

Vol. 74 Carol Taylor Torsello, Katherine Ackerley & Erik Castello (eds)
Corpora for University Language Teachers.
308 pages. 2008. ISBN 978-3-03911-639-3

Vol. 75 María Luisa Pérez Cañado (ed.)
English Language Teaching in the European Credit Transfer System. Facing the Challenge.
251 pages. 2009. ISBN 978-3-03911-654-6

Vol. 76 Marina Dossena & Ingrid Tieken-Boon van Ostade (eds)
Studies in Late Modern English Correspondence. Methodology and Data.
291 pages. 2008. ISBN 978-3-03911-658-4

Vol. 77 Ingrid Tieken-Boon van Ostade & Wim van der Wurff (eds)
Current Issues in Late Modern English.
436 pages. 2009. ISBN 978-3-03911-660-7

Vol. 78 Marta Navarro Coy (ed.)
Practical Approaches to Foreign Language Teaching and Learning.
297 pages. 2009. ISBN 978-3-03911-661-4

Vol. 79 Qing Ma
Second Language Vocabulary Acquisition.
333 pages. 2009. ISBN 978-3-03911-666-9

Vol. 80 Martin Solly, Michelangelo Conoscenti & Sandra Campagna (eds)
Verbal/Visual Narrative Texts in Higher Education.
384 pages. 2008. ISBN 978-3-03911-672-0

Vol. 81 Meiko Matsumoto
From Simple Verbs to Periphrastic Expressions: The Historical Development of Composite Predicates, Phrasal Verbs, and Related Constructions in English.
235 pages. 2008. ISBN 978-3-03911-675-1

Vol. 82 Melinda Dooly
Doing Diversity. Teachers' Construction of Their Classroom Reality.
180 pages. 2009. ISBN 978-3-03911-687-4

Vol. 83 Victoria Guillén-Nieto, Carmen Marimón-Llorca & Chelo Vargas-Sierra (eds)
Intercultural Business Communication and Simulation and Gaming Methodology.
392 pages. 2009. ISBN 978-3-03911-688-1

Vol. 84 Maria Grazia Guido
English as a Lingua Franca in Cross-cultural Immigration Domains.
285 pages. 2008. ISBN 978-3-03911-689-8

Vol. 85 Erik Castello
Text Complexity and Reading Comprehension Tests.
352 pages. 2008. ISBN 978-3-03911-717-8

Vol. 86 Maria-Lluisa Gea-Valor, Isabel García-Izquierdo & Maria-José Esteve (eds)
Linguistic and Translation Studies in Scientific Communication.
317 pages. 2010. ISBN 978-3-0343-0069-8

Vol. 87 Carmen Navarro, Rosa Mª Rodríguez Abella, Francesca Dalle Pezze & Renzo Miotti (eds)
La comunicación especializada.
355 pages. 2008. ISBN 978-3-03911-733-8

Vol. 88 Kiriko Sato
The Development from Case-Forms to Prepositional Constructions in Old English Prose.
231 pages. 2009. ISBN 978-3-03911-763-5

Vol. 89 Dorothee Heller (Hrsg.)
Formulierungsmuster in deutscher und italienischer Fachkommunikation. Intra- und interlinguale Perspektiven.
315 pages. 2008. ISBN 978-3-03911-778-9

Vol. 90 Henning Bergenholtz, Sandro Nielsen & Sven Tarp (eds)
Lexicography at a Crossroads. Dictionaries and Encyclopedias Today, Lexicographical Tools Tomorrow.
372 pages. 2009. ISBN 978-3-03911-799-4

Vol. 91 Manouchehr Moshtagh Khorasani
The Development of Controversies. From the Early Modern Period to Online Discussion Forums.
317 pages. 2009. ISBN 978-3-3911-711-6

Vol. 92 María Luisa Carrió-Pastor (ed.)
Content and Language Integrated Learning. Cultural Diversity.
178 pages. 2009. ISBN 978-3-3911-818-2

Vol. 93 Roger Berry
Terminology in English Language Teaching. Nature and Use.
262 pages. 2010. ISBN 978-3-0343-0013-1

Vol. 94 Roberto Cagliero & Jennifer Jenkins (eds)
Discourses, Communities, and Global Englishes
240 pages. 2010. ISBN 978-3-0343-0012-4

Vol. 95 Facchinetti Roberta, Crystal David, Seidlhofer Barbara (eds)
From International to Local English – And Back Again.
268 pages. 2010. ISBN 978-3-0343-0011-7

Vol. 96 Cesare Gagliardi & Alan Maley (eds)
EIL, ELF, Global English. Teaching and Learning Issues
376 pages. 2010. ISBN 978-3-0343-0010-0

Vol. 97 Sylvie Hancil (ed.)
The Role of Prosody in Affective Speech.
403 pages. 2009. ISBN 978-3-03911-696-6

Vol. 98 Marina Dossena & Roger Lass (eds)
Studies in English and European Historical Dialectology.
257 pages. 2009. ISBN 978-3-0343-0024-7

Vol. 99 Christine Béal
Les interactions quotidiennes en français et en anglais. De l'approche comparative à l'analyse des situations interculturelles.
424 pages. 2010. ISBN 978-3-0343-0027-8

Vol. 100 Maurizio Gotti (ed.)
Commonality and Individuality in Academic Discourse.
398 pages. 2009. ISBN 978-3-0343-0023-0

Vol. 101 Javier E. Díaz Vera & Rosario Caballero (eds)
Textual Healing. Studies in Medieval English Medical, Scientific and Technical Texts.
213 pages. 2009. ISBN 978-3-03911-822-9

Vol. 102 Nuria Edo Marzá
The Specialised Lexicographical Approach. A Step further in Dictionary-making.
316 pages. 2009. ISBN 978-3-0343-0043-8

Vol. 103 Carlos Prado-Alonso, Lidia Gómez-García, Iria Pastor-Gómez &
David Tizón-Couto (eds)
New Trends and Methodologies in Applied English Language Research.
Diachronic, Diatopic and Contrastive Studies.
348 pages. 2009. ISBN 978-3-0343-0046-9

Vol. 104 Françoise Salager-Meyer & Beverly A. Lewin
Crossed Words. Criticism in Scholarly Writing?
371 pages. 2011. ISBN 978-3-0343-0049-0.

Vol. 105 Javier Ruano-García
Early Modern Northern English Lexis. A Literary Corpus-Based Study.
611 pages. 2010. ISBN 978-3-0343-0058-2

Vol. 106 Rafael Monroy-Casas
Systems for the Phonetic Transcription of English. Theory and Texts.
280 pages. 2011. ISBN 978-3-0343-0059-9

Vol. 107 Nicola T. Owtram
The Pragmatics of Academic Writing.
A Relevance Approach to the Analysis of Research Article Introductions.
311 pages. 2009. ISBN 978-3-0343-0060-5

Vol. 108 Yolanda Ruiz de Zarobe, Juan Manuel Sierra &
Francisco Gallardo del Puerto (eds)
Content and Foreign Language Integrated Learning.
Contributions to Multilingualism in European Contexts
343 pages. 2011. ISBN 978-3-0343-0074-2

Vol. 109 Ángeles Linde López & Rosalía Crespo Jiménez (eds)
Professional English in the European context. The EHEA challenge.
374 pages. 2010. ISBN 978-3-0343-0088-9

Vol. 110 Rosalía Rodríguez-Vázquez
The Rhythm of Speech, Verse and Vocal Music. A New Theory.
394 pages. 2010. ISBN 978-3-0343-0309-5

Vol. 111 Anastasios Tsangalidis & Roberta Facchinetti (eds)
Studies on English Modality. In Honour of Frank Palmer.
392 pages. 2009. ISBN 978-3-0343-0310-1

Vol. 112 Forthcoming.

Vol. 113 Mihhail Lotman & Maria-Kristiina Lotman (eds)
Frontiers in Comparative Prosody. In memoriam: Mikhail Gasparov.
426 pages. 2011. ISBN 978-3-0343-0373-6

Vol. 114 Merja Kytö, John Scahill & Harumi Tanabe (eds)
Language Change and Variation from Old English to Late Modern English.
A Festschrift for Minoji Akimoto
422 pages. 2010. ISBN 978-3-0343-0372-9

Vol. 115 Giuliana Garzone & Paola Catenaccio (eds)
Identities across Media and Modes. Discursive Perspectives.
379 pages. 2009. ISBN 978-3-0343-0386-6

Vol. 116 Elena Landone
Los marcadores del discurso y cortesía verbal en español.
390 pages. 2010. ISBN 978-3-0343-0413-9

Vol. 117 Maurizio Gotti & Christopher Williams (eds)
Legal Discourse across Languages and Cultures.
339 pages. 2010. ISBN 978-3-0343-0425-2

Vol. 118 David Hirsh
Academic Vocabulary in Context.
217 pages. 2010. ISBN 978-3-0343-0426-9

Vol. 119 Yvonne Dröschel
Lingua Franca English. The Role of Simplification and Transfer.
358 pages. 2011. ISBN 978-3-0343-0432-0

Vol. 120 Tengku Sepora Tengku Mahadi, Helia Vaezian & Mahmoud Akbari
Corpora in Translation. A Practical Guide.
135 pages. 2010. ISBN 978-3-0343-0434-4

Vol. 121 Davide Simone Giannoni & Celina Frade (eds)
Researching Language and the Law. Textual Features and Translation Issues.
278 pages. 2010. ISBN 978-3-0343-0443-6

Vol. 122 Daniel Madrid & Stephen Hughes (eds)
Studies in Bilingual Education.
472 pages. 2011. ISBN 978-3-0343-0474-0

Vol. 123 Vijay K. Bhatia, Christopher N. Candlin & Maurizio Gotti (eds)
The Discourses of Dispute Resolution.
290 pages. 2010. ISBN 978-3-0343-0476-4

Vol. 124 Davide Simone Giannoni
Mapping Academic Values in the Disciplines. A Corpus-Based Approach.
288 pages. 2010. ISBN 978-3-0343-0488-7

Vol. 125 Giuliana Garzone & James Archibald (eds)
Discourse, Identities and Roles in Specialized Communication.
419 pages. 2010. ISBN 978-3-0343-0494-8

Vol. 126 Iria Pastor-Gómez
The Status and Development of N+N Sequences in
Contemporary English Noun Phrases.
216 pages. 2011. ISBN 978-3-0343-0534-1

Vol. 127 Carlos Prado-Alonso
Full-verb Inversion in Written and Spoken English.
261 pages. 2011. ISBN 978-3-0343-0535-8

Vol. 128 Tony Harris & María Moreno Jaén (eds)
Corpus Linguistics in Language Teaching.
214 pages. 2010. ISBN 978-3-0343-0524-2

Vol. 129 Tetsuji Oda & Hiroyuki Eto (eds)
Multiple Perspectives on English Philology and History of Linguistics.
A Festschrift for Shoichi Watanabe on his 80th Birthday.
378 pages. 2010. ISBN 978-3-0343-0480-1

Vol. 130 Luisa Chierichetti & Giovanni Garofalo (eds)
Lengua y Derecho. líneas de investigación interdisciplinaria.
283 pages. 2010. 978-3-0343-0463-4

Vol. 131 Paola Evangelisti Allori & Giuliana Garzone (eds)
Discourse, Identities and Genres in Corporate Communication.
Sponsorship, Advertising and Organizational Communication.
324 pages. 2011. 978-3-0343-0591-4

Vol. 132 Leyre Ruiz de Zarobe & Yolanda Ruiz de Zarobe (eds)
Speech Acts and Politeness across Languages and Cultures.
402 pages. 2012. 978-3-0343-0611-9

Vol. 133 Thomas Christiansen
Cohesion. A Discourse Perspective.
387 pages. 2011. 978-3-0343-0619-5

Vol. 134 Giuliana Garzone & Maurizio Gotti
Discourse, Communication and the Enterprise. Genres and Trends.
451 pages. 2011. ISBN 978-3-0343-0620-1

Vol. 135 Zsuzsa Hoffmann
Ways of the World's Words.
Language Contact in the Age of Globalization.
334 pages 2011. ISBN 978-3-0343-0673-7

Vol. 136 Cecilia Varcasia (ed.)
Becoming Multilingual.
Language Learning and Language Policy between Attitudes and Identities.
213 pages. 2011. ISBN 978-3-0343-0687-5

Vol. 137 Susy Macqueen
The Emergence of Patterns in Second Language Writing.
A Sociocognitive Exploration of Lexical Trails.
325 pages. 2012. ISBN 978-3-0343-1010-9

Vol. 138 Maria Vittoria Calvi & Giovanna Mapelli (eds)
La lengua del turismo. Géneros discursivos y terminología.
365 pages. 2011. ISBN 978-3-0343-1011-6

Vol. 139 Ken Lau
Learning to Become a Professional in a Textually-Mediated World.
A Text-Oriented Study of Placement Practices.
261 pages. 2012. ISBN 978-3-0343-1016-1

Vol. 140 Sandra Campagna, Giuliana Garzone, Cornelia Ilie & Elizabeth Rowley-Jolivet (eds)
Evolving Genres in Web-mediated Communication.
337 pages. 2012. ISBN 978-3-0343-1013-0

Vol. 141 Edith Esch & Martin Solly (eds)
The Sociolinguistics of Language Education in International Contexts.
263 pages. 2012. ISBN 978-3-0343-1009-3

Vol. 142 Forthcoming.

Vol. 143 David Tizón-Couto
Left Dislocation in English. A Functional-Discoursal Approach.
416 pages. 2012. ISBN 978-3-0343-1037-6

Vol. 144 Margrethe Petersen & Jan Engberg (eds)
Current Trends in LSP Research. Aims and Methods.
323 pages. 2011. ISBN 978-3-0343-1054-3

Vol. 145 David Tizón-Couto, Beatriz Tizón-Couto, Iria Pastor-Gómez & Paula Rodríguez-Puente (eds)
New Trends and Methodologies in Applied English Language Research II.
Studies in Language Variation, Meaning and Learning.
283 pages. 2012. ISBN 978-3-0343-1061-1

Vol. 146 Rita Salvi & Hiromasa Tanaka (eds)
Intercultural Interactions in Business and Management.
306 pages. 2011. ISBN 978-3-0343-1039-0

Vol. 147 Francesco Straniero Sergio & Caterina Falbo (eds)
Breaking Ground in Corpus-based Interpreting Studies.
254 pages. 2012. ISBN 978-3-0343-1071-0

Vol. 148 Forthcoming.

Vol. 149 Vijay K. Bhatia & Paola Evangelisti Allori (eds)
Discourse and Identity in the Professions. Legal, Corporate and Institutional Citizenship.
352 pages. 2011. ISBN 978-3-0343-1079-6

Vol. 150 Maurizio Gotti (ed.)
Academic Identity Traits. A Corpus-Based Investigation.
363 pages. 2012. ISBN 978-3-0343-1141-0

Vol. 151 Priscilla Heynderickx, Sylvain Dieltjens, Geert Jacobs, Paul Gillaerts &
Elizabeth de Groot (eds)
The Language Factor in International Business.
New Perspectives on Research, Teaching and Practice.
320 pages. 2012. ISBN 978-3-0343-1090-1

Vol. 152 Paul Gillaerts, Elizabeth de Groot, Sylvain Dieltjens, Priscilla Heynderickx &
Geert Jacobs (eds)
Researching Discourse in Business Genres. Cases and Corpora.
215 pages. 2012. ISBN 978-3-0343-1092-5

Vol. 153 Yongyan Zheng
Dynamic Vocabulary Development in a Foreign Language.
262 pages. 2012. ISBN 978-3-0343-1106-9

Vol. 154 Carmen Argondizzo (ed.)
Creativity and Innovation in Language Education.
357 pages. 2012. ISBN 978-3-0343-1080-2

Vol. 155 David Hirsh (ed.)
Current Perspectives in Second Language Vocabulary Research.
180 pages. 2012. ISBN 978-3-0343-1108-3

Vol. 156 Seiji Shinkawa
Unhistorical Gender Assignment in Laȝamon's *Brut.* A Case Study of a Late Stage
in the Development of Grammatical Gender toward its Ultimate Loss.
186 pages. 2012. ISBN 978-3-0343-1124-3

Vol. 157 Forthcoming.

Vol. 158 Bárbara Eizaga Rebollar (ed.)
Studies in Linguistics and Cognition.
301 pages. 2012. ISBN 978-3-0343-1138-0

Vol. 159 Giuliana Garzone, Paola Catenaccio, Chiara Degano (eds)
Genre Change in the Contemporary World. Short-term Diachronic Perspectives.
329 pages. 2012. ISBN 978-3-0343-1214-1

Vol. 160 Carol Berkenkotter, Vijay K. Bhatia & Maurizio Gotti (eds)
Insights into Academic Genres.
468 pages. 2012. ISBN 978-3-0343-1211-0

Vol. 161 Forthcoming.

Vol. 162 Patrizia Anesa
Jury Trials and the Popularization of Legal Language. A Discourse Analytical Approach.
247 pages. 2012. ISBN 978-3-0343-1231-8

Vol. 163-166 Forthcoming.

Vol. 167 Shunji Yamazaki & Robert Sigley (eds)
Approaching Language Variation through Corpora. A Festschrift in Honour of Toshio Saito.
421 pages. 2013. ISBN 978-3-0343-1264-6

Vol. 168 Franca Poppi
Global Interactions in English as a Lingua Franca. How written communication is changing under the influence of electronic media and new contexts of use.
249 pages. 2012. ISBN 978-3-0343-1276-9

Vol. 169-170 Forthcoming.

Vol. 171 Aleksandra Matulewska
Legilinguistic Translatology. A Parametric Approach to Legal Translation.
279 pages. 2013. ISBN 978-3-0343-1287-5

Vol. 172 Maurizio Gotti & Carmen Sancho Guinda (eds)
Narratives in Academic and Professional Genres.
513 pages. 2013. ISBN 978-3-0343-1371-1